BOOKS BY DR. CHRIS THURMAN

If Christ Were Your Counselor (Thomas Nelson Publishers)

It's Your Attitude (Cascade Books)

Self-Help or Self-Destruction? (Thomas Nelson Publishers)

Stop Shoulding All Over Yourself (Kharis Publishing)

The Lies Couples Believe (David C. Cook Publishers)

The Lies We Believe—30th Anniversary Edition (Thomas Nelson Publishers)

The Lies We Believe About God (David C. Cook Publishers)

The Lies We Believe Workbook—Revised Edition (Thomas Nelson Publishers)

The Truths We Must Believe (Thomas Nelson Publishers)

POP'S ADVICE

Godly Guidance for My Grandkids . . .
and Everyone Else

CHRIS THURMAN, PH.D.
A.K.A. "POP"

WESTBOW
PRESS®
A DIVISION OF THOMAS NELSON
& ZONDERVAN

WestBow Press books may be ordered through booksellers or by contacting:

WestBow Press
A Division of Thomas Nelson & Zondervan
1663 Liberty Drive
Bloomington, IN 47403
www.westbowpress.com
844-714-3454

ISBN: 978-1-6642-7822-6 (sc)
ISBN: 978-1-6642-7842-4 (e)

Print information available on the last page.

WestBow Press rev. date: 10/24/2022

To my awesome, fantastic, amazing, incredible,
wonderful, and extraordinary grandkids,
Scout, Leni, and Luke

If I had known how wonderful it would be to have grandchildren, I'd have had them first.
—Lois Wyse

Contents

Introduction

It dawned on me the other day that I'm considered "elderly" now that I'm in my late sixties. I'm kind of upset about that because it implies I'm old, something I vehemently deny. Nevertheless, reaching this point in my life got me thinking about what we psychologists call "generativity," the stage of life where we desire to create or nurture things that will outlast us and benefit those who follow, especially the younger generation.

Given that I don't know how much longer I've got left, I felt nudged by God to write a book of advice for my grandkids. Because my grandkids call me Pop, I decided to title the book *Pop's Advice*. In it, I hand down the most important things I've learned over the years about how to live life in a spiritually and emotionally healthy manner.

You might question why I think I have something of value to pass along to my grandkids, much less why you might want to read it. All I can tell you is that I have spent the last fifty-plus years as a Christian person of faith and forty-plus years as a psychologist studying what it takes to live life in the wisest and most growthful manner possible, and I want to offer what I've learned to my grandkids and to you in case it might help.

Here are some suggestions on how to read *Pop's Advice*.

First, I purposely wrote 52 chapters so you can read one chapter a week and complete the book in a year. If you are going to go through the book with your child or grandchild, set aside an hour each week to read a chapter together, discuss what you read, and complete the corresponding lesson in the workbook along the way.

Second, don't wait until the end of the book to do the workbook. I wrote the workbook because I'm a firm believer we need to put what we learn into action as quickly as possible. James 1:22 says, "Do not merely listen to the word and so deceive yourselves. Do what it says." We'd all be wise to tattoo that statement on our foreheads. Anything less than spending time each day taking what we know and acting on it isn't going to be enough to move our lives forward in a healthy and constructive way.

Third, if you're going to read the book with your child or grandchild, I encourage you to wait until he or she is middle school age (11-13) or older. I'm suggesting this particular age group because it strikes me as the time during which young people might be more likely to understand and implement the advice offered in this book. Do what you think is best given the maturity level of your particular child or grandchild. As you know, some five-year-olds are more mature than some fifty-year-olds.

Fourth, don't get discouraged if your child or grandchild thinks the book is boring or a waste of time. Just threaten to withhold their allowance, restrict their social life, load them down with chores, forbid them from playing video games, and put their cell phones in a bank vault until they're willing to go through it with you.

Fifth, if you're a grandparent wanting to read the book with your grandchild, make sure you get permission from their parents. Your grandkid's parents are their earthly authority and need to be the ones who green light doing the book. If they don't want you to do it, please respect that and just do it behind their back (I'm kidding).

Sixth, if you can't do the book with your kids or grandkids, read it for your own growth and development. The material covered in this book applies to everyone on the planet regardless of age, gender, race, ethnicity, occupation, personality type, marital status, background, talents, abilities, or life circumstances. Because it's based on biblical wisdom, this book can help everyone become a healthier, more mature adult.

Finally, if you're going to read the book for yourself, do it with a group of like-minded folks who want to live their lives in a spiritually and emotionally healthy manner. Proverbs 27:17 says, "As iron sharpens iron, so one person sharpens another," and we adults need to iron sharpen iron each other into becoming whole and complete human beings.

My grandkids mean the world to me. Nothing fills my heart with joy like being their granddad. Grandchildren are a precious gift to us, a gift like no other, and we need to do the best job we can to guide them in the right direction as they make their way through life. Edward Fays was right when he said, "There is nothing more wonderful than the love and guidance a grandparent can give his or her grandchild." Let's give our children, grandchildren, and even ourselves the guidance contained in this book, especially in light of the fact that it reflects God's love, wisdom, and guidance for us.

Blessings,
Chris

THE JOY OF BEING A GRANDPARENT

Children's children are a crown to the aged,
and parents are the pride of their children.
—Proverbs 17:6

An hour with your grandchildren can
make you feel young again. Anything
longer than that, and you start to age quickly.
—Gene Perret

I asked God for three things when I was in college. First, He would bring me a wonderful woman to be my wife. Second, He would bless me with children. And, third, He would let me live long enough to experience the joy of being a grandparent. God graciously answered all three requests, and my life has been richly blessed ever since.

While I am eternally grateful to have an amazing wife and three awesome kids, being your granddad brings me joy that goes beyond what I could have ever hoped for or imagined. Nothing I've experienced on this planet compares with how awesome it is to have you grandkids.

While you've only been here a short time, you've already given me and everyone else so much joy and happiness. One of the most enjoyable parts of that for me has been the dozens of times you've made me laugh . . . out loud. Let me give you three examples, one for each of you.

Just the other day, one of you asked me how I put on my socks and shoes. You wanted to know if I put a sock on and then a shoe on or if I

1

put both socks on and then both shoes. After I informed you that I mix things up to keep my life interesting, you seemed quite satisfied with my answer and went on to ask me about something else that interested you. I'm still smiling about that particular exchange and know that many more like it are to come.

A while back, one of you had your school picture taken. Unbeknownst to your parents and grandparents, you put a Chiquita banana sticker on your shirt the morning before you left for school. When we got the pictures back from your photoshoot, we all burst out laughing that your unbridled affinity for stickers led to you making this particular fashion choice, one that will follow you the rest of your life. Anytime I need a laugh, I pull that particular picture out of my wallet and look at it.

Finally, the newest of you let me teach you how to make inappropriate noises with your mouth. Not only did you let me teach you how to make inappropriate noises with your mouth, but we were able to do a duet together that made both of us grin from ear to ear. Your mother wasn't happy with me, but that was an experience I'll treasure for the rest of my life and look forward to repeating many times in the future.

The name I chose for you to call me is "Pop," the name I called my grandfather on my mother's side. When I refer to you collectively, I call you "munchkins" based on characters in *The Wizard of Oz*. You know, like "Come on, munchkins, we're going on a walk rather than watch five hundred more hours of cartoons" and "Munchkins, pick up all the toys you've thrown all over the house before your parents come to get you." According to Merriam-Webster, a munchkin is "a person who is notably small and often endearing." That describes you—small and often (not always, though) endearing.

Nonnie and I recently came back from Disney World with you granddaughters. I had a birthday while we were there (thanks, by the way, for singing *Happy Birthday*, at least I think it was *Happy Birthday*), and it prompted me to think about what I want to leave behind for you when my days on earth come to an end. I felt nudged by God to write a book of advice on how to live life in the wisest way possible in terms of your spiritual and emotional health.

Let me share a few thoughts with you before I start doling out advice.

First, you need to know I'm writing this book for you. I've never written a book for such a small and select group of people before, but I've learned over the years to stop worrying about how many people read what I write. Worrying about it never did any good, and most of my books have only been read by my family and close friends anyway. So, munchkins, this one's for you. If the three of you read it, I will die a happy man.

Second, you need to know I believe God provides us with wise principles for how to live life in a healthy manner that never change or go out of style. They are valid no matter what time period you live in, what part of the world you live in, or how God uniquely wired you as a human being. If you want advice that anchors itself in timeless biblical wisdom from God Himself, this book is for you.

Third, you're going to be tempted to push back on what I say in this book. As human beings, we're all prone to take the easy path, one that doesn't require hard work, sacrifice, or suffering on our part. All the advice I'm about to give you will require some degree of spiritual and emotional suffering on your part if you follow it. Please, resist the urge to run from the advice in this book because it's hard. Follow it because it's hard, not because it's easy.

Finally, I want to encourage you to listen to your parent's advice before mine. Your parents are your earthly authority, and I want you to honor and respect the advice they give you over what I have to say. If my advice differs from your parent's, listen to them. They'll be wrong, but listen to them anyway.

Munchkins, thanks for bringing such joy and happiness to our lives. I hope and pray the advice in this book will help make your life better and bring glory to God, the One who fearfully and wonderfully made you in His image and loves you with every fiber of His being.

2

HANG AROUND GOOD PEOPLE

Do not be misled: "Bad company corrupts good character."
—1 Corinthians 15:33

But mark this: There will be terrible times in the last
days. People will be lovers of themselves, lovers of
money, boastful, proud, abusive, disobedient to their
parents, ungrateful, unholy, without love, unforgiving,
slanderous, without self-control, brutal, not lovers of the
good, treacherous, rash, conceited, lovers of pleasure
rather than lovers of God—having a form of godliness but
denying its power. Have nothing to do with such people.
—2 Timothy 3:1-5

Keeping bad company is like being in a germ-
infested area. You never know what you'll catch.
—Frank Sonnenberg

Bad company is like a nail driven into a post,
which, after the first and second blow, may be
drawn out with little difficulty; but being once
driven up to the head, the pincers cannot
take hold to draw it out, but which can only
be done by the destruction of the wood.
—Saint Augustine

Throughout your life, there will be times when you're tempted to hang around bad people. For reasons I can't fully explain, bad people are exciting to be around, and we're sometimes drawn to them like a moth to a flame. But, give these people enough time, and they'll damage your soul and leave you in spiritual and psychological tatters.

There are two groups of bad people I want to warn you about, the chronically self-absorbed (also known as *narcissists*) and the militant rule-breakers (also known as *sociopaths*). The terms *narcissist* and *sociopath* don't mean anything to you now, but they will later on when you run into enough of these not-so-wonderful people. Let me give you a brief description of how these folks (pathologically) function.

The chronically self-absorbed are people who have a grandiose sense of self-importance, are preoccupied with fantasies of unlimited success and power, believe that they are special and can only be understood by other special people, require excessive admiration, have a strong sense of entitlement, take advantage of others to achieve their own ends, lack empathy for the pain others are in, often envy others and think others are envious of them, and show arrogant and haughty behaviors and attitudes—you know, the kind of guy or gal you're going to have a crush on in high school and college and want to marry. Please don't.

The militant rule-breakers are people who refuse to conform to social norms, repeatedly lie, fail to plan, act impulsively, are often irritable and aggressive, tend to disregard their safety and the safety of others, act irresponsibly, and lack remorse when they hurt others—you know, the kind of guy or gal you're going to have a crush on in high school and college and want to marry. Please don't.

While chronically self-absorbed and militant rule-breaking folks comprise a very small percentage of the human race, they cause 99.8% of the world's problems. Look back through human history at the people who caused the most damage. It's always the narcissists and the sociopaths. So, whenever you have to be around them, make sure it's for very limited periods of time and keep your boundaries firmly in place. More on that later.

Now, if you're worried you might be a chronically self-absorbed (narcissistic) or militantly rule-breaking (sociopathic) person, I can assure you you're not. We're all *deeply fallen human beings and have these two unhealthy tendencies in us*, but you were raised by healthy parents and they would never let you go too far down these pathological paths without bringing it to your attention and putting some painful consequences in place to get you back on the right path. Call them right now and thank them. Also, your grandparents, especially me, are too healthy to allow you to be this way, so call and thank us, too.

Let me speak out of the other side of my mouth for just a minute. While the title of this chapter is, *Hang Around Good People*, Jesus made it clear, "No one is good—except God alone" (Mark 10:18). So, there are no *inherently* good people on the planet, something that, unfortunately, includes you and me. Here, I'm simply trying to make a distinction between those who are bent in the direction of badness but trying to become better human beings and those who are bent in the direction of badness but don't care and are only getting worse. I *strongly* suggest you hang around the former and avoid the latter.

The reason I'm making such a big deal out of who you hang around with is that it's a big deal. God wouldn't have put "Bad company corrupts good morals" in the Bible if it weren't a big deal. I have witnessed, both personally and professionally, just how damaging the chronically self-absorbed (narcissists) and militant rule-breakers (sociopaths) can be, and my heart breaks for all of us when they act out their psychopathology at our expense.

Munchkins, the next time you're thinking about letting someone into your life as a friend, boyfriend/girlfriend, spouse, roommate, travel companion, colleague, boss, workout partner, spiritual mentor, or anything else, call me and I'll help you evaluate whether or not they cross the line when it comes to these two character-disordered personality types. If they check too many of the boxes, I'll tell you to run in the opposite direction as fast as you can and never look back. If you don't follow my advice, I'll remove you from my will and you won't receive the $47.50 that's coming your way when I go to the Great Beyond.

Bad company corrupts good morals. Please, hang around people who, by human standards, are good folks. You know, the kind of people who have empathy for your emotional pain, don't think too highly of themselves, follow the rules, give rather than take, think before they act, work hard, take responsibility for their actions, care when they hurt you, and do what they can to grow and mature. These are the kind of people who will leave your soul better off, and you'll thank the Lord you spent your time hanging around them.

OWN YOUR OWN STUFF

The man said, "The woman you put here
with me—she gave me some fruit from
the tree, and I ate it." Then the Lord God
said to the woman, "What is this
you have done?" The woman said, "The
serpent deceived me, and I ate."
—Genesis 3:12-13

So then, each of us will give an account of ourselves to God.
—Romans 14:12

It is a painful thing to look at your
own trouble and know that you
yourself and no one else has made it.
—Sophocles

The choices we make are ultimately our responsibility.
—Eleanor Roosevelt

We live in a world full of people who have mastered the blame game.
These folks spend their lives blaming their thoughts, feelings, and
actions on others, playing the victim card along the way. It all goes
back to the Garden of Eden, of course, where Adam blamed Eve for *his
choice* to take a bite out of an apple, and Eve blamed the serpent for *her
choice* to do the same.

I want to encourage you to resist blaming others for your thoughts, feelings, and actions and that you don't allow others to blame you for theirs. Let me explain.

Let's say someone calls you a derogatory name. As strange as it might sound, I want you to stop, take a deep breath, and assume *complete responsibility* for how you *think*, *feel*, and *respond* to what they said. If you do that, you won't give people power over your spiritual and emotional health from day to day. Please, don't ever blame your thoughts, feelings, and actions on the people who mistreat you. How you respond to the unkind things they say or do is completely on you, not them.

Now, let's flip this around. Let's say you call someone a derogatory name. Please, don't let the person you called a bad name blame you for how they think, feel, and act in responding to what you said. If the person you called a bad name says, "You hurt my feelings when you called me a _____ and that's why I called you a _____," don't buy it. If they blame you for their reaction, say something like, "I'm not responsible you felt hurt when I called you a bad name, and I'm not responsible that you called me a bad name in return. What I am responsible for is calling you a _____. That was rude and inappropriate. I'm truly sorry, I apologize, and I hope you will forgive me for what I did."

I know all of this sounds like semantics, but it's important that we live our lives putting ourselves completely on the hook for all the thoughts, feelings, and actions we have each day. If we fail to do this, our relationships with others are going to be a bigger mess than they already are. If we do it, we'll clean up our relationships with others and make them healthier and a lot more functional.

Now, because I know you're not listening, I want to say all this again using a different example to drive it home.

Let's say you're walking down a city street and someone sticks a gun to your head and demands your wallet. You're going to think I've lost my mind, which I have, but you're completely responsible for how you respond.

If you decide to give them your wallet, you're on the hook for that. Please don't fall into thinking or feeling "They made me give them my wallet." They didn't. You made a very wise choice to value your life over your wallet, and you need to own that. If you are healthy enough to take full responsibility for your choice, you won't give people hold over you or let them turn you into a bitter, resentful victim when they mistreat you.

At the same time, you need to hold the robber responsible for sticking a gun to your head and taking your wallet when you gave it to him. Even if you were walking in an area of town that's crime-infested (not a smart choice on your part), you're *not* responsible if someone robs you. They are. Don't fall into the mental trap, "It's my fault they robbed me." You could have hundred-dollar bills safety-pinned all over your clothes (not a smart choice on your part) and you're not responsible for someone robbing you. You're just responsible for being unwise.

So, here's how I want a situation like this to play out in your thoughts, feelings, and actions: "I chose to walk down that particular street. Someone chose to stick a gun to my head and demand my wallet. I chose to give him my wallet because my life is far more important than my wallet. He chose to take my wallet and run away with it. I chose to contact the police to let them know what happened, give them a description of the perpetrator, and ask them to do what they can about it. If they find this guy, I'm going to choose to have him prosecuted to the full extent of the law so he spends time in the Big House. In the interim, I'm going to choose to have my credit cards canceled so this guy can't use them to buy a big screen t.v., eat a meal at a five-star restaurant, or book a trip to Barbados."

I need to practice what I preach here. Just the other day, I left my charge card at a restaurant (not a good choice on my part). Whoever found it chose to go to a nearby Target and try to charge over $1100 on it (their choice). My credit card company declined the purchase (my credit card company's choice—thank you). I canceled the card and got a new one (my choice). I felt angry and resentful toward the staff at the restaurant that they didn't properly address the situation (my choice, and not a good one). And, I started thinking some very bad thoughts about all the people involved (my choice, and, again, not a good one). I think you get the point—everyone is on the hook in life for their thoughts, feelings, and actions whether they want to be or not.

Munchkins, you may think I'm making much ado about nothing here. Trust me, I'm not. If you dedicate the rest of your life to taking full responsibility for your thoughts, feelings, and actions and holding others fully responsible for theirs, you'll be a much healthier individual, you'll problem-solve situations more effectively and maturely, and you'll be less prone to victimhood and the bitterness and resentment that goes along with it. Try it, you'll like it.

TELL PEOPLE WHAT
YOU NEED

"Blessed are the poor in spirit, for theirs
is the kingdom of heaven."
—Matthew 5:3

And my God will meet all your needs according
to the riches of his glory in Christ Jesus.
—Philippians 4:19

When we ask we are owning our needs. Asking for love,
comfort or understanding is a transaction between two
people. You are saying: I have a need. It's not your problem.
It's not your responsibility. You don't have to respond, but
I'd like something from you. This frees the other person to
connect with you freely and without obligation. When we
own that our needs are our responsibility we allow others to
love us because we have something to offer. Asking is a far
cry from demanding. When we demand love, we destroy it.
—Henry Cloud

God not only loves me as I am, but also
knows me as I am. Because of this I
don't need to apply spiritual cosmetics to
make myself presentable to Him.

I can accept ownership of my poverty
and powerlessness and neediness.
—Brennan Manning

Munchkins, never apologize for being needy. Ever. We're born that way. We come into the world physically needy for air, food, water, clothes, and shelter. We come into the world spiritually needy for an intimate relationship with God. And, we come into the world psychologically needy for close relationships with other human beings. That last part, the close relationships with other human beings part, is what I want to talk about in this chapter.

You come into the world with a soul. Your soul is composed of your mind, will, and emotions. Your mind is your "thinker" and interprets, assesses, judges, perceives, and evaluates the things that happen to you. You will is your "chooser" and enables you to take a course of action in responding to the things that happen to you. Your emotions are your "feeler" and enable you to respond to the things that happen to you such that you don't walk around like an unfeeling rock. Your soul is wired by God with psychological needs (also called "attachment needs" and "relational needs"), and it's important to know that not only is it okay to have these needs but it's okay for you to want them met by others.

Your psychological needs include attention, acceptance, appreciation, affirmation, affection, comfort, encouragement, respect, security, support, and understanding. Another granddad who's a psychologist might have given you a list of fifty psychological needs and another might have given you a list of five. I'm suggesting you have these eleven psychological needs (plus or minus maybe one) and that you're going to go through life in a healthier manner if you're aware that you have them and humbly ask people to meet them.

There are four traps people fall into when it comes to having psychological needs. Some people deny they have these needs (the denial trap). Some people think it's selfish to have them (the selfish trap). Some people try to meet these needs themselves (the self-sufficiency trap). And some people think they are entitled to these needs being met by others (the narcissism trap). None of these folks are thinking correctly when it comes to their psychological needs, and they often get in their own way when it comes to living an emotionally healthy life.

The bottom line here is that when God makes us, He makes us needy. One reason God makes us needy is that He wants us to go through life *humble*—aware we're needy and can't meet these needs ourselves. We're all completely dependent on God to meet our needs each day, something we need to accept rather than stiff-arm. And, apparently, one of the best ways God keeps us humble is to make us needy rather than self-sufficient. That way we depend on Him to meet all our needs according to the vast resources He has at His disposal.

Munchkins, I was raised to think the biblical notion "poor in spirit" (Matthew 5:3) meant we're supposed to think of ourselves as worthless. In the church I grew up in, it was called "worm theology," as in "Oh, what a wretched worm am I." That's not what the concept "poor in spirit" means. Poor in spirit simply means we've accepted that we're needy at our core, are okay with it, and aren't going to spend the rest of our lives denying it, apologizing for it, or trying to be self-sufficient.

So, for the rest of your lives, be aware of the fact that you have these eleven psychological needs. And, please, work on getting better at *directly asking people to meet these needs*. Don't walk around hoping people will read your mind and give you what you need without you asking for it. Doing that gets in the way of God keeping you humble, and, believe me, you don't want to do that.

At the same time, make sure you pay attention to the other side of the coin by being willing to meet the psychological needs of others as well. Healthy relationships are always a two-way street. They require both people to do a good job of meeting each other's needs, not one person doing all the need-meeting. I've seen unhealthy relationships where both people were in take-mode, what we call a "two ticks and no dog" relationship. Save yourself a lot of heartaches and don't get involved in those kinds of relationships.

When the Bible says "Blessed are the poor in spirit, for theirs is the kingdom of heaven" (Matthew 5:3), it's trying to tell us something important—we come into the world needy, we're this way the whole time we're here, and that we go to our graves needy. As you go through life, humble yourself about your deep-seated neediness and ask people for attention, acceptance, appreciation, affirmation, affection, comfort, encouragement, respect, security, support, and understanding. And, let them ask you for the same in return.

Well, what are you waiting for? Go tell someone what you need and ask them what they need from you! Time's a-wasting!

5

THINK THE RIGHT THOUGHTS

Finally, brothers and sisters, whatever is true,
whatever is pure, whatever is lovely, whatever
is admirable—if anything is excellent or
praiseworthy—think about such things.
—Philippians 4:8

Do not conform to the pattern of this
world, but be transformed by the
renewing of your mind. Then you will
be able to test and approve what God's
will is—his good, pleasing and perfect will.
—Romans 12:2

A noble and God-like character is not
a thing of favor or chance, but is the
natural result of continued effort in right
thinking, the effect of long-cherished
association with God-like thoughts.
—James Allen

The greatest discovery of my generation is that a human
being can alter his life by altering his attitudes.
—William James

We all struggle with "stinking thinking." What I mean by that is we all have ways of looking at things that don't completely square with reality.

As you go through life, I want you to examine the way you think and be honest with yourself about whether or not you're thinking right (accurately, rationally, realistically, biblically). Hold fast to the idea that "garbage in, garbage out" when it comes to your thoughts. If you believe things that are false, irrational, inaccurate, and unbiblical, you're going to struggle more emotionally, relationally, and spiritually. If you believe things that are true, rational, accurate, and biblical, you'll handle the trials and tribulations of life in a healthier and more mature manner.

Here are a few of the deadliest beliefs you can fall into, lies if you will. These are toxic ways of thinking that many of us struggle with, ways of thinking we wouldn't wish on our worst enemy. Whatever you do, make sure these toxic beliefs don't take up residence in your mind.

I must be perfect. Perfectionism is one of the deadliest ways of thinking we humans buy into. It stiff-arms the painful reality that we're all noticeably imperfect and that everything we think, feel, and do falls significantly short of God's perfect perfectness.

I'm worthless. A lot of people walk around feeling they have no worth as human beings, the main reason being that many folks tie their worth to performance. Since our day-to-day performance fluctuates, our sense of worth automatically fluctuates along with it.

I must have everyone's approval. For many of us, our emotional health depends way too much on whether or not others approve of us. This leads to wasting a lot of time anxiously seeking everyone's approval and being willing to throw our integrity out the window to have it.

Life should be easy, fair, and just. In a deeply broken world like ours, we're going to run into our share of difficulty, unfairness, and injustice. We need to accept the fact that life is hard, unfair, and unjust at times and respond with as much decency and civility as possible.

Now, let's turn our attention to some of the most important truths, truths we need to spend the rest of our lives internalizing in the deepest nooks and crannies of our minds. These beliefs are the ones you want to soak your mind in each day because they have the power to foster emotional, relational, and spiritual health.

I have worth because I'm fearfully and wonderfully in God's image. If you want a proper basis for worth, anchor it in the fact that God fearfully and wonderfully made you in His image (Psalm 139:14). The fact that God made you in His image gives you and every other human being on the planet inherent, priceless, permanent worth.

It is more blessed to give than to receive. It is important to focus on serving others rather than being served by them. Trust that if you serve others, God will do everything He can in the context of a fallen world to make sure your needs are met along the way as well.

To err is human. Accept the fact that you're a noticeably imperfect human being who will make a lot of mistakes throughout your life. Accept that life is about learning from your mistakes, growing and improving along the way, and being excellent rather than perfect.

Life is difficult. On this side of heaven, difficult problems and challenges are always nipping at our heels and frequently trigger physical, emotional, and spiritual pain in life. Don't forget that "Each day has enough trouble of its own" (Matthew 6:34), and try to accept this important truth about life rather than whine, moan, or complain about it.

The victory is in the effort, not the result. The world we live in focuses on results, not effort. Focus on effort, not results. We only have control over our effort, not the outcome. Keep your head held high when you give something your best shot and don't look at the scoreboard to assess how you did.

You can't please everyone. If you're like most people, you care way too much about whether or not people like you. While we're not supposed to intentionally displease or antagonize others, we aren't supposed to seek their approval either. We are only supposed to seek the approval of God and focus on pleasing Him, not the approval of people and worry about pleasing them.

Munchkins, don't ever forget—garbage in, garbage out; good stuff in, good stuff out. Spend as much time as you can thinking about what is true, pure, noble, right, and worthwhile so that your feelings and actions grow to be healthier over time. The truth will set you free, but you need to dedicate your life to running it through your mind day and night and acting on it. Your mind is too important to waste on false, impure, unprincipled, wrong, and worthless thoughts. Let the truth set you free.

PRACTICE GOOD BOUNDARIES

Do not make friends with a hot-tempered
person, do not associate with one
easily angered, or you may learn their
ways and get yourself ensnared.
—Proverbs 22:24-25

"All you need to say is simply 'Yes' or 'No'; anything
beyond this comes from the evil one."
—Matthew 5:37

When we begin to set boundaries with people we love,
a really hard thing happens: they hurt. They may feel
a hole where you used to plug up their aloneness, their
disorganization, or their financial irresponsibility.
Whatever it is, they will feel a loss. If you love them,
this will be difficult for you to watch. But, when you are
dealing with someone who is hurting, remember that your
boundaries are both necessary for you and helpful for
them. If you have been enabling them to be irresponsible,
your limit setting may nudge them toward responsibility.
—Henry Cloud

You best teach others about healthy
boundaries by enforcing yours.
—Bryant H. McGill

You're going to need healthy boundaries as you go through life, and please don't let anyone tell you otherwise. Some pop psychology/new age folks, and even some misguided people of faith, seem to think that loving others means having no boundaries and that you're always supposed to passively turn the other cheek no matter how badly people treat you. That's false and foolish from about a hundred different perspectives. Benjamin Franklin was right when he said, "Love your neighbor, yet don't pull down your hedge."

As you go through life, you're going to need to have your physical, emotional, financial, and spiritual boundaries in place and do what you can to keep people from violating them. A phrase I heard growing up, attributed to poet Robert Frost, was, "Good fences make for good neighbors," and there's a great deal of truth to that. Fences, not walls, between us and others, help us to know where we begin and end and where our neighbor begins and ends.

I have been blessed over the years to have good neighbors. I hope they felt I was a good neighbor in return. But, for the sake of discussion, let's say that along the way one time I had a particularly bad neighbor. Let me tell you what that would look like from a "violating your boundaries" perspective.

A bad neighbor walks into your garage and borrows things without asking. A bad neighbor drops in uninvited and talks your ear off for hours and hours about their problems. A bad neighbor yells at your children when they misbehave. A bad neighbor tells you that you can't plant a certain kind of tree in your yard because they don't like it. A bad neighbor parks their car in your driveway (leaking oil, of course) without asking because they want to leave room in their driveway for their family and friends to use. A bad neighbor comes over to borrow a cup of this and a gallon of that and never thinks about returning the favor. A bad neighbor lets their kids come over to your house uninvited and walk in acting like they own the place. I could go on.

The point I want you to hear in all this is that you can't afford to go through life without proper boundaries given that everybody is imperfect and will unknowingly, or even knowingly, violate your boundaries along the way. Fences, not walls, make for good neighbors, and you need to make sure you have a pretty sturdy fence between you and others.

The flip side of all this is allowing people to have healthy boundaries with you when you're the one out of line. Sometimes, we're the fly in the ointment when it comes to not treating people respectfully and need to be properly called on the carpet for it. It's hypocritical of us to have firm boundaries with others but not let them have firm boundaries with us.

I keep saying "fences, not walls" because sometimes our boundaries with others are too rigid and impenetrable. Going back to my earlier description of a bad neighbor, what if I was the kind of neighbor who never let anyone borrow my lawnmower, never let people drop in to talk about their problems, never let others bring my children's misbehavior to my attention, planted hundred-foot-tall sequoia trees that caused my neighbor's grass to die, never made my driveway available to my neighbor when they needed it, and always expected something in return when giving my neighbor a cup of this or a gallon of that?

Sometimes, in an effort to have good boundaries, we erect a concrete wall between ourselves and others, a wall that gets in the way of being a truly good neighbor. Sometimes, our boundaries are so rigid and unyielding that we fall far short of fulfilling the second greatest commandment, "Love your neighbor as yourself" (Mark 12:31).

Admittedly, healthy boundaries are a hard thing to figure out at times. It's difficult to know when to say yes and when to say no. It's difficult to know when to be passive in reacting to others, turning the other cheek, and when to be assertive and "clear the temple." Nevertheless, I want you to work on this along the way because you're sure going to need appropriate boundaries if you're going to be a healthy, functional adult.

Munchkins, good fences make for good neighbors. Even if your neighbor doesn't understand or feels hurt about your boundaries, make sure you have them at the right time and in the right way. If your neighbor comes over and wants to borrow your car for five years and expects you to pay for the gas, say no whether they like it or not. But, if your neighbor comes over uninvited because they're going through something traumatic, say yes to listening to them pour their heart out and then do what you can to get them some help.

Real estate folks say "location, location, location." As you go through life dealing with *relational* real estate, we need to say two things, "love, love, love" and "boundaries, boundaries, boundaries." The two always go hand in hand.

LISTEN MORE THAN
YOU TALK

To answer before listening—that is folly and shame.
—Proverbs 18:13

My dear brothers and sisters, take note
of this: Everyone should be quick to listen,
slow to speak and slow to become angry, . . .
—James 1:19

Deep listening is miraculous for both listener and speaker.
When someone receives us with open-hearted, non-
judging, intensely interested listening, our spirits expand.
—Sue Thoele

Deep listening is the kind of listening
that can help relieve the suffering
of another person. You can call it
compassionate listening. You listen
with only one purpose: to help him
or her to empty his heart.
—Nhat Hanh

In general, people don't listen very well. As Stephen Covey put it, "Most people do not listen with the intent to understand; they listen with the intent to reply."

I want you to be different. I want you to be the kind of person who offers others the "compassionate listening" mentioned above, the kind of listening that helps "relieve the suffering of another person" and helps them to "empty their heart."

I grew up hearing the saying, "God gave you two ears and one mouth because He wants you to listen more than you talk." There's a lot of wisdom in that statement.

At the same time, if God wanted to really drive home the point that we're to listen a lot more than we talk, He would have given us fifty ears and one mouth. That would have made all of us truly unpleasant to look at, so God cut us a lot of slack when He didn't go to that extreme to emphasize listening over talking. We need to thank Him for that.

Theologian Paul Tillich said, "The first duty of love is to listen." When we listen to others, we're loving them in one of the most important ways possible. Even when we can't do anything directly to help a person with their problems, just the fact that we listened deeply and compassionately helps more than we realize.

Munchkins, I want to give you some specific tips on how to be a better listener and encourage you to work on these listening skills for the rest of your life.

> #1: Maintain good eye contact. Look into a person's eyes when you're talking to them, not at the top of their shoes. As pediatrician Thomas Phaer observed, "The eyes are the windows of the soul," and we would be wise to look into people's eyes as a deeper way to listen to their souls.

> #2: Remove all distractions and don't multi-task when you're listening to others. Turn the television off, put your cell phone and computer away, and don't work on getting other things done. Psychiatrist M. Scott Peck wisely noted, "You cannot truly listen to anyone and do anything else at the same time."

> #3: Avoid judging what people say. Accept people's thoughts and feelings *as they are* whether you agree with

them or not. Theologian Dietrich Bonhoeffer rightly noted, "Judging others makes us blind, whereas love is illuminating."

#4: Don't try to fix or solve people's problems. We are to "Carry each other's burdens" (Galatians 6:2) by reaching out a helping hand, but "each one should carry their own load" (Galatians 6:5) by facing their own problems. Returning to M. Scott Peck's insightful observation, "It is only because of problems that we grow mentally and spiritually. It is through the pain of confronting and resolving problems that we learn."

#5: Ask clarifying questions. Don't assume you understand what others are saying. Ask them to tell you what they're thinking and feeling from as many different angles as possible. As psychiatrist Arthur Bloch noted, "Every clarification breeds new questions." Clarifying questions facilitate a deeper understanding of the inner experience of the person you're listening to.

#6: Try to feel what the other person is feeling. It's called "empathy," and it means walking compassionately in the other person's shoes to more deeply experience what they're going through. Psychologist Marshall Rosenburg defined empathy as "a respectful understanding of what others are experiencing" and that it "calls upon us to empty our mind and listen to others with our whole being."

#7: Pay attention to non-verbal clues. Experts suggest the vast majority of interpersonal communication is non-verbal (facial expressions, gestures, tone of voice, posture, body language). We need to pay special attention to this aspect of interacting with others. Leonard Mlodinow wisely noted, "Nonverbal communication forms a social language that is in many ways richer and more fundamental than our words."

#8: Listen for what's underneath a person's words. Psychologists call this "listening with your third ear," which means listening for the meaning behind people's words and even listening for what they're *not* saying. Peter Senge stated, "To listen fully means to pay close attention to what is being said beneath the words."

#9: Don't interrupt. When we interrupt others, we're communicating that we're not really listening. Let people finish what they're saying, even if it takes a while.

#10: Tell the person what you heard them say and provide feedback. To let someone know you're really listening, you need to state back to them what you heard them say, see if it was close enough for horseshoes as to what they were actually saying, and then give them your honest feedback without putting them down or being judgmental.

Munchkins, make listening deeply and compassionately a top priority. In a world of eight billion people, so many folks are emotionally starving to death for someone to truly listen and care about what they're going through. When you're in the presence of another human being, make sure you give them your full, undivided attention and offer them a compassionate and understanding heart.

8

PLEASE MIND YOUR MANNERS

Remind the people to be subject to
rulers and authorities, to be
obedient, to be ready to do whatever
is good, to slander no one,
to be peaceful and considerate, and
always gentle toward everyone.
—Titus 3:2

Be wise in the way you act toward
outsiders; make the most of every
opportunity. Let your conversation be
always full of grace, seasoned with salt, so
that you may know how to answer everyone.
—Colossians 4:5-6

Good manners: The noise you don't
make when you're eating soup.
—Bennett Cerf

I am a stickler for good manners, and I believe
that treating other people well is a lost art.
In the workplace, at the dinner table, and walking
down the street—we are confronted

> with choices on how to treat people nearly
> every waking moment. Over time these
> choices define who we are and whether we
> have a lot of friends and allies or none.
> —Tim Gunn

My Mom passed away over forty years ago when I was in my mid-twenties. She would have taken such delight in her grandkids (my kids, your parents) and been head-over-heels obsessed with you great-grandkids had she lived long enough to know you.

My Mom raised her four sons to practice good manners, no easy task given that we were typical boys who were pretty rough around the edges. While I didn't fully appreciate it at the time, I'm thankful my Mom cared about us turning out well in this particular area of life. I think she understood that if you are going to send your children into the world, you need to make sure they are well-versed in good manners.

For my Mom, good manners meant the following:

- Saying "Yes, sir" and "No, mam" not "Yea" or "Nah"
- Saying "Excuse me" and "I'm sorry, would you mind saying that again?" not "What!" or "Huh"
- Saying "Please" when you want something
- Saying "Thank you" when you get what you want
- At the dinner table, chewing with your mouth closed, pulling up to the table, keeping your elbows off the table, letting others be served first, never reaching across the table for food (ask someone to hand it to you), never talking with your mouth full, never slurping, always using a napkin, not rushing to eat and leave the table, participating in dinner conversation, having proper dinner conversation (no talking about gross stuff), and using utensils rather than your fingers
- Not talking too loudly, interrupting people, or dominating conversations
- Never using foul language, something Pop does on occasion even though he knows better

- Never burping or passing gas in public, something you munchkins find great delight in
- Saying "excuse me" when you need someone to move out of the way, not "move it or lose it" like some people in our family are prone to say
- Holding doors open for others
- Arriving on time out of respect for the fact that other people's time is as valuable as yours
- Paying attention to good hygiene—no one likes bad breath or body odor
- Offering your seat to those who are elderly, disabled, or physically compromised
- Not chewing gum in formal settings or smacking gum in any setting
- In movie theaters, never talking during a film, putting your feet on the chair in front of you, overreacting to what's happening on the screen, or being irritating in any way
- Not gossiping about others (either tell them to their face or keep it to yourself)
- Not touching or taking things that belong to someone else without their permission
- Cleaning up after yourself
- Not inviting yourself over to someone's house or presuming to stay too long when invited
- Standing up when adults enter the room and looking them in the eye
- Shaking hands firmly, not like a wet fish, when meeting or greeting someone
- Smiling at people rather than frowning
- Telling people what you like, not what you don't like
- Not commenting on how other people look unless you're paying them a compliment
- Knocking on closed doors and waiting for a response (unless you want to shock yourself and those inside the room you're entering)
- Not calling people mean names or making fun of them

- Covering your mouth or nose when you cough or sneeze
- Not grumbling when someone asks you to do them a favor
- Returning what you borrow
- Not yelling from across the house—finding the person you want to talk to and going to them
- Whether it seems sexist or not, if you're a man, holding doors open for women and pulling chairs out for them (yes, I know women are quite capable of doing these things for themselves, but my Mom taught me that doing this was good manners and I'm going to honor that)
- Always hugging and kissing your grandparents when you arrive and when you leave (that wasn't from my Mom, it was from me)

Munchkins, I could go on and on (as if I haven't gone on too much already!). I think you get the point—good manners are important and serve as your international passport to better relationships with others. Whether your peers, bosses, teachers, coaches, parents, or grandparents practice good manners or not, make sure you do—you'll never regret it.

WITHDRAW AND PRAY

But Jesus often withdrew to lonely places and prayed.
—Luke 5:16

Rejoice always, pray continually, and
give thanks in all circumstances;
for this is God's will for you in Christ Jesus.
—1 Thessalonians 5:17

Solitude is the furnace of transformation.
Without solitude we remain victims
of our society and continue to be entangled
in the illusions of the false self.
—Henri Nouwen

If you are not praying, then you are quietly
confident that time, money, and
talent are all you need in life. You'll always
be a little too tired, a little too busy.
But, if like Jesus, you realize you can't do
life on your own, then no matter how
busy, no matter how tired you are, you
will find the time to pray.
—Paul E. Miller

Each day, take some time to get away from the maddening crowd to quiet your soul and connect with God. Some of us do this so infrequently that weeks, even months, go by before we spend time alone with God.

There are two major mistakes we make when it comes to spending time with people rather than God. One is to be around people *too much* and not spend enough time with God. The other is to be around people *too little* and spend too much time with God. The idea that you can spend too much time with God may sound wrong, even heretical, but there are people who do just that. They take spending time with God (and studying the Bible) to such an obsessive level that they fall into the trap Oliver Wendell Holmes described, "Some people are so heavenly minded that they are of no earthly good."

Munchkins, try to find your sweet spot in all this. If you're the kind of person who likes to be around people all the time, *decrease* the amount of time you spend with others, get away by yourself more often, and spend more time connecting with God. If you're the kind of person who would be happy to spend all day by yourself, *increase* the amount of time you spend with others, get away by yourself a little less often, and spend more time connecting with God.

Related to the issue of spending time with God, I read an interesting article a long time ago that talked about how Jesus spent His day. The author (whose name I can't remember, otherwise I'd give him credit for writing the article) suggested that Jesus started His day by Himself in quiet places with God the Father, followed that by spending time with His disciples and then spent time ministering to the crowds who followed Him. Jesus's relational pecking order each day appears to have been God the Father, inner circle, outer circle.

I'm sure there were days Jesus didn't do things in this particular order, but it wouldn't surprise me if this was how He typically spent each day. I also wouldn't be surprised if after being with the crowd Jesus finished His day by spending time with His disciples and then spent time alone with God the Father. If this was the case, Jesus spent each day in the following order: God the Father, inner circle, outer circle, inner circle, God the Father. I'm making a lot of assumptions here, but this makes a lot of sense given what we know about the way Jesus lived His life.

I hope you will practice the same relational pecking order by beginning your day with God, spending time with loved ones, interacting with the crowd, spending time with loved ones, and ending the day with God. If you do, your life will be so much more emotionally, relationally, and spiritually healthy and your energy level will be renewed each day in ways that will probably surprise you.

Easier said than done, right? If you're like me, you're tired in the morning and don't feel like getting up early enough to spend time with God. If you're like me, you're tired in the morning and don't necessarily feel like interacting with loved ones. If you're like me, you're tired throughout the day and don't feel like interacting with all the folks who need your help. If you're like me, you're tired when you get home and don't feel like being around your family. And, if you're like me, you don't feel like ending the day being with God. All of these are reasons why I hope you're not like me.

Whether you feel like it or not, try to spend your day the way Jesus probably spent His—God, inner circle, outer circle, inner circle, God. Do whatever you can to get out of bed early enough to go off to a quiet place and spend time with God. Before you go to work (even if you're a stay-at-home mom or dad), connect with your family, even if it's just for fifteen minutes at the breakfast table. At work, pour yourself out as a drink offering to the people who need your help. Once you return home, reconnect with your family, even if it's just for fifteen minutes at the dinner table. Finally, before your head hits the pillow, withdraw to a quiet place and connect with God.

I wish I had practiced what I'm preaching here sooner in my life. When it comes to "withdraw and pray," I've spent most of my life as a workaholic focusing on the crowd first, my family second, friends third, and God fourth. My relational pecking order up until the last few years was outer circle, inner circle, God. All this did was lead to a life of exhaustion, guilt, and shallow relationships with everyone. Still, it's never too late to let God help you turn this around and get things in the proper pecking order.

You'll notice that I'm leaving something out here—time by yourself to just relax and refuel. It's important that you try to find time each day to go off by yourself for the purpose of putting some gas back in your tank—listening to music, taking a walk, reading a good book, enjoying a hobby, watching a good show, and the like. Tweaking the biblical idea to withdraw and *pray*, here I'm suggesting you withdraw and *play*.

Do yourself a favor, munchkins. Start your day with God, follow that by spending time with family and friends, follow that by spending time with people you serve at work, follow that by spending time with your family, and then follow that by spending time with God. And, somewhere in the midst of it all, do something fun by yourself for the pure enjoyment of it. Live this way, and you'll have a lot more energy for living life in an abundant manner.

LAUGH . . . A LOT

A cheerful heart is good medicine, but a
crushed spirit dries up the bones.
—Proverbs 17:22

There is a time for everything . . . a time to laugh . . .
—Ecclesiastes 3:1,4

Laugh my friend, for laughter ignites a fire within
the pit of your belly and awakens your being.
—-Stella McCartney

Laughter is the best medicine for a long
and happy life. He who laughs lasts!
—Wilferd Peterson

This bit of advice is something I don't really need to give you, but I'm going to give it to you anyway. None of you munchkins have trouble laughing, which is one of your more endearing qualities. In fact, there are times I can't get you to stop laughing, which I find really irritating.

I'm happy you enjoy a good laugh, I truly am. I'm old enough to remember reading *Reader's Digest* magazine as a kid, and it had a section called, *Laughter is the Best Medicine*, where there were funny jokes (at least most of them were funny). Laughter truly is the best medicine, and we need to laugh and laugh a lot as we go through life. So, I'm really happy you laugh as often as you do.

The reason I'm giving you the advice to laugh a lot is that life has a way of knocking all the laughter out of us over time. I'm not trying to be an Eeyore here, I'm simply saying that on this side of heaven things are often difficult and painful, and, if we're not careful, we stop laughing along the way. Don't let life do that to you.

Even in the midst of painful times, laugh. I'm not asking you to detach from reality by laughing about things that aren't funny. I simply want you to try to find the humor in situations no matter how dire or dark they may be. As Laura Ingalls Wilder put it, "A good laugh overcomes more difficulties and dissipates more dark clouds than any other one thing." Comedian Bob Hope put it this way: "I have seen what a laugh can do. It can transform almost unbearable tears into something bearable, even hopeful."

A related piece of advice—learn to laugh at yourself. You munchkins have gotten on me at times because I laughed at some of the funny things you've said or done. And, turncoat that you are, you told your parents "Pop was mean to me today" when they came to pick you up just because I laughed about something that came flying out of you. Nevertheless, I want you to be able to laugh at the fact that you're a delightful mess of a human being, have all kinds of funny flaws and foibles, and not get defensive about it.

Laugh at yourself—your mistakes, defects, irrational points of view, bad habits (like picking your nose) . . . you know, everything about you that makes you a human being and not a robot. Don't ever take yourself so seriously that you don't laugh at the fact that you are just like the rest of us . . . noticeably imperfect. You often say and do some pretty funny things, and I hope you'll be okay with laughing about it as your life unfolds.

For example, it was reported to me recently that one of you held up seven fingers and proceeded to say, "This is seven. When you take away two, it's five. When you take away five, it's two. It's hard to explain." That's hilarious. Out of the mouth of babes comes the funniest stuff on the planet, and we all thank you for that.

So, every day, take time to laugh at yourself, not in a denigrating way but in a self-compassionate, "Ain't I human like everyone else" way. Martin Niemoller said, "If you can laugh at yourself, you are going to be fine. If you allow others to laugh with you, you will be great." He's right. Rick Warren agrees, saying, "We take ourselves way too seriously, and we don't take God seriously enough. It is not by accident that humor and humility come from the same root word. If you can laugh at yourself, you'll always have plenty of good material."

Related to laughing a lot, associate with people who have a good sense of humor. Try not to be around too many dour, humorless folks—all they're going to do is bring you down. I've been blessed to have friends who make me laugh, something that always leaves my soul refreshed. There are times I've laughed so hard at what my friends have said or done that it made my stomach hurt. I will never be able to thank them enough.

Munchkins, you have a great sense of humor. Please hang on to it. Frankly, you're not all that good at laughing at yourself yet, so keep working on that. The next time I laugh at something you say or do, cut me some slack that I'm laughing *with* you, *not at you*. That way you won't turn me into your parents for being mean when I really wasn't.

I agree with Charles Swindoll when he said, "Of all the things God created, I am often most grateful He created laughter." Can you imagine life without it? I can't. Laugh every day, even about painful things. Laugh at yourself without putting yourself down. Laugh with others, not at them. Look for things to laugh about.

Laugh . . . a lot.

P.S. Don't let your parents talk you out of laughing at my "Dad jokes." I think I've got a great sense of humor, but your parents don't. They're wrong. I'm going to tell a lot of "Dad jokes" when I'm around you (you can call them "Pop jokes"), and I want you to laugh out loud so your parents stop being mean to me.

CRY . . . A LOT

There is a time for everything . . . a time to weep . . .
—Ecclesiastes 3:1,4

Jesus wept.
—John 11:35

To weep is to make less the depth of grief.
—William Shakespeare

There is a sacredness in tears. They are not
the mark of weakness, but of power.
They speak more eloquently than ten thousand
tongues. They are the messengers
of overwhelming grief, of deep contrition,
and of unspeakable love.
—Washington Irving

Not only are you going to laugh about a lot of things that happen in life, but you're also going to cry about a lot of things as well. At least you need to cry about them. Losses, failures, setbacks, and disappointments come our way while we're here, and our tears are the way we express the sadness we feel about these painful things.

Tears are a normal part of life, and you don't need to apologize when you cry about things that are worth crying about. Author Elizabeth

Gilbert is right when she says, "Do not apologize for crying. Without this emotion, we are only robots."

One of the keys to emotional health is to cry about the things we're supposed to cry about and not about the things that don't warrant our tears. I didn't allow myself to cry about my Mom's death when I was in my twenties, something I was supposed to cry about and remains ungrieved to this day. But I've "cried" far too often about all kinds of things that don't really matter, like the Texas Longhorns losing a football game.

Given that it's important to cry about the things we're supposed to cry about, I want to suggest that you cry about the following:

- Death of a loved one (especially when I pass away)
- Failing to achieve something you worked hard on
- People treating you badly
- Being laid off from a job you love
- Someone you love being unwilling to work on improving their relationship with you
- Sins you commit that hurt the heart of God, harm others, and damage your soul
- Suffering from a chronic illness
- Not having emotional support from others
- Not finding someone to be in an intimate relationship with

On the flip side, may I suggest that you *not* cry about the following:

- People not making you the center of the universe
- Life not giving you everything you want
- Not achieving unlimited success
- People not agreeing with everything you say
- Not getting your way all the time
- People calling you on the carpet when you've said or done something mean or selfish
- People ending a relationship with you when you won't stop mistreating them

- Being made to pay the consequences for your sinful actions
- Others being smarter, more talented, and more competent than you

What I'm trying to say here is that there is a time to cry and a time not to cry, and you need to be discerning about the difference. The same thing is true when it comes to other primary emotions—there's a time to be happy and a time not to be happy, there's a time to be angry and a time not to be angry, there's a time to be afraid and a time not to be afraid, and there's a time to feel guilty and a time not to feel guilty. Wisdom and maturity involve knowing the difference.

When you're not sure if your feelings about a particular event or situation are appropriate, ask around. The Bible says, "Plans fail for lack of counsel, but with many advisers they succeed" (Proverbs 15:22). I'm going to tweak that a little bit and say, "Without counsel, we aren't likely to understand if what we're feeling is appropriate. With input from many wise people, we will know."

One final thought about being sad and crying. Make sure you pull up alongside others when they're sad and help them cry it out (if they want you to—obviously, we don't ever force ourselves on someone who's sad). If we are going to be good friends to others, we need to "Rejoice with those who rejoice; mourn with those who mourn" (Romans 12:15).

On this side of heaven, there are a lot of things to be sad about—losses, failures, setbacks, and disappointments. When these kinds of things happen, allow yourself a good cry. Make sure you do, because stifling your tears can lead to being an emotionally unhealthy person. Susan Tamaro wisely observed, "Unshed tears leave a deposit on your heart. Eventually they form a crust around it and paralyze it, the way mineral deposits paralyze a washing machine."

Munchkins, don't let unshed tears form a crust around your heart. Don't let unshed tears paralyze your emotional "washing machine." When it's time to cry, give it all you got. As Charles Dickens noted, doing so "opens the lungs, washes the countenance, exercises the eyes, and softens down the temper; so cry away."

12

STAY IN THE HERE-AND-NOW

Therefore do not worry about tomorrow, for tomorrow will
worry about itself. Each day has enough trouble of its own.
—Matthew 6:34

Forget the former things; do not dwell on the past.
—Isaiah 43:18

Do not wait for life. Do not long for
it. Be aware, always and at every moment,
that the miracle is in the here and now.
—Marcel Proust

Disabused of our illusions by much travel
and travail, we awaken one day to find
that the sacred center is here and now -
in every moment of the journey,
everywhere in the world around us, and
deep within our own hearts.
—Parker J. Palmer

The here-and-now is hard to stay in, even though it's all we got. Unlike
Marty McFly in the movie, *Back to the Future* (yes, I'm dating myself
here—you probably aren't familiar with the movie I'm talking about),
we don't have the luxury of going back in time to shape how things turn
out or into the future to try to control them.

The tendency to mentally go back in time often leads to a lot of regrets, sadness, bitterness, guilt, and even self-condemnation. The tendency to project into the future often leads to becoming overly idealistic about how awesome things might be or overly anxious about how bad they might turn out.

Far too often, we look back in time and rub our faces in the mistakes we've made or rub other people's faces in the mistakes they've made. When we look ahead to the future, it is often with unrealistic expectations (delusions, really) about how everything is going to be sunshine, lollipops, and rainbows or full-blown panic about the possibility that everything is going to be a dumpster fire. Neither creates a sense of peace and confidence about the here-and-now that allows us to focus on the issues at hand. This, in turn, makes us less productive and effective in our day-to-day endeavors.

Out of the other side of my mouth, I would say there are times it's appropriate to look back in time and look ahead to the future. Let me explain.

While there are numerous legitimate reasons to look back in time, let me highlight two. First, it is healthy to look back in time to heal from past wounds. If we can find the courage to face the traumatic things that happened to us in the past, we can forgive those who wounded us and set ourselves free from what they did. Second, it is appropriate to look back in time to do what twelve-steppers call a "fearless moral inventory" where we take responsibility for the ways we've mistreated others, learn from it, and make amends where possible.

While there are numerous legitimate reasons to look ahead to the future, let me highlight two. First, we need to look ahead to the future to plan for what is coming our way. John J. Beckley said, "Most people don't plan to fail, they fail to plan." For example, we need to look into the future to plan for how much to put away for our children's education. Second, we need to look ahead to the future to decide what kind of boundaries to have with those who mistreat us in the here-and-now. It's unhealthy to allow people to mistreat us, and we need to make sure future interactions with these folks look a whole lot different if they continue to be abusive.

As a psychologist, I've seen clients who frequently don't do the things I'm talking about here. I've seen clients who refuse to look back in time to heal from their wounds, and they tend to stay embittered and unforgiving toward those who hurt them. I've seen clients who won't look back in time to take responsibility for how they've hurt others, and they tend to stay defensive and unrepentant. I've seen clients who won't look into the future to wisely plan for important things to come, and they tend to be impulsive and out of control. And I've seen clients who won't look into the future to create firm boundaries with those who have been abusive, and they tend to play the victim card.

Munchkins, try to avoid making these mistakes in life. Have the courage to look back in time to heal from the things that wounded you. Look back in time to take responsibility for how you wounded others and seek their forgiveness. Look ahead to wisely plan for the future. And look ahead so you can put firm boundaries in place with those who mistreat you.

One of my favorite writers, Henri Nouwen, once said, "Patience asks us to live the moment to the fullest, to be completely present to the moment, to taste the here and now, to be where we are. When we are impatient, we try to get away from where we are. We behave as if the real thing will happen tomorrow, later, and somewhere else. Let's be patient and trust that the treasure we look for is hidden in the ground on which we stand." I hope that as you live your life you will do as Nouwen suggests, patiently live the moment to the fullest, taste the here and now, and be where you are.

Munchkins, the treasure you're looking for in life is hidden in the ground on which you stand. Try to live in the here and now as much as you possibly can. When you look back in time or ahead to the future, do it for the purpose of living more fully in the moment. Forgive yourself and others for past mistakes and move on. Take the worries and fears you have about the future and do what you can to be ready for them should they happen. Leave everything else in the hands of God.

BE GRATEFUL, EVEN
FOR YOUR PROBLEMS

Give thanks to the Lord, for he is good.
His love endures forever.
—Psalm 136:1

Consider it pure joy, my brothers and sisters,
whenever you face trials of many kinds,
because you know that the testing of your faith
produces perseverance. Let perseverance
finish its work so that you may be mature
and complete, not lacking anything.
—James 1:2-4

Gratitude, like faith, is a muscle. The more
you use it, the stronger it grows.
—Alan Cohen

To be grateful is to recognize the love of God in everything.
—Thomas Merton

A spirit of entitlement runs rampant throughout our world today, and it's killing people's gratitude for the good things of life they already possess. Because many of us think we're entitled to "the good life" while we're here, we don't appreciate the wonderful things God blesses us with each and every day. And, to make matters worse, we feel bitter and resentful when God allows (not causes) bad things to happen.

Every human being has some degree of entitlement in them. None of us are completely free from thinking in this life-destroying way. It shows up when we think we're entitled to love, respect, fairness, kindness, justice, or a life free of bumps and bruises. Nothing will atrophy gratitude in the human heart faster than thinking we're entitled to the good things of life.

You munchkins are no different. So far, you seem to feel entitled to watch as many hours of cartoons as you want, eat as many snacks as you want, have as much fun as you want, get a new toy at Target whenever you want, and irritate Pop as often as you want—you know, normal kid stuff. I want you to start working NOW on trying to eliminate any spirit of entitlement that has found its way into your heart so that you will be more grateful as your life unfolds.

I grew up singing a song in church, *Count Your Many Blessings*. It was written by Johnson Oatman in 1897 (isn't that a perfect name for someone who lived in the 1800s?). The chorus of the song is "Count your blessings, name them one by one; Count your blessings, see what God hath done; Count your blessings, name them one by one; Count your blessing, see what God hath done." I'm glad we sang that song growing up because it reminded me to be grateful for all the blessings God showered me with along the way—family, education, health, friends, physical provision, hobbies, sports, and a hundred other wonderful things.

William Penn was right when he said, "The secret of happiness is to count your blessings while others are adding up their troubles." So true. Far too often, we're adding up all our troubles and only paying attention to the things we lack rather than the wonderful blessings we already have in life.

You're going to think I've lost my mind with what I'm about to say next. Not only do we need to be thankful for our blessings, we also need to be thankful for our problems and the suffering that goes with them. "Pop, come on, you can't be serious! Do you want me to be thankful for my problems and the suffering they cause? Have you lost your mind?"

Yes, I've lost mind mind. But I'm serious about how we need to be grateful for the painful problems that come our way. You see, problems help us grow. Without problems, all of us would stay immature, unappreciative, entitled little munchkins who never grow into full-fledged adults.

Psychiatrist M. Scott Peck wisely said, "It is in the whole process of meeting and solving problems that life has meaning. Problems are the cutting edge that distinguishes between success and failure. Problems call forth our courage and our wisdom; indeed, they create our courage and our wisdom. It is only because of problems that we grow mentally and spiritually." That's telling it like it is, don't you think?

All this reminds me of when Job was having a terrible, horrible, no good, very bad day back in Old Testament times. Job lost everything—his children, servants, livestock, and physical health. Yet, here's how Job responded to the terrible, horrible, no-good things that came his way, words that echo throughout human history: "Shall we accept good from God, and not trouble?" (Job 2:10). WWWWWHHHHHAAAAATTTTT? You gotta be kidding me! Yep, that's what he said. Maybe Job had lost his mind.

I don't think so. I think Job understood he wasn't *entitled* to the blessings of God, something that made him grateful for all of God's goodness and helped him handle adversity in the mature way he did. That's the heart of gratitude we're supposed to have in life. We're supposed to be grateful for all the good things that come from God, and we're supposed to accept and grow from the painful things that come from living in a fallen world that God wants to use to facilitate our growth into mature human beings.

It's important we don't get caught up in the spirit of entitlement that permeates our world today. Because so many people think they're entitled to all the good things of life, they don't truly appreciate all the good things they already have. For some folks, life is a never-ending, insatiable desire for more, and all they feel is miserable and unhappy.

Munchkins, count your blessings, name them one by one. Also, count (not add up) your problems, and name them one by one. Be grateful for both your blessings and your problems. As Ralph Waldo

Emerson put it, "Cultivate the habit of being grateful for every good thing that comes to you, and to give thanks continuously. And because all things have contributed to your advancement, you should include all things in your gratitude."

STAY HUMBLE

All of you, clothe yourself with humility
toward one another, because, "God opposes
the proud but shows favor to the humble."
—1 Peter 5:5

When pride comes, then comes disgrace,
but with humility comes wisdom.
—Proverbs 11:2

It is almost impossible to overestimate the value
of true humility and its power in the spiritual life.
For the beginning of humility is the beginning of
blessedness and the consummation of humility is the
perfection of all joy. Humility contains in itself the
answer to all the great problems of the life of the soul.
It is the only key to faith, with which the spiritual life
begins: for faith and humility are inseparable. In perfect
humility all selfishness disappears and your soul no
longer lives for itself or in itself for God: and it is lost
and submerged in Him and transformed into Him.
—Thomas Merton

> True humility is not an abject, groveling,
> self-despising spirit; it is but a right
> estimate of ourselves as God sees us.
> —Tryon Edwards

I once heard someone say that life has a way of taking your trophies from you. What I think they meant is that a lot of things come our way in life that take us down a notch or two and reveal us to be noticeably imperfect and flawed human beings who aren't as awesome as we, or others, might think we are. Some people allow this trophy-taking process to humble them, while others become more arrogant and prideful.

Munchkins, I want you to be prepared for the inevitable humbling that's coming your way. It's going to happen across numerous areas of life. Let me highlight seven.

First, life will humble you relationally. We're all noticeably imperfect when it comes to being able to develop close relationships with others. Every relationship we're in reveals just how flawed we are interpersonally when it comes to our ability to bond with others, and this painful reality is supposed to keep us humble.

Second, life will humble you intellectually. During our brief stay on this planet, we constantly run into the fact that we don't know very much and don't understand very much of what we know. Compared to an all-knowing, all-understanding God, we're all intellectual pipsqueaks (bet you haven't heard that word in a long time . . . if ever). That's supposed to keep us humble about how intelligent *we aren't*.

Third, life will humble you psychologically. We come into the world with a broken psyche (pronounced "sigh-key"), and we prove that all the time by not coping with the trials and tribulations of life in a mentally healthy manner. Each day is a test of our ability to cope well emotionally with the challenges of life, and we often come up short. That's supposed to keep us humble about our psychological health as we go through life.

Fourth, life will humble us when it comes to how talented and gifted we are compared to others. Each day is another reminder that there are lots of people out there who are significantly more talented and gifted than we are and lots of people who are more talented and gifted than them. That's supposed to keep us humble about the finite level of talent and ability we bring to the table while we're here.

Fifth, life will humble you in terms of how incompetent you are at the daily tasks of life. We're all incompetent to some degree at *everything* we do given we do everything in a noticeably imperfect manner. If you don't think that's true, you haven't gone through a drive-through lately and gotten home to find that they royally messed up your rather simple, hard-to-royally-mess-up order. None of us hit the ball out of the park when it comes to being fully competent workers, partners, parents, friends, citizens, and the like. That's supposed to keep us humble.

Sixth, life will humble you when it comes to your moral shortcomings. No one comes close to the moral perfection of Jesus Christ, not by a long shot. According to the Bible, our most righteous acts are like filthy rags in God's eyes (Isaiah 64:6) given that they are always stained by some degree of selfishness and impure motives. And, like it or not, we are going to commit major moral failures along the way, some that end up exposed to the general public (who, in their right mind, wants to be a celebrity and have their dirty laundry aired in public?). That's supposed to keep us humble.

Finally, life will humble you related to getting older. Everybody ages, but not everybody ages gracefully. I, for example, have not aged gracefully. It bugs the starch out of my shirts that I can't see as well, remember people's names (including my own), hear as well, and don't have the energy I once had (my get up and go got up and went). Our bodies fall apart as we get older, something that is supposed to keep us humble.

James Barrie, the novelist who created Peter Pan, said, "Life is a long lesson in humility." So true. We can rail against that fact, or we can eat humble pie and try to be at peace with it. The choice is ours, but I would strongly encourage you to go the humble pie route.

Munchkins, be humble when it comes to your interpersonal skills, intelligence, psychological health, talents and abilities, competence, moral integrity, and physical acumen. Don't think too highly of yourself, but don't think too lowly of yourself either. As English cleric Charles Caleb Colton put it, "He that places himself neither higher nor lower than he ought to do exercises the truest humility." Humbly accept the truth about everything you are—the good, the bad, and the ugly—and keep working on improving all of it before God takes you home.

HAVE COMPASSION FOR YOURSELF AND OTHERS

When Jesus landed and saw a large crowd,
he had compassion on them, because they
were like sheep without a shepherd.
—Mark 6:34

Be kind and compassionate to one another . . .
—Ephesians 4:32

There never was any heart truly great and generous,
that was not also tender and compassionate.
—Robert Frost

Spirituality is recognizing and celebrating
that we are all inextricably connected
to each other by a power greater than all
of us and that our connection to
that power and to one another is grounded
in love and compassion.
—Brené Brown

As I mentioned earlier, real estate agents are known for saying, "location, location, location," when it comes to selling homes. Here, I want to suggest that "compassion, compassion, compassion" is the proper mantra if you want to be a healthy human being.

Author and playwright Jane Stanton Hitchcock was right when she said, "Compassion is the most necessary ingredient in all relationships. Everything depends on it." I agree and would go further by saying that whether or not we have compassion toward others is the most important way to assess where our heart is at. As comedian Bob Hope put it, "If you haven't got any charity in your heart, you have the worst kind of heart trouble."

What is compassion? Timothy Miller suggests, "Compassion is the intention to see each human being as no better or worse than yourself, neither more nor less important, and as fundamentally similar to yourself." Henri Nouwen says, "Compassion asks us to go where it hurts, to enter into the places of pain, to share in brokenness, fear, confusion, and anguish. Compassion challenges us to cry out with those in misery, to mourn with those who are lonely, to weep with those in tears. Compassion requires us to be weak with the weak, vulnerable with the vulnerable, and powerless with the powerless. Compassion means full immersion in the condition of being human." Put these two statements together, and I think you have a pretty good idea of what compassion is all about.

Compassion is most frequently taught as something we are supposed to have for others, and that is certainly true. If we lack compassion for other people's struggles and pain, we're not living life in a spiritually and emotionally healthy manner. Each day, we need to redouble our efforts to have compassion for the suffering of others given that it is one of the main ways God draws us out of our unhealthy self-absorption.

At the same time, very few of us are taught to have compassion for ourselves. Just like airlines will tell you to put the oxygen mask on yourself first, we need to put the emotional oxygen mask of compassion on ourselves first to experience deeper compassion for others. Compassion for our own pain and suffering in life is just as important as compassion for the pain and suffering of those around us. As author Jack Kornfield put it, "If your compassion does not include yourself, it is incomplete."

We fall into a lot of misconceptions about compassion. We think it means pitying others. We think it means we're acting like we're better than others. We think we shouldn't have compassion toward those who live life in ways we find loathsome. We think that having compassion for ourselves means we're being selfish. All of this is nonsense, lies if you will.

First, compassion is not pity but *empathy* for the suffering others experience. Second, compassion doesn't imply we think we're better than others because we're not. It means we understand the suffering and pain they're going through as fellow human beings. Third, we're to have compassion for others regardless of how deplorably they act. Even if a person lives life in a way we find reprehensible, we're still supposed to have compassion for them as fellow human beings. And, finally, having compassion for ourselves is not selfish but humble and kind.

Take time each day to offer yourself compassion about the fact that your life has a lot of painful, challenging, and stressful things in it. As weird as it sounds, offer yourself compassion that you have hard things to do each day, people let you down and hurt you, you don't get enough appreciation and support, and on this side of heaven life is a contact sport that will knock you on your backside fairly often.

At the same time, take time each day to offer compassion to your fellow human beings that all this is true for them as well. Before you criticize or condemn someone for the way they live, try to have compassion they are struggling with life just like you. Try to have a humble, "There but for the grace of God go I" response to what others go through and how they are struggling to cope with life.

Something else. Compassion isn't just a feeling—it's supposed to lead to action. "Compassion is a verb" according to religious leader Nhat Hanh. He's right. It's great if you *feel* compassion for others, but it is even more important that you *express* compassion toward others by giving them attention, comfort, encouragement, support, and understanding and that you do acts of kindness to help them out. Don't tell people you feel compassion for them, show them.

Nelson Mandela observed, "Our human compassion binds us the one to the other—not in pity or patronizingly, but as human beings who have learnt how to turn our common suffering into hope for the future." That's right.

Munchkins, compassion for ourselves and others helps us stay humble about the fact that, as struggling human beings, we're all in this together . . . as equals. Offer compassion to yourself and others each day and you'll help make the world a better place to live.

16

DO THE HARD THINGS FIRST

Then he said to them all: "Whoever
wants to be my disciple must
deny themselves and take up their
cross daily and follow me.
—Luke 9:23

The word of the Lord came to Jonah son
of Amittai: "Go to the great city of Ninevah
and preach against it, because its wickedness
has come before me." But Jonah ran away
from the Lord and headed for Tarshish.
—Jonah 1:1-3

Avoiding problems you need to face is
avoiding the life you need to live.
—Paulo Coelho

Life is a series of problems. Do we want to
moan about them or solve them?
—M. Scott Peck

I'm not going all Freudian on you here, but old Siggy was right when he observed that people's natural bent is to seek pleasure and avoid pain. It's called the "pleasure principle." Given that life is a never-ending series of painful problems, we have a natural bent as human beings to run from our problems and the pain that goes along with them.

Tarthang Tulku wisely observed, "When a child encounters something he or she does not want, that child has all kinds of maneuvers to avoid it, such as crying, hiding, or fighting. . . Unless we are taught to face our problems directly and work through them, the pattern of avoidance will be repeated; it can be a natural, accepted way to act." For far too many of us, running from our problems in a childish manner is a natural, accepted way to act.

That's not good, and there are two primary reasons why.

First, when we run from our problems, they only get worse. Psychiatrist R. D. Laing was right when he said, "Pain in this life is not avoidable, but the pain we create avoiding pain is avoidable." Running from your problems is a fool's errand because ultimately the bill comes due down the road and is much higher.

Second, when we run from our problems, we get in the way of developing into more mature human beings. Psychiatrist M. Scott Peck noted, "When we avoid the legitimate suffering that results from dealing with problems, we also avoid the growth that problems demand from us." Being a problem avoider means you're a growth-avoider.

So, it's a doubly bad thing when we run from our problems—we suffer at a much higher level down the road and we delay growing into full-fledged adults. These two reasons alone ought to motivate us to face our problems every day.

Munchkins, I'm preaching to myself here. I can't tell you how many times I've run from my problems only to bring more suffering into my life and delay becoming a more mature adult. Let me give you just one example.

One time I heard some critters banging around up in my attic. What did I do about it? Nothing. This went on for over a month before I noticed a dark, smelly stain on the ceiling. Finally, I decided to face my problem as a homeowner and called the pest control folks. They came out and laid some traps. Three days later, they came back and removed three of the biggest honking raccoons from my attic that I had ever seen in my life.

What's my point? Well, my point is that had I called the pest control people the first day I heard those terrorists ransacking my attic, I would have only been out $300 and a couple of hours of my time. Because I waited for over a month, I was out a lot more money and a lot more time to deal with the tornado-like damage they caused in my attic. By the way, the smelly brown stain was from them using the bathroom in the same place over and over.

There's a biblical example of what I'm talking about here that involves the infamous problem-avoider, Jonah. God told Jonah to go preach to the wicked city of Ninevah. Ninevah was Las Vegas on steroids. Jonah didn't want to do such a painful thing because he understandably feared he wouldn't be well received. So, he boarded a boat and traveled in the direction of Tarshish. If you've ever looked at a map for that time period, and, I'm concerned about you if you have, Tarshish is in the opposite direction from Ninevah.

What did Jonah get for all his problem-avoiding ways? He got tossed overboard by the men who were taking him to Tarshish and ended up spending three days in the belly of a large fish (I was told as a kid it was a whale, but we don't know that for sure). Plus, he ended up going to Ninevah anyways.

Take a step back and look at what happened to Jonah. He ran from his problem (preaching to the folks in Ninevah), got tossed overboard and spent time inside a fish (unnecessary suffering he brought on himself), and ended up preaching to the not-so-wonderful folks in Ninevah anyway (the legitimate suffering he was supposed to experience the first time). Sometimes, we're our own worst enemies, something that was certainly true of Jonah that day.

Nonnie and Pop were determined as parents to not let our kids run from their problems. That's why we called one summer the "Summer of Hard Things First." That whole summer, much to their chagrin, our kids had to do painful things first before they could do anything pleasurable. They didn't particularly like that summer, but it was one of the best they ever had from a personal growth standpoint. I believe that particular summer laid the foundation for them to be as successful as they are as adults. I think they would agree.

Everywhere we turn, we're going to have difficult, painful problems. That's called life. What separates the men from the boys and the women from the girls is whether or not we face our problems and resolve them or run in the opposite direction and avoid them.

Munchkins, do yourself a favor and learn to do the hard things first. Do the painful things before you do the pleasurable things. Do your chores before you play video games, get some exercise before you wolf down a dozen donuts, and do your homework before you watch television. Fight that part of you that would allow running from your problems to ruin your life. Do the hard things first so your suffering in life will be the healthy kind that helps you grow into a mature adult. You don't want to end up in the belly of a large fish for three days, do you?

STRIVE FOR EXCELLENCE,
NOT PERFECTION

There is no distinction, for all have sinned
and fall short of the glory of God . . .
—Romans 3:22-23

I do not understand what I do. For what I want
to do I do not do, but what I hate I do.
—Romans 7:15

Sometimes you think that you need to be
perfect, that you cannot make mistakes ...
realize you are a human being - like everyone
else capable of reaching great potential but
not capable of being perfect.
—Susan Polis Schutz

Perfectionism is the voice of the oppressor; the enemy
of the people. It will keep you insane your whole life.
—Anne Lamott

We've already talked about it, but one of the things to watch out for in
life is trying to be perfect. Very few things will cause you more anxiety,
depression, and self-condemnation than trying to be something you
can't be. Samuel McChord Crothers wisely observed, "Try as hard as we
may for perfection, the net result of our labors is an amazing variety of

imperfectness. We are surprised at our own versatility in being able to fail in so many different ways."

That's right. Like it or not, our whole life is going to be "an amazing variety of imperfectness" and example after example of how "to fail in so many different ways." Please, accept how imperfect you are rather than spend your whole life trying to be perfect only to discover that, as author Hugh Prather put it, "perfectionism is slow death."

Pop has spent the bulk of his life trying to be perfect and that is why he's always been such an anxious, sad, and shame-based human being (even though he's a psychologist—figure that!). When I was a kid, I used to do homework assignments over if I had any erasures. When I was a little league baseball player, I was upset after hitting a home run because it hit the top of the outfield fence before going over (not perfect enough!). As someone who plays a lot of golf, I put myself under constant pressure to hit every shot perfectly, something that only makes my shots worse and my score climb higher than the national debt.

May I offer you an alternative to perfectionism? Excellence. Excellence is a mindset that will actually help you along the way rather than harm you. As psychologist Harriet B. Braker put it, "Striving for excellence motivates you; striving for perfection is demoralizing."

Let me distinguish between perfection and excellence in five different ways. I stole this from another mental health professional decades ago but can't remember who it was. Otherwise, I would give him credit for being so wise about how to live life in a healthy manner.

Perfectionism is idealistic, excellence is realistic. Perfectionists think about how things "should" be in an ideal world and set goals at an unreachable level. People who strive for excellence think about how things actually are in the real world and set goals that are challenging but within reach.

Perfectionism is product-minded, excellence is process-minded. Perfectionists postpone happiness, joy, and a sense of victory until they've accomplished what they're working on. People who strive for excellence focus on the process, pay attention to what they can do in the here-and-now, and believe that the joy is in the journey and not arriving at the destination.

Perfectionism is about being the best, excellence is about being your best. Perfectionists often compare themselves with others to see how they stack up against the competition and feel that they have to be #1. People who strive for excellence couldn't care less about being the best and simply try to be the best version of themselves they can be. The old Army slogan, "Be all that you can be" makes sense to those who want to be excellent.

Perfectionism avoids feedback, excellence welcomes it. Perfectionists don't like feedback about how they could do things better. In fact, they often resent it. People who strive for excellence want feedback because it helps them get better at the things they do. They know that apart from accurate feedback they are not likely to improve or become the best person they can be in the various roles they play in life.

Perfectionism ties worth to performance, excellence ties worth to being made in the image of God. Since our performance goes up and down, a perfectionist's sense of worth goes up and down with it. People who strive for excellence anchor their worth in being made in the image of God, something that never fluctuates. Consequently, their sense of worth never fluctuates.

G. K Chesterton was right when he said, "If it's worth doing, it's worth doing badly." He understood that "To err is human" and we need to do the best we can no matter how badly we mess things up. At the same time, we need to balance Chesterton's statement with Josh Jenkins' humorous take, "To err is human, but when the eraser wears out ahead of the pencil, you're overdoing it." Somewhere between Chesterton and Jenkins is the sweet spot we need to find in life—knowing we are going to make mistakes but trying to do the best we can.

One other thing about perfectionism. Underneath it you will frequently find toxic feelings of shame and self-hatred related to growing up in a wounding, conditionally loving world. Some of us falsely believe that, if we could just be perfect, we would finally be acceptable to others, have nothing to feel insecure about, and be worthy of their love.

It just doesn't work that way. Even if you were perfect, which is impossible, people would still treat you badly. Case in point: Jesus Christ. Christ was perfect in every way but people frequently condemned Him and treated Him hatefully. Being perfect doesn't eliminate people treating you badly—it usually invites more of it. So, in a weird way, it's actually a good thing we can't be perfect. Think of all the abuse we avoid.

Munchkins, strive to be excellent, not perfect. One is doable, the other is delusional. Don't let the unhealthy pursuit of perfection drive you into anxiety attacks, depression, despair, self-condemnation, shame, and hopelessness. Excellence is within reach each day and doesn't carry all the toxic emotional baggage of perfectionism with it.

But, please, be careful not to let your eraser wear out ahead of your pencil.

FORGIVE OTHERS . . .
AND YOURSELF

Be kind and compassionate to one another, forgiving
each other, just as in Christ God forgave you.
—Ephesians 4:32

Bear with each other and forgive one
another if any of you have
a grievance against someone. Forgive
as the Lord forgave you.
—Colossians 3:13

By far the strongest poison to the human spirit is the
inability to forgive oneself or another person. Forgiveness
is no longer an option but a necessity for healing.
—Caroline Myss

He that cannot forgive others breaks the
bridge over which he must pass himself;
for every man has need to be forgiven.
—Thomas Fuller

You can't go through life and not be wounded by others. And, you can't
go through life and not wound others. It's called being human. All of
us are far too fallen (selfish, lazy, and immature) to not do things that
wound each other.

The real issue here is whether or not we are going to forgive those who hurt us and seek forgiveness from those we hurt. Henri Nouwen put it beautifully when he said, "Forgiveness is the name of love practiced among people who love poorly. The hard truth is that all people love poorly. We need to forgive and be forgiven every day, every hour increasingly. That is the great work of love among the fellowship of the weak that is the human family."

The struggle to forgive is tied to the fact that we have a lot of misconceptions about what forgiveness really means. Here are seven of the deadliest misconceptions we have about forgiving others.

Some people wrongly believe that we only forgive a person if they are truly sorry for what they did and have made amends.

Some people wrongly believe that forgiveness means forgetting the wrong that was done.

Some people wrongly believe that to forgive means we're saying what the other person did was no big deal.

Some people wrongly believe forgiving others means we're saying their actions didn't hurt.

Some people wrongly believe that forgiving others is "a moment in time" that permanently resolves the issue.

Some people wrongly believe that to forgive someone means we shouldn't let negative consequences come their way for what they did.

And, some people wrongly believe forgiving others means we automatically reconcile with them.

All this is false and gets in the way of choosing, *as an act of will*, to forgive others for the wrongs they commit against us.

True forgiveness isn't tied to whether or not a person admits they did something wrong, is sorry for having done it, or has made amends. With some folks, we're going to wait a long time, if not a lifetime, for them to take responsibility for what they did, be genuinely sorry for their hurtful actions, and help heal the wound they inflicted.

True forgiveness doesn't mean we forget what a person did. We can't forget the deeply hurtful things people do; we simply choose not to hold what they did against them.

True forgiveness involves acknowledging something was a big deal and too hurtful to ignore. If what a person did wasn't a big deal, we don't need to forgive them for it.

True forgiveness is both a specific moment-in-time decision and a lifelong process of forgiving over and over again.

True forgiveness doesn't get in the way of letting the natural consequences come down on the person who did the hurtful thing. In general, people need to pay the consequences for the wrong and hurtful things they do.

True forgiveness doesn't automatically lead to reconciliation. Reconciliation takes two people, one who is genuinely sorry for what they did wrong and one who is willing to forgive them for it. There are times in relationships when reconciliation isn't possible or even wise. If a person isn't sorry for what they did, reconciliation can't take place. If a person is unwilling to forgive someone for what they did wrong, reconciliation can't take place.

Munchkins, please don't let anything get in the way of forgiving people for the wrongs they do to you. Forgiveness is a choice, and it's a choice you make so you can break free from what the person did. As Lewis Smedes said, "To forgive is to set a prisoner free and discover that the prisoner was you."

There's another side to the issue of forgiveness that's important to mention. We need to forgive ourselves for the wrong things we have done. We all do immoral things that hurt others. Not only do we stand in need of their forgiveness, but we need to forgive ourselves for what we did as well. Ruth Carter Stapleton was right to say, "Self-forgiveness is essential to self-healing." Don't withhold forgiveness from yourself as if your standards are higher than God's. They aren't. If God forgives you for all the wrong things you've done, forgive yourself for them as well.

Corrie Ten Boom, who survived the horrors of Nazi concentration camps during World War II, observed, "Forgiveness is the key that unlocks the door of resentment and the handcuffs of hatred. It is a power that breaks the chains of bitterness and the shackles of selfishness." Do yourself a favor and forgive others for how they have mistreated you, forgive yourself for how you've mistreated others, and seek forgiveness from those you've mistreated.

Poet Alden Nowlan observed, "The day the child realizes that all adults are imperfect, he becomes an adolescent; the day he forgives them, he becomes an adult; the day he forgives himself, he becomes wise." Choose to be both an adult and wise by forgiving others and forgiving yourself. There's no other healthy way to live.

STAND UP TO EVIL

When it was almost time for the Jewish Passover,
Jesus went up to Jerusalem. In the temple courts, he
found people selling cattle, sheep, and doves, and
others sitting at tables exchanging money. So he made
a whip out of cords, and drove all from the temple
courts, both sheep and cattle; he scattered the coins
of the money changers and overturned their tables.
—John 2:13-15

There are six things the Lord hates, seven
that are detestable to him: haughty
eyes, a lying tongue, hands that shed
innocent blood, a heart that devises
wicked schemes, feet that are quick to
rush into evil, a false witness who
pours out lies, and a person who stirs
up conflict in the community.
—Proverbs 6:16-19

Silence in the face of evil is evil itself.
—Dietrich Bonhoeffer

The only thing necessary for the triumph of
evil is for good men to do nothing.
—Edmund Burke

This was a hard chapter to write. No parent or grandparent I know wants to talk to young'uns about there being evil in the world, much less challenge them to be ready, willing, and able to stand up to it when necessary. Nevertheless, we live in a world where "our struggle is not against flesh and blood, but against the rulers, against the authorities, against the powers of this dark world and against the spiritual forces of evil in the heavenly realms" (Ephesians 6:12). So, we gotta talk about it.

Munchkins, I'm going to bunny trail a little and then wrap up by challenging you to have the courage to oppose evil whenever you feel called to do so. I say "whenever you feel called to do so" because evil is too widespread and deeply entrenched in our world for any of us to oppose it every time and everywhere we see it rear its ugly head.

First, I encourage you to distinguish between *evil deeds* and an *evil person*. All of us commit evil (sinful) deeds, but doing so doesn't make us an evil person. An evil person is someone who militantly refuses to acknowledge their "dark side," unrepentantly commits one evil deed after another, and has no remorse about it. On a worldwide scale, think of Adolf Hitler, Joseph Stalin, and Pol Pot (look them up).

For example, all people lie (evil/sinful deed) but not all people are pathological liars (evil person). It's the pathological liars who are evil people because all that comes out of their mouths is one lie after another, and they couldn't care less. It's why we know Satan is an evil spiritual entity—he's the "father of lies," lying is his native tongue, and he is utterly remorseless about being a pathological liar (John 8:44).

Second, it is important to understand what makes something an evil deed. Being ten minutes late meeting someone for lunch is not an evil deed, it's just inconsiderate (unless you have a good reason for why you're late). If you want to know what makes something an evil deed, refer to the Ten Commandments (Exodus 20:2-17), the seven things God hates (Proverbs 6:16-19), and the description of a "lover of self" in 2 Timothy 3:1-5. These three passages give us a pretty good sense of what God considers to be an evil/sinful deed. When you run into a person doing something that *doesn't* make these lists, you might want to ask yourself if what they did was evil or just insensitive, rude, or inconsiderate.

Third, and this goes back to the chapter about hanging around good people, don't hang around evil people. Ever. Bad company corrupts good morals, and evil people are the worst kind of bad company to keep. Don't hang around those who chronically do evil things, have no remorse about it, and never repent. While you may need to be in their presence at times, don't make a habit of being around them. Evil people will always take you down with them.

Fourth, be willing to let God show you your dark side and the evil/sinful deeds you commit. We all have a dark side that leads us to do sinful things. In the Bible, it's called the "flesh." If you find yourself running from admitting that you are as fallen as the rest of us, call me and I'll talk you into facing your defects and repenting of them.

Fifth, try not to project your dark, sinful side onto others. I spent years projecting my anger issues onto others rather than facing the fact that I was the one with the anger problem. Ask God to help you be more honest about how dark some of your feelings, thoughts, and actions are at times, and let Him help you take the plank out of your own eye before you look at the speck in someone else's.

Sixth, be aware of the fact that evil people are skilled at making bad look good and good look bad. Swedish playwright and novelist August Strindberg correctly observed, "Now I know the full power of evil. It makes ugliness seem beautiful and goodness seem ugly and weak." Evil people are the kind of folks the Bible warns about, saying "Woe to those who call evil good and good evil, who put darkness for light and light for darkness, who put bitter for sweet and sweet for bitter" (Isaiah 5:20). If you spend too much time around evil people, you'll get pretty confused about what's up and what's down morally. Don't—have nothing to do with them.

Finally, stand up to evil people when and where you feel called to do so, but don't try to talk an evil person into taking responsibility for their actions or being repentant. It never works. It's pearls before swine. If someone is an evil person, they're never going to admit it and will resent the fact that you think they're that way. Evil people are good at "gaslighting" others, which means they're good at getting others to think they're evil when it's actually them.

Munchkins, I wish the world wasn't so full of evil deeds and evildoers, but it is. Make sure you face your fallen bent toward doing sinful *deeds* and make sure you stand up against evil deeds and evildoers at the right time and in the right way. Like it or not, we are constantly under attack from spiritual forces of darkness, and they do everything they can to get us to play along with their malevolent agenda to kill, steal, and destroy all of us who occupy the planet together. Align with the God of light, not the god of darkness.

READ A LOT OF REALLY GOOD BOOKS

Blessed is the one who does not walk in
step with the wicked or stand in the
way that sinners take or sit in the company
of mockers, but whose delight
is in the law of the LORD, and who
meditates on his law day and night.
—Psalm 1:1-2

For the word of God is alive and active.
Sharper than any double-edged sword,
it penetrates even to dividing soul and
spirit, joints and marrow; it judges the
thoughts and attitudes of the heart.
—Hebrews 4:12

Read the best books first, or you may not
have a chance to read them all.
—Henry David Thoreau

To read is to fly: it is to soar to a point of vantage
which gives a view over wide terrains
of history, human variety, ideas, shared
experience and the fruits of many inquiries.
—A.C. Grayling

I'd put this chapter right up there with the "Hang Around Good People" chapter. As author Paxton Hood put it, "Be as careful of the books you read, as of the company you keep; for your habits and character will be as much influenced by the former as the latter."

Let me start with some statistics about people's reading habits in the United States. Apparently, a lot of Americans don't value reading all that much.

- 23% of adults haven't read a book in the last 12 months
- Americans aged 20 to 34 spend just 6 minutes reading a day
- Romance is the most popular genre
- The average literacy rate in the United States ranges from seventh to eighth grade
- The average number of books Americans read has been declining over the years, recently dropping to 12.6 books a year
- In 2018, the literacy rate in the United States was 28th compared to other countries (I would give you more current data, but, for the life of me, I couldn't find any)

To encourage you to read more, I want to talk about Belle, the central character in the film, *Beauty and the Beast*. If you remember the movie, Belle was made fun of because she loved to read. All the townspeople thought she was odd because of her passion for books. When she returned a book to the local bookshop, she always got another one even if she had read it before. Belle had a voracious appetite for books.

Belle's harshest critic in *Beauty and the Beast* was the town's leading misogynist, Gaston. Gaston was the stereotypical "tall, dark, and handsome" town stud who the women swooned over (except for Belle, who couldn't stand him) and the men wanted to emulate. Gaston could kill anything he shot at, eat five dozen eggs a day to stay "as large as a barge" (who would want to be as large as a barge other than a narcissist?), and was "especially good at expectorating" (who would want to be especially good at spitting other than a narcissist?).

Gaston was bothered by two things when it came to Belle—that she wasn't the least bit interested in him and that she read so much. One of the iconic lines in *Beauty and the Beast* is when Gaston scolds Belle for her reading habits saying, "The whole town is talking about it! It's not right for a woman to read! Soon she starts getting ideas . . . and thinking!" Gaston thought it was abhorrent that a woman would read, get ideas, and start thinking! How Belle wasn't drawn to someone as awesome as Gaston is beyond me!

Belle responds to all this by calling Gaston "primeval." Given that he is not the least bit well-read, Gaston thinks it's a compliment and thanks her. Belle's love of reading put her light years ahead of Gaston in terms of being a thoughtful, wise, and mature human being, and she was understandably not interested in spending the rest of her life with someone like him.

I could be stretching things here, but I believe one of the reasons Belle was an *internally* beautiful person is because she read so much. I think that's the impact good books have on us. I think Gaston was an internally ugly human being because he probably hadn't cracked a book his whole life. That Belle read so many books is one of the main reasons she was wise enough to not fall into the arms of such a toxic human being like Gaston.

Munchkins, God gave you a good mind and wants you to use it. To use your mind well, here's some advice. First, read a lot of books. Second, try to make sure the books you read are good ones. Third, read each book as deeply and thoroughly as you can. And, fourth, read the great books over and over again. As Francis Bacon put it, "Some books are to be tasted, others to be swallowed, and some few to be chewed and digested."

I'm not going to give you a list of books to read other than I think you should read all the ones I've written, especially this one. Seriously, what you read is up to you. I would suggest you read the Bible every day and twice on Sunday. Franklin D. Roosevelt wisely said, "A thorough reading of the Bible is worth more than a college education."

I would tweak that a little by saying, "A thorough, Holy Spirit-led reading of the Bible is worth more than a college education." The reason I say this is that there are a lot of people who have thoroughly read the Bible but who put it to malevolent use, leaving the world much worse off in the process. For example, people used the Bible to justify slavery.

That, alone, ought to tell you how important it is that the Holy Spirit guides your reading of the Bible.

Matthew Henry wisely noted, "If you take a book into your hands, be it God's book, or any other useful good book, rely on God to make it profitable to you. Do not waste time reading unprofitable books. When you read, do so not out of vain curiosity but with love for God's kingdom, compassion for human beings, and the intent to turn what you learn into prayers and praises."

Munchkins, do yourself a favor and read a lot of really good books. You don't want to turn out like Gaston, do you?

ACCEPT YOURSELF AND OTHERS, WARTS AND ALL

Accept one another, then, just as Christ accepted
you, in order to bring praise to God.
—Romans 15:7

Therefore let us stop passing judgment on one
another. Instead, make up your mind
not to put any stumbling block or obstacle
in the way of a brother or sister.
—Romans 14:13

Acceptance is simply love in practice. When you love,
you accept, when you lack love, you judge.
—Abhijit Naskar

The older I get, the more I believe that the
greatest kindness is acceptance.
—Christina Baker Kline

A lot of us go through life refusing to accept others because they have flaws and defects. We let the fact that people have bad qualities get in the way of fully accepting them "warts and all."

Our refusal to accept people's warts is one of the most unloving things we can do in our relationships with others. Rejecting others because of their flaws unconsciously puts us in the morally superior position of thinking we're better than them. Nothing could be further from the truth. We're not better than others, and others aren't better than us, at least not compared to Jesus Christ.

Our refusal to accept other's flaws and deficiencies is often tied to the erroneous notion that if we accept people as they are, we're saying we're okay with their negative qualities. That's not what accepting other's defects means. Accepting other's peccadillos means we're not going to let the fact that others have negative qualities get in the way of having a relationship with them as fellow human beings struggling to make their way through life.

Truth be told, we aren't supposed to like everything about a person because everything about a person isn't likable. Some things about human beings are not only unlikeable but deplorable. Nevertheless, we're supposed to accept and love people *as they are* however dark things may be about how they think, feel, and act. We've heard it a thousand times, but we are to love the sinner, not the sin.

This applies to ourselves as well. We often refuse to accept ourselves until we eliminate all of our flaws and imperfections. "I'm only going to accept myself when I am free of all the deficiencies and defects that have plagued my life" is a common attitude many of us have. Unfortunately, if we refuse to accept ourselves or others until we all get our act together, we are going to wait forever. No one ever completely gets their act together on this side of heaven.

Another painful truth is that we often reject others because they have the same flaws we do. Let me put that differently. When we criticize and reject a person for their flaws, we usually have the same flaws. For example, I often find myself criticizing selfishness in others when that is something I struggle with on a daily basis.

Accepting our own and other people's messsedupness (that's not a word, but I like it and am going to use it) doesn't mean we're okay with having flaws or not going to do anything about correcting them. It just means we're not going to spend the rest of our lives refusing to accept others or ourselves until everyone is flaw-free. NONE OF US ARE EVER GOING TO BE FLAW-FREE!

We human beings simply can't pull off perfection in our own power. Even with God's power, we are still going to be highly messed up folks.

We've got to learn how to accept the reality of our own and other people's messedupness while having the courage to grow and improve as human beings.

Strangely enough, we sometimes struggle to accept the *positive things* about people as well. We let jealousy and envy get in the way of accepting the good qualities others have. Sadly, it can be too threatening to our ego to fully accept the positive attributes people have that we don't possess. Not good.

Related to this, some of us have a hard time accepting our own good qualities, erroneously thinking that we're being prideful or arrogant if we acknowledge we have strengths, abilities, talents, positive traits, likable qualities, and moral integrity we can feel good about. I've seen far too many people refuse to accept the upside side of who they are while simultaneously refusing to accept their downside as well.

We face quite a dilemma as we go through life, and it goes something like this: "Am I going to fully accept others and myself warts and all, or am I going to reject myself and others because we're all so deeply flawed?" The answer to that question will make or break our relationship with others, our relationship with ourselves, and even our relationship with God. God accepts us warts and all, but even He can't have a close relationship with us if we run from Him because we're a big honking mess.

Munchkins, I want you to accept others as they are and accept yourself as you are. Please, stop rejecting yourself and others just because of how fallen and broken we are. The world is full of nothing but fallen and broken people, every one of whom thirsts to be fully accepted as they are before anyone challenges them to get their act together.

Author Robert Greene wisely noted, "The most effective attitude to adopt is one of supreme acceptance. The world is full of people with different characters and temperaments. We all have a dark side, a tendency to manipulate, and aggressive desires . . . Some people have dark qualities that are especially pronounced. You cannot change such people at their core, but must merely avoid becoming their victim. You are an observer of the human comedy, and by being as tolerant as possible, you gain a much greater ability to understand people and to influence their behavior when necessary." Now, those are some words to live by.

22

STOP SHOULDING ALL OVER YOURSELF

"Do not judge, or you too will be judged."
—Matthew 7:1

You, therefore, have no excuse, you who
pass judgment on someone else, for at
whatever point you judge another, you are
condemning yourself, because you who
pass judgment do the same things.
—Romans 2:1

Shoulds' come only from leftover thinking.
If we are truly in this moment (the
only one there really is), we don't should
on ourselves. It's a great freedom.
—Kelly Corbet

Should is my all-time least favorite word.
It's this sort of guilt-inducing,
finger-wagging word that we use to
beat up others and ourselves.
—Frank Beddor

This chapter is my most self-indulgent because I wrote a book on this particular topic, *Stop Shoulding All Over Yourself.* No one read it, but I wrote it. So, if you will permit me, I'd like to pontificate for a couple of pages about the evils of shoulding all over yourself and others as you go through life.

First, there are very few words in the English language that are more toxic than "should" and "shouldn't." Any time these two words bang around in your head much less come out of your mouth, you have just left the reality of what's actually going on and are going to bring shame and self-condemnation on yourself and others. As Margaret Atwood put it, "*Should* is a futile word. It's about what didn't happen. It belongs in a parallel universe. It belongs in another dimension of space."

Second, one of the main reasons should and shouldn't are such toxic words is that they lead us to stiff-arm reality just because it's not how we want it to be. When we say, "I shouldn't have missed my exit," we're refusing to accept the painful reality that we missed our exit, something we didn't want to happen. When we refuse to accept things as they are, our mental health goes flying out the window and we're not going to deal with setbacks and miscues in an emotionally healthy manner.

Third, when we should all over ourselves, we're talking to ourselves in a way that is condemning and shaming. We're putting ourselves down for being fallen human beings who prove our fallenness every day by doing the misguided and foolish things we do. Should and shouldn't are words that guarantee a life of self-hatred and self-rejection.

Fourth, shoulding all over ourselves causes us to miss out on one of the most important truths of all, "What should have happened did." For example, when you're four lanes over and texting on your cell phone, *you should have missed your exit and did*. What would have been more surprising in a situation like that is you actually making your exit, not missing it. "I should have . . ." or "I shouldn't have . . ." forces us to completely deny and ignore the fact that all the internal and external stars were aligned for us to do exactly what we did.

Fifth, shoulding all over ourselves leads to shoulding all over others. Anytime we get on our own case for being human, we're so much more likely to get on the case of others for being human as well. We're going to should all over every person we know if we don't stop doing it to ourselves. Just like we need to offer ourselves compassion and acceptance first to be able to offer them more fully to others, we need to stop shoulding all over ourselves first in order to stop shoulding all over the folks who occupy the planet with us.

Sixth, shoulding all over ourselves is especially likely when we commit a major moral failure. It's one thing to miss an exit, but it's a whole different matter when we break one of the Ten Commandments like murdering someone, committing adultery, or bearing false witness about someone that damages their reputation. If we should all over ourselves about the small stuff, we're going to should all over ourselves ten times worse about the big stuff.

Let me quickly walk you into one of the deadliest shoulds of all, "People should always give me what I want when I want it." This is one of the most narcissistic shoulds we have in life, and is extremely damaging to our mental health and the mental health of those around us. Why is this such a toxic way to think about things? A few reasons come to mind.

First, just because you want something doesn't mean the rest of the world is going to suddenly stop and deliver the goods. Everyone has their own life and needs to attend to, and no healthy person is going to meet your every wish and whim just because you want them to.

Second, some of the things you want are selfish, unhealthy, and immoral, and no one in their right mind would give those things to you. Let's say you want someone to worship the ground you walk on or agree with everything you say. Neither are legitimate wants, and people are only demeaning and denigrating themselves to give you these things.

Third, thinking people should give you what you want when you want it keeps you from being grateful when they deliver the goods. Why? Because "should" implies you think you're *entitled* to others meeting your needs, and you're not. When you feel entitled to your wants and needs being met, all you can say in your mind when people give you what you want is, "That's what they should have done." That's not gratitude.

Munchkins, I hope and pray you will work hard to eliminate the words should and shouldn't from your vocabulary. If you do, you'll find a great deal of psychological, relational, and spiritual health waiting for you on the other side.

23

BE ANGRY BUT DON'T ACT THE FOOL

"In your anger do not sin": Do not let the sun
go down while you are still angry . . .
—Ephesians 4:26

My dear brothers and sisters, take note
of this: Everyone should be quick to listen,
slow to speak and slow to become angry,
because human anger does not produce
the righteousness that God desires.
—James 1:19-20

When angry, count four. When very angry, swear.
—Mark Twain

Anger is a valid emotion. It's only bad when it takes control
and makes you do things you don't want to do.
—Ellen Hopkins

I'm probably the last one on the planet to give you advice about managing your anger. I've spent my life struggling with a bad temper and have acted the fool on more occasions than I care to remember. Let me share one especially embarrassing example.

My two older brothers and I were playing baseball in our backyard one Saturday. I was five or six years old at the time. One brother was pitching, the other was catching, and I was batting. The incident that triggered my anger that day was my brothers having the nerve to call me out on three strikes.

Now, you might wonder why that bothered me. Let me explain. At the time, I was under the false impression that you got four strikes and three balls in baseball (obviously, I had confused balls and strikes), so I thought my brothers were being mean and ripping me off.

Being a hothead, I marched up to the *glass* door at the back of our home and proceeded to drive my fist through it, cutting my *wrist* badly enough that my parents had to rush me to the hospital and have it stitched up. Eight stitches later, my parents brought me home wondering how they were going to survive a kid with that bad of a temper.

I say all this to be honest about my lifelong battle with anger and share with you what I've learned along the way about how to handle this particular emotion in a more mature manner. So, let me give you some things to consider.

First, you need to know that anger is a legitimate emotion. I grew up thinking all anger was bad. That's simply not true. There are times in life you're supposed to feel angry and it would be unhealthy for you *not* to.

Second, you need to know that, in general, two things trigger (not cause) anger. One thing that triggers anger is when an event blocks or frustrates your goal. If you're trying to get across town and you run into a traffic jam, you're likely to get frustrated/angry because your goal is being blocked. The other thing that triggers anger is when people mistreat you, someone you love, or another human being somewhere on the planet. Here, anger is an internal signal to you that someone is not being treated right (fairly, justly, lovingly), and it energizes your will to do what you can to address the wrong being done.

Third, anger is perhaps the most difficult emotion to handle in a mature manner. When something blocks a goal or someone mistreats you or another human being, it's hard to handle it like a mature adult. In those moments, we're prone to either stuff our anger, spew our anger or let it out passive-aggressively, all of which are unhealthy ways to handle anger.

Finally, on a more encouraging note, even if you have a bad temper and can be easily triggered like me, you can learn to handle your anger better over time. With that in mind, let me give you some tips about how to handle your anger in a healthier way.

Tip #1: Breath. When you find yourself feeling angry, you're breathing becomes rapid and shallow. Take a minute or two to regulate your breathing when you become angry.

Tip #2: Buy some time. When you're angry, buy as much time as you can before reacting. Thomas Jefferson noted, "When angry count to ten before you speak. If very angry, count to one hundred." Stoic philosopher Seneca observed, "The greatest remedy for anger is delay."

Tip #3: Take a new view. We often get angry because we misinterpret the things that happen to us (for example, taking things personally). As Adam Grant wisely noted, "Anger and frustration are rarely caused by other people's actions. They're caused by how you interpret their actions. To change your reactions, question your explanations. You know what they did, but not why. New interpretations pave the way to new emotions."

Tip #4: Figure out what unmet needs are underneath your anger. More often than not, the anger you feel is trying to tell you that one or more of your eleven psychological needs (attention, acceptance, appreciation, affirmation, affection, comfort, encouragement, respect, security, support, and understanding) has gone unmet. Make sure you use your anger to figure out which psychological needs went unmet so you can be more "emotionally intelligent" in understanding your anger and how to handle it better.

Tip #5: Own your anger. More often than not, we blame our anger on the person or event that triggered it. Author Thibaut Meurisse noted, "Friendly reminder. If you ever lose your temper, it is your fault. Always. Your emotional responses are never the responsibility of any other human being." Take full responsibility for your emotions, anger included.

Tip #6: Assert yourself. When you're angry, see if you can do anything to be assertive about the situation. Focus on the problem, not the person, and "speak the truth in love" (Ephesians 4:15) about what might help resolve what happened and leave the two of you at peace with one another.

Aristotle was right when he said, "Anybody can become angry — that is easy, but to be angry with the right person and to the right degree and at the right time and for the right purpose, and in the right way — that is not within everybody's power and is not easy." So true.

Ecclesiastes 7:9 says, "Do not be quickly provoked in your spirit, for anger resides in the lap of fools." Munchkins, keep working on being angry toward the right person, to the right degree, at the right time, and for the right purpose so you don't act the fool.

PRACTICE GENEROSITY

Good will come to those who are
generous and lend freely . . .
—Psalm 112:5

A generous person will prosper; whoever
refreshes others will be refreshed.
—Proverbs 11:25

You have not lived today until you have done
something for someone who can never repay you.
—John Bunyan

Children must early learn the beauty of
generosity. They are taught to
give what they prize most, that they may
taste the happiness of giving.
—Charles Eastman

Munchkins, I'm going to brag on your parents for a minute.

We were at a restaurant in New York City a while back, and, when it came time to pay the bill, they all grabbed the check rather than hand it over to Nonnie and Pop expecting us to pay it as so many adult children do. Not only did they fight over who was going to pay the check, I saw them huddling with each other over what size tip to give.

In my day, back when the earth was still cooling, tips were typically in the range of 10-15%. So, if your bill came to $50, you were supposed to tip anywhere from $5-$7.50. Apparently, your parent's generation doesn't think that's enough. They decided to give the waitress a 100% tip. Yes, you heard me right. And, because there were eight of us eating that night at a fancy-schmancy restaurant, that was no small tip.

On top of that, your parents wanted to leave the restaurant before the server could come back to see her tip. Not me. I wanted to sit there and bask in the glow of their generosity. They, on the other hand, couldn't leave the restaurant fast enough. Carol Ryrie Brink said, "The most truly generous persons are those who give silently without hope of praise or reward." Your parents get that. I don't.

Your parents have many wonderful qualities, and one of them is generosity. They are incredibly generous people who are always on the lookout for how to give to others with no desire to receive any praise or reward. And, it's not just their money they're generous with—they're just as generous with their time, talents, and heart.

When it comes to generosity, try to be like your parents. Model yourself after them when it's time to give generously of the resources you have at your disposal. Spend the rest of your life looking for ways to sacrificially give, the kind of giving that has an "ouch" to it and has no expectation of anything in return.

Let me pat you munchkins on the back about this for a minute as well. While you're not very old, I've already seen you be generous with each other, schoolmates, and us adults, something that warms my heart. I've seen you give your time, share your favorite toy, and provide help when others needed it. You will never know the smile you put on your parent's and grandparents' faces when we see you being generous in those ways.

A specific example of your generosity that I especially appreciate is that you give me your waffle fries when we go to Chick-Fil-A. I'm ashamed to say this, but I know you like the fruit cup that comes with a kid's meal more than the waffle fries, and there have been many times I "helped" you with your order by suggesting you get the waffle fries instead of the fruit cup. I do this because I know you aren't going to eat the fries and will hand them over to me. Bad Pop.

A word of caution about generosity, though. Be careful not to be too generous with people, especially those who are selfish and exploitive like me. There are people out there who, if you give them an inch, will take a mile and keep asking for more and more until your time, talent, and treasures are exhausted. Avoid these folks if you can. Just don't apply this standard to me when it comes to your waffle fries.

If we practice generosity with others, it often comes back our way sooner or later, even if it's just seeing the smile on the face of the person we gave to. In general, when you give generously, the generosity you expressed often comes back in your direction in some form or fashion. We don't give generously for that reason, of course, but it's a nice little perk God seems to have wired into human relationships.

Being generous just makes sense because you can't take anything with you anyway. Not to be morbid, but we're all going to die, and it is irrational and even wrong to withhold things from others that we don't need, don't use, or can give to those who lack. Henri Nouwen was wise to observe, "When we face death with hope, we can live life with generosity." The hope of there being an afterlife ought to spur us to live life with generosity in the here-and-now.

When it comes to generosity, it's important to remember the words of Jesus, "From everyone who has been given much, much will be demanded; and from the one who has been entrusted with much, much more will be asked" (Luke 12:48). Many of us have been blessed with so much; let's make sure we give back just as much as we've been given.

Finally, don't fool yourself into thinking that you'll be more generous later on when you have more to give. William Swan Plummer was right when he said, "He who is not liberal with what he has, does but deceive himself when he thinks he would be liberal if he had more." Give generously of what you have now, and don't wait until sometime down the road when you have more. What you can give today is more than enough.

Your parent's generosity over the years has inspired me to be more generous. I appreciate that about them. You'd be wise to model yourself after your parents in this very important way. For sure, don't model yourself after me in this area. I *take* generously (your waffle fries) rather than give generously to you guys when we're at Chick-Fil-A. Although now that I think about it, Nonnie and I pay for your meal, but there I go again wanting credit for my generosity. You guys are already way ahead of me because you give generously and don't expect any praise or reward. Maybe you should have written this chapter.

SEEK WISE COUNSEL

Plans fail for lack of counsel, but with
many advisers they succeed.
—Proverbs 15:22

The way of fools seems right to them,
but the wise listen to advice.
—Proverbs 12:15

A fool despises good counsel, but a
wise man takes it to heart.
—Confucius

Without good direction, people lose their way; the more
wise counsel you follow, the better your chances.
—Eugene H. Peterson

We all need advice, whether it's about finances, occupational choices, ways to improve our relationships with others, or how to grow into a spiritually mature person. The primary reason we all need advice is that none of us are all-knowing, not anywhere close. Because we're not all-knowing, we need to tap into what other people know so we can make wiser choices.

If you can admit to not knowing very much, you are going to be more open to seeking input from the people you trust. On the other side of the coin, if you think you know a lot, you're going to be your own advisor and royally mess your life up. As Hunter S. Thompson put it, "He that is taught only by himself has a fool for a master." I would tweak that and say, "He or she who only looks to themself for advice has a fool for an advisor."

That we all need advice is a given in life. The more important issue is this: Who are we going to turn to for advice? Rasheed Ogunlaru rightly noted, "Choose your counsel, company and companions wisely: beware seeking wise words of advice from a fool or expecting informed opinions or decisions from the ignorant." Sophocles stated, "No enemy is worse than bad advice." We need to make sure we seek advice only from those who actually know what they are talking about.

So, here are just a few guidelines when you're thinking about who to turn to for advice.

First, get advice from people who practice what they preach. Douglas Adams said, "The quality of any advice anybody has to offer has to be judged against the quality of life they actually lead." That's right. If the person giving you advice isn't living a relatively high-quality life, take everything they say with a huge grain of salt.

Second, get advice from people who know you well. Some of the worst advice comes from those who haven't taken the time to know you and understand how you're wired. John Gottman wisely pointed out, "Human nature dictates that it is virtually impossible to accept advice from someone unless you feel that that person understands you." If someone hasn't taken the time to understand your situation, how you tick, and what you've already tried, their advice will be off the mark and you would be wise not to listen to it.

Third, make the person giving you advice explain their reasons for it. Don't just let them throw stuff against the wall to see what sticks. Have them tell you why they gave you the advice they did. If they can't explain their advice, don't take it all that seriously. As Frank Sonnenberg put it, "Before acting on any recommendation, know the rationale." Following advice for which there is no rationale usually means you're headed in a bad direction.

Fourth, when someone tells you their advice is 100% true, run in the opposite direction. We need to avoid people who are prideful enough to think their advice is foolproof and completely trustworthy. Mehmet

Murat ildan observed, "The best advice is the one that presents the given advice not as an absolute truth, but as just an idea to consider!"

Fifth, make sure you're willing to hear good advice. Not only do we need to make sure the advice we're getting is good, but we need to make sure we have ears to hear it. Hesiod stated, "That man is best who sees the truth himself. Good too is he who listens to wise counsel. But who is neither wise himself nor willing to ponder wisdom is not worth a straw."

Sixth, act on the advice if it's good. Don't let good advice drop to the ground unheeded. Sallust stated, "Get good counsel before you begin; and when you have decided, act promptly." Sometimes, we get good advice but don't implement it, much to our detriment.

Seventh, get advice from well-written books. There are a lot of pretty smart people out there who have put a lot of time and energy into understanding things at a deep level. Reading good books, something we've already talked about in a previous chapter, is one way to ensure you're getting wise advice.

As a person of faith, I believe the Bible is the best book to read on a daily basis for wise counsel. Hebrews 4:12 says, "For the word of God is alive and active. Sharper than any double-edged sword, it penetrates even to dividing soul and spirit, joints and marrow; it judges the thoughts and attitudes of the heart." Whatever else you read for wise input on how to live your life, read the Bible.

Munchkins, make sure you seek the wise counsel of as many people as possible, especially when the stakes are high regarding the decision you need to make. When it comes to things like what career path to take, who to marry, how to manage your finances, and how to be an emotionally and spiritually healthy human being, get as much advice as possible from as many reputable sources as possible.

Make sure the folks you listen to practice what they preach, provide a proper rationale for why they think the way they do, have deeply studied the subject matter at hand, and are humble enough to admit they might be wrong. Make sure you are humble enough to listen to what they say and courageous enough to act on good advice when it's given to you.

26

BE ANXIOUS BUT DON'T WORRY

Therefore I tell you, do not worry about your life, what you will eat or drink; or about your body, what you will wear. Is not life more than food, and the body more than clothes?
—Matthew 6:25

Therefore do not worry about tomorrow, for tomorrow will worry about itself. Each day has enough trouble of its own.
—Matthew 6:34

Worry does not empty tomorrow of its sorrow, it empties today of its strength.
— Corrie Ten Boom

Blessed is the person who is too busy to worry in the daytime and too sleepy to worry at night.
— Leo Aikman

I'm a worrywart. Dictionary.com defines a worrywart as "a person who tends to worry habitually and often needlessly." Yea, that's me.

I've spent my whole life worrying about pretty much everything. Along the way, I've worried about making good grades, finding a spouse, having children, getting through graduate school, becoming a psychologist, making a good living, putting a roof over my family's head, having grandchildren, coming down with serious health issues, hitting a golf ball safely on a green, having an automobile accident, my clients getting better, and people liking me.

So, it is with some degree of fear and trembling that I'm giving you advice on how not to worry given that I worry all the time.

First, make a distinction between anxiety and worry. We're supposed to be anxious about things in life that pose a genuine threat to our physical, emotional, relational, financial, and spiritual health. For example, if someone is walking toward you with a knife and a menacing look, for goodness' sake, be anxious. Worry is the unhealthy mental component of anxiety where you take what you're anxious about, ruminate and obsess about what might happen, freeze up, and fall into what we psychologists call "borrowing problems from the future."

Second, while it is healthy and functional to feel anxious about things that pose a genuine threat to your life, worry is almost always unhealthy and dysfunctional. All worry does is make you lay on the floor, curl up in a fetal position, and hope the threatening situation will go away. The Dalai Lama was right when he said, "If a problem is fixable, if a situation is such that you can do something about it, then there is no need to worry. If it's not fixable, then there is no help in worrying. There is no benefit in worrying whatsoever." Wise words we all need to listen to.

Third, worry is really bad for your physical and emotional health. When I was growing up, I heard people say things like, "Frank worried himself to death." That happens. Oscar Auliq-Ice noted, "Perpetual worry will get you to one place ahead of time—the cemetery." Marty Rubin said, "Death kills us once; worry kills us every day." So true.

Fourth, most of the things you worry about never happen. Mark Twain said, "I am an old man and have known a great many troubles, but most of them have never happened." Sadly, many of us are prone to think "worst-case scenario" about what the future might hold and imagine all kinds of horrible things coming our way. The vast majority of the time the horrible things we worry about don't happen. Even when they do, we're often surprised by how God helped us get through them and come out on the other side better off.

Fifth, worry is a form of pride. It reflects we think we have control over things. We don't. As June Hunt said, "Worry is most often a prideful way of thinking that you have more control over life and its circumstances than you actually do." Also, when you worry, you're presuming to know more about the future than you do. Terence McKenna said, "Don't worry. You don't know enough to worry. That's God's truth. Who do you think you are that you should worry, for crying out loud? It's a total waste of time. It presupposes such a knowledge of the situation that it is in fact a form of hubris."

Sixth, worry negatively reflects on how we see God. Worry presumes that God doesn't know what's going on, doesn't care about your situation, or isn't doing what he can to look out for you. Nothing could be further from the truth. As George Foster rightly said, "Worry is common, it's not good for us, it accomplishes little, and it dishonors the God who cares for us. Worry may be our most enduring form of unbelief."

Seventh, worry often leads to inaction. Whereas truly threatening situations trigger a much-needed fight or flight response in our bodies, worry tends to trigger an immobilizing freeze reaction. As Michael Corthell put it, "The worst worry habit is sitting in your worry doing nothing...sweep the floor." When you find yourself worrying, get up and do something, even if it's sweeping the floor.

Eighth, don't worry alone. We have a tendency when we worry to pull away from others because it's embarrassing to admit something is getting to us. John Ortberg noted, "Never worry alone. When anxiety grabs my mind, it is self-perpetuating. Worrisome thoughts reproduce faster than rabbits, so one of the most powerful ways to stop the spiral of worry is simply to disclose my worry to a friend."

Munchkins, worry seems like it's constructive, doing you some good, and giving you some control over the situation. It's not. As Wayne Bennett wisely observed, "Worry is like a rocking chair. It gives you something to do but gets you nowhere." If you can do something about a situation, there's no need to worry. If you can't, there's no need to worry. Let yourself be anxious about the truly threatening things that happen in life, but, please, refuse to worry about them.

27

DON'T PLAY TO THE CROWD

They came to him and said, "Teacher, we
know that you are a man of integrity. You
aren't swayed by others, because you pay no
attention to who they are; but you teach the
way of God in accordance with the truth."
—Mark 12:14

Am I now trying to win the approval of human beings,
or of God? Or am I trying to please people?
—Galatians 1:10

I much prefer the sharpest criticism of a single intelligent
man to the thoughtless approval of the masses.
— Johannes Kepler

What does it mean to get someone else's approval?
Usually, it means lowering and debasing yourself.
— Marty Rubin

Throughout your life, you're going to be tempted to "play to the crowd"
in order to gain their approval. Don't. There are very few things that
will damage your integrity as a human being more than seeking the
approval of others.

There is a difference between wanting *acceptance* and seeking
approval. As we talked about in an earlier chapter, we all have a pre-wired

psychological need to be accepted "warts and all" by others, something we don't need to apologize for as we go through life.

Approval is a whole different ball of wax. Wanting people's approval can take us down the garden path of not remaining true to who God meant us to be. Mark Manson noted, "Seeking approval and people-pleasing forces you to alter your actions and speech to no longer reflect what you actually think or feel."

When we seek the approval of others, we're showing ourselves to be people who don't have a solid internal sense of worth and value. Vernon Howard noted, "A truly strong person does not need the approval of others any more than a lion needs the approval of sheep."

The need for approval gives people tremendous power over how we think, feel, and act. Trish MacGregor wisely observed, "Don't seek approval. This may be the toughest suggestion for you to follow — and the most important. Whether you're a teenager seeking approval from your peers, a middle-aged parent seeking the approval of your kids, or a man or woman seeking the approval of a partner, it all amounts to the same thing. You're giving your personal power away every time you seek validation from someone else for who you are."

The need for approval can be an addiction. If your "drug" is approval, you need others to supply that drug to you every day, otherwise, you go through an emotionally and even physically painful withdrawal that makes you desperate for more approval. Harriet B. Braiker said, "If you are an approval addict, your behavior is as easy to control as that of any other junkie. All a manipulator need do is a simple two-step process: Give you what you crave, and then threaten to take it away. Every drug dealer in the world plays this game."

The need for approval submarines your uniqueness. Everyone on the planet is unique. Even if you're an identical twin, there is no one else exactly like you. When you seek approval from others, you allow life to chip away at your uniqueness and can become indistinguishable from everyone else. Suzy Kassem was right when she said, "Stay true to yourself. An original is worth more than a copy." You're an original. Please, don't seek the approval of others such that you become a boring copy.

Another thing about approval to watch out for—it's pretty flaky. Oliver Cromwell said, "Do not trust the cheering, for those very persons would shout as much if you and I were going to be hanged." The crowd will cheer you as long as you think, feel, and act like they want you to, but it will turn on you pretty quickly if you don't, even to the point of having you hanged.

You see people playing to the crowd across various aspects of life—racially, politically, religiously, and the like. It's rare to see a man or a woman have enough personal integrity to say what they really think in these various areas, especially if it might cost them their jobs, livelihoods, and approval by those in their circle of friends

What we desperately need going forward is men and women of character who, regardless of their stance on things, have the courage to tell us what they *really* think, even if they pay dearly for it. Sadly, so many people say whatever they need to in a desperate attempt to hang on to approval as long as they can.

If we're going to seek someone's approval, we need to seek the approval of God. I'm not talking here about seeking the love of God. God *is* love, and we can't do anything to raise or lower His love for us. That being said, God's *approval* of our actions goes up and down based on whether or not our actions are good or bad. Craig D. Lounsbrough said, "I would rather have the approval of God over the accolades of men. For while men might 'lift' me up, God is the only One who can 'take' me up."

Munchkins, don't play to the crowd. Doing so means you're debasing yourself and throwing your integrity out the window. Play to the audience of one—God. Enjoy the unchanging love and worth you have in God, and spend the rest of your life acting in ways that please Him and gain His approval.

28

BE CONTENT WITH LITTLE

I am not saying this because I am in need, for
I have learned to be content whatever the
circumstance. I know what it is to be in
need, and I know what it is to have plenty.
I have learned the secret of being content
in any and every situation, whether well fed
or hungry, whether living in plenty or want.
—Philippians 4:11-12

But if we have food and clothing, we
will be content with that.
—1 Timothy 6:8

He who is not contented with what he has, would not be
contented with what he would like to have.
— Socrates

But if I'm content with little, enough is as good as a feast.
—Isaac Bickerstaffe

Contentment is a misunderstood concept. Some wrongly believe it to be
a bad thing. They believe that if you're content you won't keep striving
for greater heights in life. That's not what contentment means.

Contentment is a byproduct of being grateful for what you already
have. It is an outgrowth of counting all the blessings in your life. Let me

put this differently. If you aren't content, you're probably not grateful for the many blessings that already permeate your life each day. Charles Spurgeon put it this way: "You say, 'If I had a little more, I should be very satisfied.' You make a mistake. If you are not content with what you have, you would not be satisfied if it were doubled."

All this raises the million-dollar question, "How is it possible to be content in a world that never seems to be satisfied with what it already has?" How do we live in a fundamentally ungrateful and discontented world and not fall into the same trap? Here are some suggestions.

First, take time each day to express gratitude to God for all the things in your life that are good. As weird as it might sound, be grateful for the air you breathe, the water you drink, the food you eat, the people in your life who love you, the home you live in, the car you drive, the freedoms you enjoy, the beauty of nature, the job you get paid to do, the hobbies you get to pursue, the fun you get to have, and four million other positive things that enrich your life.

Second, don't pursue things that are either unhealthy to pursue (being perfect, having everyone's approval, unlimited wealth and power) or unlikely to occur (running the 100-yard dash in 9 seconds when people have to time you with a calendar, being a world-class singer when you can't carry a tune in a bucket, becoming a Nobel laureate in mathematics when you can't balance your checkbook). Unhealthy pursuits and unlikely-to-happen pursuits are a surefire prescription for being chronically discontented. P.D. James rightly observed, "The secret of contentment is never to allow yourself to want anything which reason tells you you haven't a chance of getting."

Third, tap the breaks on what you desire in life. The notion that "You can have it all" is utter nonsense. Every "Yes" to one thing is a "No" to something else, and that's the main reason you can't have it all in life. So, don't try. Be selective when prioritizing what you want in life. John Stuart Mill said, "I have learned to seek my happiness by limiting my desires, rather than in attempting to satisfy them."

Fourth, pay more attention to what you already have, not what you don't have. Ann Brashares said, "Do not spoil what you have by desiring what you have not." Far too many of us are constantly thinking about the things we want in life that we don't have, and the result of thinking this way is greater discontentment.

Fifth, realize that there is so much in life you can live without. The Apostle Paul got his wants and needs down to a rather shocking level, "But if we have food and clothing, we will be content with that" (1 Timothy 6:8). Walt Whitman put it more starkly when he said, "Whoever is not in his coffin and the dark grave, let him know he has enough." About ninety-nine times out of a hundred, you'll realize after the fact that you weren't going to die if you never had the things in life you so desperately wanted. Immanuel Kant was right when he said, "We are not rich by what we possess but by what we can do without."

Sixth, accept that becoming a more contented person is a lengthy process. Alain de Botton said, "Being content is perhaps no less easy than playing the violin well and requires no less practice." If you want to become a more contented human being over time, you have to patiently practice gratitude each day, get your desires down to a healthy level, stop pursuing things that are inherently unhealthy or highly unlikely to happen, and pay more attention to what you have and less attention to what you don't.

Seventh, without putting yourself down, let feelings of discontentment be a signal to you that you are, most likely, ungrateful for what you already have. Most people see their lack of contentment as the problem. It's not. The real problem is ingratitude. Own it and ask God to help you break free from it.

Eighth, don't hang around discontented people. While it's not literally true, I believe discontentment is a disease you can catch from others. Try to avoid people who complain about what they don't have. Hang around people who are "content with little" and truly thankful for however little or much they currently have.

Munchkins, contentment is an incredibly rare and precious thing. Very few people have it, and those who do are the richest folks in the world. John Balguy wisely said, "Contentment is a pearl of great price, and whoever procures it at the expense of ten thousand desires makes a wise and a happy purchase." Genuine contentment is the greatest kind of wealth, and you'd be wise to pursue it for the rest of your life.

I'll leave you with a final quote. Wayne Trotman observed, "Contentment comes from wanting what we need, not needing what we want." Take some time today to think about what you truly *need* in life, and spend the rest of your days *wanting* that. Take some time today to think about what you *want* in life, and spend the rest of your life not *needing* that. Do yourself a big favor—work on becoming a more contented person. You'll never regret it.

29

WATCH YOUR MOUTH

Likewise, the tongue is a small part of the
body, but it makes great boasts.
Consider what a great forest is set on fire
by a small spark. The tongue also
is a fire, a world of evil among the parts
of the body. It corrupts the whole
body, sets the whole course of one's life on
fire, and is itself set on fire by hell.
—James 3:5-6

Do not let any unwholesome talk come out of
your mouths, but only what is helpful
for building others up according to their needs
that it may benefit those who listen.
—Ephesians 4:29

Guard your tongue, and use it for good instead
of evil. How many marriages or friendships
have been destroyed because of criticism that
spiraled out of control? How many relationships
have broken down because of a word spoken
thoughtlessly or in anger? A harsh word can't be
taken back; no apology can fully repair its damage.
— Billy Graham

Verbal abuse is as damaging as physical abuse,
and in some cases, it does even more
damage to a child. Insulting names, degrading
comments and constant criticism all
leave deep emotional scars that hinder feelings
of self-worth and personal agency.
— Susan Forward

Just like it wasn't enjoyable to talk about evil, I don't like talking about verbal abuse either. Nevertheless, we have to talk about how deadly the human tongue can be for inflicting all kinds of emotional and spiritual damage on others. This is a two-way street, of course, us being verbally abusive to others and others being verbally abusive to us.

There are numerous versions of verbal abuse we could talk about. Here, I'm going to highlight ten.

BLAMING. When we blame others for our feelings and actions, saying things like "You made me mad" and "It's your fault I punched a hole in the wall," we're being verbally abusive and need to stop.

CRITICISM. We are being verbally abusive when we criticize others rather than give them constructive feedback. "You never do anything right" and "You're always upset about something" are abusive statements aimed at making a person feel bad about themselves.

GASLIGHTING. Gaslighting is an effort to get a person to question their view of reality and doubt their own sanity. Saying, "Of course, I told you about the appointment, you just have a really bad memory," in an effort to make someone think they're the one with the memory problem (when they don't have one) is verbally abusive.

JUDGING. Judging involves looking down on someone as inferior. "You were raised on the wrong side of the tracks" and "You never know what you're talking about" are examples. It's abusive to look down your nose at someone in an effort to make them feel small.

NAME-CALLING. This involves using abusive, derogatory language aimed at making a person feel worthless.

THREATS. Making statements that are meant to manipulate, frighten, bully, and control the other person, like "If you don't get your act together, I'm going to leave and take the kids." It's abusive to threaten others in an effort to get them to give you what you want.

WITHHOLDING. Refusing to interact with and/or meet the needs of another person. It's abusive to not be willing to talk with someone (unless you're taking a much-needed "time out"), refuse to make eye contact, or act in a cold and indifferent manner.

ACCUSATIONS. Accusing someone of doing something wrong when you don't have any valid evidence, like "I know you're cheating on me and just too much of a coward to admit it." When you don't have evidence to support an accusation, you're being abusive to make one.

CIRCULAR ARGUMENTS. Constantly disagreeing with someone and going around in circles to avoid admitting you're wrong. It's abusive to refuse to admit you're wrong when you are and to argue with someone in a way that clouds the issue.

CONDESCENSION. Being sarcastic, patronizing, and disdainful toward others in an effort to make them feel small. "Let me see if I can explain this in a way that you will understand" is abusive.

Let me pass along some tips for how to do a better job of reigning in your tongue when interacting with others. These tips are based on various quotes I came across when writing this chapter. I hope you find them helpful.

Tip #1: Avoid saying things you don't want following you around for the rest of your life. "Okay, let's put this another way—if what you're about to say wouldn't look good permanently engraved on your tombstone, *bite your tongue*" (Richelle E. Goodrich).

Tip #2: If you feel like you're going to explode if you don't say something, it's probably better to remain quiet. "The best time for you to hold your tongue is the time you feel you must say something or bust" (Josh Billings).

Tip #3: Actions speak louder than words. If you're talking too much, you're probably not backing up your words with action. "Hold your tongue and live your life, for it is in the way that you live that you speak the loudest" (Craig D. Lounsbrough).

Tip #4: Keep in mind that what comes out of your mouth reflects what's going on in your heart. Let the words you speak diagnose where your heart is at. "For the mouth speaks what the heart is full of" (Jesus Christ).

Munchkins, I mean this in the most respectful way possible, but, watch your mouth. Be careful to watch the things you say to others. The tongue is a fire and can burn down everything in its path. Avoid its misuse as much as possible.

ASK OTHERS TO CORRECT YOU

Whoever heeds life-giving correction
will be at home among the wise.
—Proverbs 12:31

Whoever disregards discipline comes to poverty and shame,
but whoever heeds correction is honored.
—Proverbs 13:18

Being open to correction means
making ourselves vulnerable, and
many people are not willing to do that.
— Myles Munroe

To admonish is better than to reproach
for admonition is mild and friendly, but
reproach is harsh and insulting; and
admonition corrects those who are doing
wrong, but reproach only convicts them.
— Epictetus

Because we're all prideful and defensive to some degree, we struggle when it comes to allowing others to correct us. As Nouman Ali Khan put it, "If someone corrects you, and you feel offended, then you have an ego problem."

Our defensive reaction to correction shows up in different forms. Let me offer three.

"How dare you correct me! You're no better!" It may very well be the case that the person correcting you isn't any better than you, but, out of respect, you still need to hear what they have to say.

"You don't know what you're talking about!" It may very well be the case that the person correcting you doesn't know much about you, your situation, or the issue at hand, but, out of respect, you still need to listen to what they have to say.

"I'm sorry, I didn't know!" Sometimes, we hide behind the fact that we didn't know that what we did was wrong, as if ignorance is bliss and lets us off the hook. If you take a right turn on a red light in New York City (which is illegal), please don't tell the cop you didn't know it was illegal—just let him or her hand you a ticket and be on your way.

Let me give you twelve tips on how to correct someone properly. These tips not apply to how you need to act when correcting others and but how they need to act when correcting you.

> Tip #1: Do it in private if possible. There's no need to embarrass someone by correcting them in front of others.
>
> Tip #2: Don't correct those over whom you have no authority. If you live in New York City and see someone take a right turn on red, don't correct them unless you're a cop.
>
> Tip #3: Question your motives. Are you correcting someone out of love (to help them grow), or are you correcting them out of ego (to make yourself feel superior)?
>
> Tip #4: Focus on the person's behavior, not their personhood. Don't give someone corrective feedback about their character, just their behavior. Focus on the sin, not the sinner.

Tip #5: Watch your tone. A condescending, passive-aggressive tone takes us from kindly correcting someone to being critical, shaming, and abusive.

Tip #6: Correct someone publicly if their actions could hurt others. If someone says drinking bleach cures cancer, correct them publicly so others won't act on their ignorance.

Tip #7: Correct with evidence, not with opinion or feeling. Make sure you have the proper data, evidence, and cultural norms to back up correcting someone. "I feel . . ." and "It's just my opinion . . ." are insufficient.

Tip #8: Admit the correction you're offering reflects the way *you* see things. Even if you have all the data and evidence on your side, you want to be humble and acknowledge that you see things the way you do and could be wrong.

Tip #9: Start with the positive. Before you correct someone, start with what they are doing right. "Dwight, I see you treating people kindly all the time. I just want to mention that it's not okay to steal people's lunches from the office refrigerator."

Tip #10: Avoid sounding authoritative. Even if you've studied something thoroughly and have lots of data on your side, it doesn't make you an infallible expert. Be humble in spirit when giving others corrective feedback, and try to avoid sounding like an authoritative expert.

Tip #11: Ask questions to facilitate the conversation. Try to avoid passive-aggressive questions like, "Sue, do you ever look at the clock when you get to work, because you're always late?" Ask something like, "Sue, you look tired when you get to work in the morning. Is everything okay?"

Tip #12: Offer help. When you correct someone, be ready to offer help. For example, if you're about to correct someone for poor interpersonal skills, be prepared to share what you know about emotional intelligence and the resources that could help them make improvements in that area.

One final tip. Don't make others have to find you to correct you. Don't make people have to hire a private detective to serve you with a correction subpoena. On a regular basis, go to the people you trust and ask them to give you corrective feedback about your behavior. Seek them out—it'll shock their socks off and may inspire them to do the same with you.

Munchkins, I hope all this helps. Try not to let your ego get in the way of receiving correction from others, and try not to let your fears get in the way of offering correction to others. Proverbs states, "Wounds from a friend can be trusted, but an enemy multiplies kisses" (Proverbs 27:6). Humbly receive and offer the wounds of correction, helping everyone to grow into the mature and loving people God meant all of us to be.

31

LISTEN TO A LOT OF
REALLY GOOD MUSIC

My heart, O God, is steadfast, my heart is
steadfast; I will sing and make music.
—Psalm 57:7

Whenever the spirit from God came on Saul, David would
take up his lyre and play. Then relief would come to Saul;
he would feel better, and the evil spirit would leave him.
—1 Samuel 16:23

Life seems to go on without effort
when I am filled with music.
– George Eliot

A great song should lift your heart, warm
the soul and make you feel good.
– Colbie Caillat

I have a confession to make. I listened to a lot of really bad music when
I was growing up. I don't like to admit it, but it's true.

The apex of my bad music listening tendencies involved listening to
a group popular in the early 1970s, Black Sabbath. I mean, what was I
thinking? The group's name was BLACK SABBATH for crying out loud!
Why, in my most delusional moment as a music lover, would I turn my
ear in the direction of a heavy metal band that peppered its songs with
occult themes and horror-inspired lyrics? YIKES!

Thankfully, I listened to a lot of good music as well, and I am convinced that the good music I listened to helped soothe my soul along the way. There were more than a few thousand times when music was my best friend and comforter. I identify with Jane Austen when she said, "Without music, life would be a blank to me."

So far, you munchkins seem to be listening to good music. As have zillions of other people your age, you have taken quite passionately to Disney music. That being said, I would ask you to never sing "Let it Go" from the movie, *Frozen*, again. It's a great song, but if I hear it one more time, I'm going to pull my hair out!

Also, if Nonnie and Pop ever go to Disney World with you again, which I hope we will, I'm not going on the "It's a Small World" ride. I'm still trying to get that particular (tortuous) song out of my head from our last trip. My biggest Disney World nightmare is that the boat we're in breaks down during the ride and that we're stuck there for hours. Yikes!

You munchkins have already fallen into butchering the lyrics to the songs you love, something that makes me laugh out loud. One of you loves the song by Justin Timberlake, *Can't Stop the Feeling*, a catchy little pop fest if there ever was one. There's a line in the song, "I've got this feeling in my *body*." You thought it said, "I've got this feeling in my *bottom*," and we had to get you to stop singing that before you embarrassed yourself and your family any further.

Music has a profound effect on your body and psyche, and there are a ton of benefits to listening to it regularly. Music can: 1) stimulate brainwaves to resonate in sync with the beat, and, when you're listening to a faster beat, help with concentration and alert thinking; 2) change brainwave activity and help the brain shift speeds more easily; 3) bring positive benefits to your state of mind even after you stop listening; 4) activate your relaxation response; 5) help prevent the damaging effects of chronic stress; 6) keep depression and anxiety at bay; and 7) help lower blood pressure, boost immunity, and ease muscle tension.

I think all of this is true unless you're listening to Black Sabbath. When I listened to them, all it did was elevate my blood pressure, make me more depressed and anxious, deactivate my relaxation response, and make me want to jump off the top of a tall building. So, we need to be discerning about what kind of music we're listening to if we want the positive effects of music to come our way.

Let me say that one more time in case you weren't listening. Just like we need to read a lot of *good* books (as opposed to reading a lot of *bad* books), it's important to listen to a lot of *good* music as well. I've heard songs blaring out of people's cars lately that aren't fit for human consumption. I know I'm sounding like an old geezer here, but, back in my day when dinosaurs still roamed the earth, we didn't have "Parental Advisory Warning" labels on the music we listened to. Now, you see those labels all the time. All that to say, be very careful when it comes to your listening preferences.

Let me close by sharing some of the best quotes I came across regarding the positive effect of (good) music. Here goes.

"Music gives a soul to the universe, wings to the mind, flight to the imagination and life to everything." (Plato)

"My heart, which is so full to overflowing, has often been solaced and refreshed by music when sick and weary." (Martin Luther)

"Music is the divine way to tell beautiful, poetic things to the heart." (Pablo Casals)

"After silence, that which comes nearest to expressing the inexpressible is music." (Aldous Huxley)

"Music is the movement of sound to reach the soul for the education of its virtue." (Plato)

"Music is an agreeable harmony for the honor of God and the permissible delights of the soul." (Johann Sebastian Bach)

Munchkins, I highly recommend that you spend the rest of your life listening to good music. Choose your music wisely, for it will play a very important role in affecting your body, soul, and spirit.

At this point in Pop's life, Black Sabbath music is bad and harmful, as is "Let It Go" and "It's a Small World After All." "Can't Stop This Feeling," on the other hand, is good and helpful as long as you guys don't butcher the lyrics.

32

FACE YOUR DEATH

Who can live and not see death, or who
can escape the power of the grave?
—Psalm 89:48

Just as people are destined to die once,
and after that to face judgment . . .
—Hebrews 9:27

The most obvious, the most easily apprehended
ultimate concern is death. We
exist now, but one day shall cease to be.
Death will come, and there is no
escape from it. It is a terrible truth, and we
respond to it with mortal terror.
—Irvin Yalom

Life is hard. Then you die. Then they
throw dirt in your face.
Then the worms eat you. Be grateful
it happens in that order.
—David Gerrold

Well, I've talked about not hanging around the chronically self-absorbed
(narcissists) and militant rule-breakers (sociopaths), standing up to evil
when you're called to do so, and refraining from any and all forms of

verbal abuse, so I might as well talk about another unpleasant topic—death. Sorry, but we've got to talk about it, too.

One day, and none of us know when, we are going to pass out of this life into another. The issue here isn't "Are we going to die?" That's a given. The issue is "How are we going to live." William Wallace, as portrayed in the movie, *Braveheart*, put it this way, "Every man dies—not every man really lives."

You may think I've lost my mind, but I think it's a good thing we're going to die. Why? For the simple reason that if we had an unlimited amount of time here on earth, we'd be so much more likely to fritter our lives away and waste them on the endless pursuit of pleasure. The quality of our lives would regress to something truly pathetic if the clock weren't ticking, don't you think? Elisabeth Kubler-Ross rightly observed, "It's only when we truly know and understand that we have a limited time on earth – and that we have no way of knowing when our time is up – that we will begin to live each day to the fullest as if it was the only one we had."

I would add that it's also a good thing we're not coming back. Why? Well, just like we'd be tempted to waste time if we had all the time in the world, we'd be tempted to waste time if we were going to come back an unlimited number of times. That we only get one shot at life is what makes it even more important to live as fully as possible. Emily Dickenson put the most positive spin on this I've ever heard, saying, "That it will never come again is what makes life so sweet."

So, let's talk about living life to the fullest so we won't worry about death.

First, devote your life to making the world a better place. Whether it's in your vocation, avocation, or both, keep in mind the second greatest commandment is to love your neighbor as yourself. Anytime you're loving your neighbor, you're putting your life to good use. Anytime you meet the physical, emotional, and spiritual needs of others or act in a way that helps them grow into mature adults, you're loving your neighbor and using your time here on earth well. Corazon Aquino said, "I would rather die a meaningful death than to live a meaningless life."

Second, create something positive and constructive that will outlast you, not for propping up your ego but for the betterment of others and the glory of God. Chuck Palahniuk said, "We all die. The goal isn't to live forever, the goal is to create something that will." This is what we psychologists call "generativity." I hope this book falls into the "will outlast me" category given that I'm writing it for you, your munchkins, and your munchkin's munchkins in an effort to help all of you live better lives.

Third, live each day like it's your last. Part of living each day fully is not only to leave the world better off but to commit to learning new things each day. We never know when the final bell is going to toll, but we're in the classroom the whole time and need to learn as much as we can along the way. Mahatma Gandhi said, "Live as if you were to die tomorrow. Learn as if you were to live forever." Wise words.

Fourth, don't let being young fool you into thinking you'll start living life more fully later on after you've accomplished your goals. Benjamin Franklin was right when he said, "Many people die at twenty-five and aren't buried until they are seventy-five." Far too many of us are a "dead man walking" in how we live life, especially those who think we have a lot of time ahead of us. Don't presume you have even one more day of life. Live life as fully and meaningfully in the here-and-now as you can, not pausing to look behind too often and not pausing to look ahead too often.

Fifth, don't let things die inside of you that God meant you to be. God meant you to be passionate, excited, energetic, enthusiastic, and hopeful about life. Sometimes, we let all those important qualities get knocked out of us because painful problems come our way. Don't. Norman Cousins wisely noted, "Death is not the greatest loss in life. The greatest loss is what dies inside us while we live."

Sixth, go after the deeper things of life while you're here. The world we live in encourages the pursuit of power, possessions, and pleasure. While we have to live in this world, we don't have to live the way the world does. Strive for things that really matter, not all the superficial glittery stuff that's offered up on a daily basis. Ralph Waldo Emerson said, "It is not length of life, but depth of life." Anaïs Nin said, "People living deeply have no fear of death." Anyone can live a shallow life of self-indulgent excess, but very few live a life of quality and depth.

Finally, live life in such a way that people are going to miss you when you're gone. Again, we're not to do this for ego reasons but for the betterment of others. Loving others in a deep manner leads to leaving an imprint on the human heart that will make those you leave behind wish you were still here. As humorist Mark Twain put it, "Let us endeavor so to live that when we come to die even the undertaker will be sorry."

Munchkins, you're going to die. Accept it, even embrace it, so that your life will be marked by passion, enthusiasm, purpose, and depth.

GUARD YOUR HEART

Above all else, guard your heart, for
it is the wellspring of life.
—Proverbs 4:23

Create in me a pure heart, O God, and
renew a steadfast spirit within me.
—Psalm 51:10

Your heart is sacred land. Don't let just
anything enter it. Guard it with your life.
—Yasmin Mogahed

Guard your heart and mind against double-
minded pretentious beings. Do not
allow infiltration beyond the surface.
If their influence travels on the inside,
they become like an incurable disease.
—Amaka Imani Nkosazana

You need to guard your heart while you're here. Failure to do so leads to a life of self-destruction that allows others to be destructive to you as well.

Guarding your heart is typically thought of as guarding your emotions, but it is so much more than that. Guarding your heart means guarding *everything about you* that makes you a human being—your body, soul, and spirit. Let me explain.

Guarding your heart means guarding your *body* against anything or anyone who would cause it harm, including you. You're guarding your heart when you take good care of your body by eating right, exercising regularly, and avoiding unhealthy physical risks like running into traffic without looking both ways. You're also guarding your heart when you don't allow others to harm your body by being physically abusive.

Guarding your heart means guarding your *soul* against anything or anyone who would cause it harm. Your soul is comprised of your mind, will, and emotions, so you're guarding your heart when you protect these three from harm. Let's explore that a little further.

You're guarding your heart when you guard your *mind* against thoughts, attitudes, and beliefs that are false, worthless, impure, and ugly. That's why the Bible says, "whatever is true, whatever is noble, whatever is right, whatever is pure, whatever is lovely, whatever is admirable—if anything is excellent or praiseworthy—think about such things" (Philippians 4:8).

You're guarding your heart when you guard your *emotions* against toxic, life-destroying feelings like bitterness, resentment, contempt, and rage. That's why the Bible says, "Get rid of all bitterness, rage and anger, brawling and slander, along with every form of malice" (Ephesians 4:31). At the same time, you're properly guarding your heart when you let yourself feel all the healthy emotions, whether they be pleasurable (happy, content, joyful, peaceful) or painful (sad, angry, hurt, guilty).

You're guarding your heart when you guard your *will* by choosing to act wisely and morally and choosing not to act foolishly or immorally. What the Bible calls our "flesh" is a reference to our fallen, sinful bent toward sin (a word that isn't used very much these days although it still applies), and, anytime you ask God to empower you by His grace to not willfully indulge your sinful desires, you're guarding your heart. This is why the Bible says to "walk by the Spirit, and you will not gratify the desires of the flesh" (Galatians 5:16).

Finally, guarding your heart means deciding who you are going to follow spiritually, the God of light or the god of darkness. Bob Dylan, songwriter extraordinaire from my generation (look him up), wrote a song called, *Gotta Serve Somebody*. The chorus to the song goes:

> But you're going to have to serve somebody, yes indeed
> You're going to have to serve somebody
> Well, it may be the devil or it may be the Lord
> But you're going to have to serve somebody

Bob Dylan was right. Everyone serves somebody, it's just a matter of who. The Bible agrees, which is why Joshua challenged Israel in the Old Testament, "But if serving the LORD seems undesirable to you, then choose for yourselves this day whom you will serve, whether the gods your ancestors served beyond the Euphrates, or the gods of the Amorites, in whose land you are living. But as for me and my household, we will serve the LORD" (Joshua 24:15).

Who you choose to follow spiritually is the single most important decision you make in life. Get that one wrong and you do more damage to your heart than you can imagine. I don't say this to scare you, simply to warn you. And, I don't say it to imply that those who follow God aren't just as messed up as human beings as those who don't. They are. Choosing to believe in and follow God is simply the first and most crucial step in guarding your heart against the harm living in a broken world can cause.

One other thing about guarding your heart. Guard your heart by being careful who you hang around with. We've talked about it before, but bad company corrupts good morals, and you're leaving your heart unprotected if you hang around people who are unrepentantly self-absorbed (narcissistic) and anti-authority (sociopathic). Hang around as many decent people as possible, folks who are good for you.

Henry Cloud wisely observed, "Boundaries help us to distinguish our property so that we can take care of it. They help us to 'guard our heart with all diligence.' We need to keep things that will nurture us inside our fences and keep things that will harm us outside." In your interactions with others, keep people inside your fences who are good for you, and keep people outside your fences who would cause you harm.

Munchkins, I'm sure you're beginning to understand that guarding your heart is a complex and difficult thing. It means guarding your body, soul (mind, will, and emotions), and spirit (who you follow), and it means guarding against being around bad company. As with everything else in this book, this is all easier said than done. But, please do it. You will always be glad you guarded your heart given that it is the "wellspring of life" (Proverbs 4:23) and will enable you to experience life in full.

34

WAIT FOR IT, WAIT FOR IT

Better a patient person than a warrior, one with
self-control than one who takes a city.
—Proverbs 16:32

The end of a matter is better than its beginning,
and patience is better than pride.
—Ecclesiastes 7:8

A waiting person is a patient person. The
word patience means the willingness to
stay where we are and live the situation
out to the full in the belief that something
hidden there will manifest itself to us.
— Henri Nouwen

Inner peace is impossible without patience.
Wisdom requires patience.
Spiritual growth implies the mastery
of patience. Patience allows
the unfolding of destiny to proceed
at its own unhurried pace.
— Brian Weiss

There's a well-known story about a butterfly that has been passed around for decades. The author is unknown. It's about the importance of patience, and I'm going to retell it for you here.

The story goes that a man found a cocoon of a butterfly, and, one day, a small opening appeared at the end of the cocoon. The man watched for several hours as the butterfly tried to force its way through the small hole. The butterfly seemed to have stopped making progress through the opening and appeared to have gotten as far as it could. After waiting a while, the man decided to help the butterfly and enlarged the hole. The butterfly emerged easily. Unfortunately, it was not able to unfurl its wings and fly away. The butterfly had come out of the cocoon with a swollen body and shriveled wings. The man kept watching, hoping that the butterfly's wings were able to expand and support its body. Sadly, neither happened. The butterfly spent the rest of its life crawling around with shriveled wings and a swollen body. In what he thought was an act of kindness, the man didn't understand that the butterfly getting through the narrow opening of the cocoon was nature's way of forcing fluid from the body of the butterfly into its wings. Had the butterfly been allowed to make the journey through the small hole, it would have been ready for flight and achieved true freedom from the cocoon.

Munchkins, whether you like it or not, every important area of life requires patience. If you do anything to artificially sped up the journey through the "small opening," you won't develop properly and will never take flight. Let's explore some examples.

Education requires patience. Learning is a lifelong process, analogous to putting a million-piece puzzle together. We have to patiently put one piece of knowledge together with another and another until the big picture begins to emerge. Cut corners on your education, and you're not going to know the things you need to know, you're not going to properly stretch your mind, and you will be ill-equipped to make a positive contribution to the world you live in.

Close relationships require patience. Falling in love with someone is a spontaneous moment in time where you temporarily lose your mind and become completely unmoored from reality. You foolishly buy into the delusion that the person you're in love with is perfect and that your time together is going to be walking on sunshine wonderful. Truth be told, we're all deeply fallen human beings, and we have to patiently work hard over a long period of time to develop a healthy closeness with others.

Physical fitness requires patience. You didn't get out of shape overnight, and you're not going to get back in shape overnight. The fitness club I work out at is packed in January, but it is semi-empty in February. Many people grow impatient with the laborious process of shedding weight and getting in shape, and they throw in the towel. Mahatma Gandhi was right when he said, "To lose patience is to lose the battle

Psychological health requires patience. Our psyche is deeply broken. None of us think, feel, or act appropriately on a consistent basis. If we just focus just on our "thinker" for a second, we're going to need to spend the rest of our lives working on "renewing your mind" (Romans 12:2) by constantly thinking about what is true, lovely, pure, and worthwhile (Philippians 4:8). As we explored in an earlier chapter, we all suffer from "stinking thinking" and need to be patient when it comes to overcoming the lies we believe. Deeply internalizing the truths we need to believe for a spiritually and emotionally healthy life is a lifelong homework assignment.

Patience requires patience. Craig Lounsbrough said, "Patience is where we realize that to rush something is to compromise it to its own destruction. Maturity is to realize that the most effective way to stop the destruction is by beginning to develop patience. And the first place that we need to do that is with ourselves." Be patient about developing patience.

Mindfulness expert Jon Kabat-Zinn observed, "Patience is a form of wisdom. It demonstrates that we understand and accept the fact that sometimes things must unfold in their own time." Tattoo "unfold in their own time" on your forehead, because letting things unfold in their own time is what you have to do in life to not mess things up.

That's what the man in the story got wrong—he didn't understand the butterfly had to painfully make its way through a narrow opening to be able to fully develop and fly away in all its majesty. That's how we are to see life—it's a narrow opening we must struggle through in order to become fully mature human beings. Anything we or others do to artificially enlarge the small opening is going to keep us from properly developing and taking flight in life.

Munchkins, keep working on developing more patience. Jim Berg rightly noted, "Impatience is a particularly dangerous habit of the heart because everything worthwhile takes time. Good marriages take time. Spiritual maturity takes time. Financial stability takes time. Effective ministry takes time. Wisdom takes time. People who are not willing to take time cannot have any of the above." Or, as Pierre Teilhard de Chardin put it, "Above all, trust in the slow work of God."

35

GO FLY A KITE

So, whether you eat or drink, or whatever
you do, do all to the glory of God.
—1 Corinthians 10:31

So I commend the enjoyment of life,
because there is nothing better
for a person under the sun than to
eat and drink and be glad.
—Ecclesiastes 8:15

Try new hobbies. Develop new interests.
Pursue new experiences. When you
expand your interests, you increase your
opportunities for happiness.
— Richelle E. Goodrich

Hobbies are great distractions from the worries
and troubles that plague daily living.
—Bill Malone

"Go fly a kite" used to be how we old-timers told people to get lost, buzz off, get out of our space, and leave us alone. I say "Go fly a kite" to encourage you to get some hobbies so you can enjoy life more.

Merriam-Webster defines a hobby as "a pursuit outside one's regular occupation engaged in especially for relaxation." That sounds right. If it is, I want to encourage you to make sure to have a hobby or two as your life plays out.

Right now, your life is pretty much one big hobby because you don't have an occupation (other than making us laugh). Enjoy that while you can, because once you have a profession, marry, and have some kiddos of your own, your free time is going to shrink and you're going to have to be careful not to let all your hobbies slip away.

When I was your age, my favorite hobbies were building model cars and airplanes, fiddling around with a telescope, riding my bike, making things with a chemistry set (that didn't blow our house up), and reading. Now that I'm an old guy, I love yard work, playing golf, irritating you grandkids, watching movies, and listening to music. I'm thankful for how these hobbies have helped me keep my sanity and brought happiness to my life.

First, here's a list of the positive effects of having a hobby.

- Make you more interesting
- Promote mindfulness and staying present
- Improve your confidence and self-esteem
- Provide additional income
- Relieve stress (unless you get too obsessive/compulsive about it)
- Help you give back to the world you live in
- Promote good stress (called "eustress")
- Transition you to retirement
- Enable you to explore yourself and your talents
- Encourage you to take a break
- Help you become more patient
- Help ward off depression
- Prevent you from wasting time and developing bad habits (unless your hobby is a bad habit)
- Help you be better at your job
- Allow you to meet new people
- Help keep you physically healthy
- Strengthen your relationship with others
- Enrich your perspective
- Help you sleep better
- Improve your memory

Second, here are 20 hobbies (out of hundreds) that could make your life better and more enjoyable:

- Hiking
- Reading
- Crafting
- Owning a pet
- Playing a musical instrument
- Learning a language
- Sculpture
- Chess
- Horseback riding
- Cooking
- Gardening
- Sports (running, golf, tennis, swimming, skiing)
- Writing
- Meditation
- Online classes
- Martial arts
- Juggling
- Dancing
- Woodwork
- Bodybuilding

Right now, no one has to tell you to develop any hobbies because you have a lot of them. Down the road, make sure you hang on to some of the hobbies you enjoy that make your life richer and fuller. Dale Carnegie put it this way, "Today is life—the only life you are sure of. Make the most of today. Get interested in something. Shake yourself awake. Develop a hobby. Let the winds of enthusiasm sweep through you. Live today with gusto."

Munchkins, I mean this is the best way possible, but go fly a kite.

NEVER GIVE UP

Let perseverance finish its work so that you may
be mature and complete, not lacking anything.
—James 1:4

For this very reason, make every effort to add to your
faith goodness; and to goodness, knowledge; and to
knowledge, self-control; and to self-control perseverance;
and to perseverance, godliness; and to godliness,
mutual affection; and to mutual affection, love
—2 Peter 1: 5-7

It does not matter how slowly you go
as long as you do not stop.
— Confucius

Whenever you make a mistake or get knocked down by
life, don't look back at it too long. Mistakes are life's way
of teaching you. Your capacity for occasional blunders
is inseparable from your capacity to reach your goals.
No one wins them all, and your failures, when they
happen, are just part of your growth. Shake off your
blunders. How will you know your limits without an
occasional failure? Never quit. Your turn will come.
—Og Mandino

There are going to be times in your life when you're tempted to give up on the things that really matter. Don't.

I'm talking here about things like developing closer relationships with others, pursuing educational goals, achieving work aspirations, becoming a more psychologically healthy human being, achieving financial goals, and growing into a spiritually mature person. These are all worthy callings, and I want to encourage you to *never* give up on pursuing them.

Because all the really important things in life take time, we have a tendency to grow weary and quit. Call it perseverance, persistence, determination, diligence, resolve, drive, tenacity, grit, doggedness, tirelessness, devotion, or steadfastness, we have to decide on a daily basis whether or not we are going to stay the course in pursuing our dreams and aspirations or call it a day and tap out.

I want to turn the word perseverance into an acronym, PERSEVERANCE, and walk you through the key characteristics of this crucial quality in life. I'm proud to say that this is one of the few things I didn't steal from someone else and came up with on my own. I hope you're sufficiently impressed.

> **P**atience: We have to be patient and allow things to play out in their own time.
>
> **E**ndurance: We have to bear the pain along the way involved in achieving what we want.
>
> **R**esilience: We have to bounce back up when we experience a setback.
>
> **S**acrifice: We have to be willing to give time, energy, and talent to achieve what we're after.
>
> **E**ffort: We have to put in a great deal of effort and avoid lethargy and laziness at all costs.
>
> **V**ision: We have to have a clear vision of what we're trying to accomplish.
>
> **E**xperience: We have to execute our plan and learn from setbacks along the way.

Relationships: We need to involve others in our efforts to accomplish our goals.

Attitude: We have to have a realistic and optimistic attitude in pursuing our aspirations.

Necessity: We need to do whatever it takes, within moral constraints, to achieve our goals.

Courage: We need to courageously press on when we experience a setback or roadblock.

Enthusiasm: We need to be energetic and passionate about our goals, "bring the juice."

I hope you're as impressed as I am with the fact that I came up with this. Anyway, these are the qualities we need to exhibit in life if we want to achieve our goals. Lack any of these twelve attributes, and our chances of being successful drop off considerably.

Let me speak out of the other side of my mouth for just a minute. I don't buy the idea that winners *never* quit and quitters *never* win, at least not as a categorical imperative. Like we've talked about before, there are times it's wise to quit, like when you pursue things you're not capable of accomplishing (running the 100-yard dash in eight seconds), highly unlikely to achieve (earning a Nobel Prize in microbiology when you and science are water and oil), not within your capabilities (being perfect), or immoral/unethical (greedily amassing as much wealth and power as you can).

That might be hard to hear, and it can certainly be difficult to discern when it's time to stay the course and when it's time to quit. Nevertheless, try to be wise about whether or not your goals fall into these various categories. Simply put, you don't want to persevere in the name of achieving something that isn't possible or appropriate to achieve. As W.C. Fields put it, "If at first you don't succeed, try, try again. Then quit."

Take a minute to write down the goals you want to accomplish in life. Be as specific as you can. After you do that, put each of the goals in one of the following categories: 1) reasonable and doable; 2) impossible; 3) highly unlikely; and 4) immoral. After you do that, agree with yourself that you are only going to pursue goals that fall into the first category. Even then, it will be hard to persevere in the pursuit of those goals, but at least you're not defeating yourself before the race even begins.

Let me close with some quotes about the importance of perseverance.

"The three great essentials to achieve anything worthwhile are, first, hard work; second, stick-to-itiveness; third, common sense." (Thomas A. Edison)

"Most of the important things in the world have been accomplished by people who have kept on trying when there seemed to be no hope at all." (Dale Carnegie)

"By perseverance the snail reached the ark." (Charles Spurgeon)

"It's always too soon to quit!" (Norman Vincent Peale)

"The only guarantee for failure is to stop trying." (John C. Maxwell)

Munchkins, never give up on your reasonable, doable, and moral goals in life. Never.

37

KEEP YOUR PROMISES

All you need to say is simply 'Yes' or 'No' anything
beyond this comes from the evil one.
—Matthew 5:37

Above all, my brothers and sisters, do not
swear—not by heaven or by earth or by anything
else. All you need to say is a simple "Yes" or
"No." Otherwise you will be condemned.
—James 5:12

Your word is your honor. If you say you're going
to do something, then you need to do it.
—Joyce Meyer

Keep every promise you make, and only
make promises you can keep.
— Anthony Hitt

As you go through life, do everything you can to make your word
your bond. If you tell someone you're going to do something, do
it. Otherwise, you will lose their respect and your integrity in the
process.

Keeping your word is tied to big promises, small promises, and
everything in between. In our world, we tend to pay the most attention to
the big promises people make. The big promises we break are especially

devastating to others and to our own integrity. Breaking big promises sends shockwaves through your life and the lives of others.

Related to how breaking a big promise hurts others, Richard Paul Evans said, "Broken vows are like broken mirrors. They leave those who held to them bleeding and staring at fractured images of themselves." Related to how breaking big promises damages your own integrity, Brian Tracy said "Integrity is the most valuable and respected quality of leadership. Always keep your word."

At the same time, it's important to not minimize when we break small promises. If someone can't trust us to follow through on our small promises, how are they going to trust us to follow through on the big ones? So, whether it's telling someone we'll call them back, write a letter of recommendation, meet for lunch, pick them up at the airport, or take them to get their car at the repair shop, we need to make sure we follow through on our promises.

A few other things to keep in mind related to the promises you make.

First, don't make promises you don't have the *time* to carry out. For example, if you already have a thousand things on your plate, don't tell a friend you'll come over to paint their house or watch their kids five nights a week. If you don't have the time, don't make a promise you can't follow through on.

Second, don't make a promise you don't have the *ability* to carry out. For example, don't promise a friend you'll help them with their computer if you have no computer skills. All you're going to do is waste their time and embarrass yourself.

Third, under-promise and over-deliver. Football coach Lou Holtz said, "Don't ever promise more than you can deliver, but always deliver more than you promise." Far too often we over-promise and under-deliver, doing harm to others and ourselves in the process.

Fourth, be careful to avoid quickly responding to someone's needs. Ask for time to think it over so that you don't impulsively say yes to things that, upon further review of the play, you had neither the time nor ability to do. Jean-Jacques Rousseau was wise to observe, "Those that are most slow in making a promise are the most faithful in the performance of it."

Fifth, say no as often as you say yes. You want to avoid the extremes here and not always say yes or always so no. Carl Jung noted, "The man who promises everything is sure to fulfill nothing, and everyone who promises too much is in danger of using evil means in order to carry out his promises and is already on the road to perdition."

Sixth, once you make a promise, carry it out as soon as you can. Don't put off until tomorrow what you can do today. As Norman Vincent Peale humorously put it, "Promises are like crying babies in a theater; they should be carried out at once."

Seventh, make sure you see a promise as something sacred, holy ground if you will. God's promises are sacred—that's how seriously He takes what He promises us. God wants us to see our promises as sacred as well. John David Rockefeller wisely observed, "I believe in the sacredness of a promise, that a man's word should be as good as his bond; that character — not wealth or power or position — is of supreme worth."

Eighth, don't put others in the position of having to remind you of a promise you made or get you to fulfill it. That's not their job. Write down the promises you make, who you made them to, and when you are going to fulfill them.

Finally, always keep in mind the positive impact of fulfilling a promise to others. As mentioned above, breaking a promise leaves people "bleeding and staring at fractured images of themselves." The flip side of all this is that keeping a promise can help give people a sense of stability and value in a world that offers very little of either. Lewis Smedes put it this way, "Some people still make promises and keep their word. When they do, they help make life around them more stably human."

People need a sense of safety and security in the world. When we keep our promises, we help others to have that sense of safety and security. When we don't, we make other people's lives unsafe and insecure.

Don't ever lose sight of the fact that keeping promises and personal integrity go hand in hand. Stephen Covey said, "Integrity is conforming reality to our words - in other words, keeping promises and fulfilling expectations." Integrity is "conforming reality to our words." I like that, and, when you make a promise, I want you to make sure you conform reality to your words so that you hold on to your integrity as a human being.

Munchkins, do the best job you can to fulfill the promises you make. Try to make your yes your yes and your no your no in life (Matthew 5:37). Make promises you have the time and ability to carry out. Make promises you can over-deliver on. Make promises that are well-considered before you make them. Make promises and don't make promises in as balanced of a way as possible. Make promises that you follow through on quickly. Remind yourself of the promises you make and when you're going to fulfill them. And, when you make a promise, keep in mind how it will impact others if you don't follow through.

38

LET OTHERS TOOT
YOUR HORN

Let someone else praise you, and not your own
mouth; an outsider, and not your own lips.
—Proverbs 27:2

In God we make our boast all day long, and
we will praise your name forever.
—Psalm 44:8

He thinks the sun comes up just to hear him crow.
— Charles Martin

Much of someone's real character lies in
what they don't say about themselves.
— Joyce Rachelle

Let others sing your praises. Never toot your own horn. Ever.

Never toot your own horn about your intelligence. If you find yourself singing your own intellectual praises, you're probably not that smart.

Never toot your own horn about your interpersonal skills. If you find yourself praising your relational skills, you're probably not all that good at relationships.

Never toot your own horn about your looks. If you find yourself praising your looks, you're probably insecure about your physical appearance.

Never toot your own horn about having talent or ability. If you find yourself praising your abilities and talents, you probably don't appreciate where they came from (God) and they probably don't compare very favorably to that of others.

Never toot your own horn about life experiences you've had. If you find yourself praising yourself for the things you've been fortunate enough to experience, you probably don't appreciate who helped make them possible (God) and feel insecure about the experiences others have had.

Never toot your own horn about your education. If you find yourself praising yourself for the number of degrees you have, you're probably insecure about what you know.

Never toot your own horn about what you've accomplished. If you find yourself praising yourself for all your accomplishments, you probably don't appreciate all the people whose shoulders you stood on to get where you are and are envious of the accomplishments of others.

Never toot your own horn about how much money you make. If you find yourself praising yourself for making a lot of money, you're probably an insecure narcissist who doesn't appreciate that "to whom much is given, much is required" (Luke 12:48) and selfishly putting money to use for your own pleasure and glory.

Never toot your own horn about being wise. If you find yourself praising your level of wisdom, you probably don't realize how big of a fool you are.

Never toot your own horn when it comes to possessing positive character traits. If you find yourself praising yourself for having positive character traits, you probably don't have them.

Never toot your own horn about being morally superior to others. If you find yourself praising your moral superiority, you're showing how morally inferior you are because you lack the most important moral trait of all—humility.

Never toot your own horn when it comes to how much you get done in a given day. If you find yourself praising your productivity, you're probably a workaholic, something you don't want to boast about.

Never toot your own horn about who you married or how your kids turn out. If you find yourself praising yourself about either, you're probably not thankful that someone actually married you and wrongly taking credit for your *kid's* wise choices.

Never toot your own horn about anything—your intelligence, interpersonal skills, looks, talent, ability, life experiences, education, all you've accomplished, how much money you make, being wise, your positive character traits, level of morality, how much you get done, who you married, or how your kids turn out.

There are dozens of reasons to refrain from tooting your own horn. Let me mention just a few.

First, it makes you hard to be around. No one likes a blowhard, and, unless you want to be friendless, don't subject others to tooting your own horn. Richelle Goodrich wisely noted, "A session of boasting won't attract any real friends. It will set you up on a pedestal, however, making you a clearer target."

Second, if you're confident that positive things are true about you, you don't need to say anything. Michael Bassey Johnson said, "If roses could talk, they would not boast of their beauty, because they know that they have always been beautiful."

Third, when you boast, you're trying to cover up your insecurities and inadequacies. Kilroy J. Oldster put it honestly when he said, "Narcissistic pleasure-seekers routinely avoid developing the humility required to manufacture a life of full measure. Shallow persons such as me hide their insecurities behind a false persona of bravado, boasting of their inconsequential deeds, pyrrhic victories, and adamant refusals to tackle any task that they fear."

Fourth, when you boast about yourself, you're boasting about the wrong person. Everything you're blessed with comes from God, "Every good and perfect gift is from above" (James 1:17). Shaila Touchton put it this way, "An egotistic man loves boasting about his positions, titles, achievements, and accomplishments before others. Boasting steals the credit from the one to whom it is due. We need to boast about God, not about ourselves."

Lord Chesterfield said, "The only sure way of avoiding these evils [vanity and boasting] is never to speak of yourself at all. But when, historically, you are obliged to mention yourself, take care not to drop one single word that can directly or indirectly be construed as fishing for applause."

Munchkins, never toot your own horn. Let others do it for you, even if it means some positive things about you or what you've accomplished goes unnoticed. If you're going to boast, boast about God and all the wonderful talents, abilities, and blessings He has given you.

39

DON'T TAKE THINGS
PERSONALLY

Jesus said, "Father, forgive them, for they
do not know what they are doing." And they
divided up his clothes by casting lots.
—Luke 23:44

When I was a child, I talked like a child, I
thought like a child, I reasoned like
a child. When I became a man, I put the
ways of childhood behind me.
—1 Corinthians 13:11

Not taking things personally is a true sign of maturity.
— Robert Celner

People will love you, people will hate you, and
none of it will have anything to do with you.
—Esther Hicks

You come into the world taking everything personally. It's called
"egocentric thinking." This faulty way of looking at reality haunts
us throughout our lives and is one of the most difficult distorted
thinking styles to overcome. Sadly, too many people not only don't
overcome this way of thinking but end up more deeply in bondage
to it.

When you first get here, you erroneously think everything is about you. Not only do you think you're the center of the universe in terms of your needs being the most important thing, but you take how others treat you as if that is about you as well.

If you were fortunate enough to grow up in a loving family, your childhood egocentrism led you to think your family loving you was about you and that you must be pretty awesome ("These people think I'm pretty awesome, so I must be pretty awesome!"). If you were unfortunate enough to grow up in an unloving, abusive family, your childhood egocentrism led you to think that family members being abusive was about you and that you must be an awful human being to have caused such mistreatment. How a young child grows to view themselves is strongly tied to how their egocentrism interacted with their upbringing.

You munchkins are blessed because you have parents, grandparents, aunts, uncles, cousins, friends, and various others who think you are God's gift to the planet and treat you that way. Couple that with your egocentrism (thinking that how all of us treat you is a reflection of your awesomeness rather than our awesomeness), and you're getting a good head start on a deep-seated sense of worth as you move forward in life. Call all of us today and thank us for that.

Nevertheless, even when you're raised in a loving family, your fallen mind is still going to take a lot of things personally. Especially when people mistreat you, you're going to be tempted to fall back into thinking that what they did (or didn't do) was all about you. Doing that only sets the stage for you to badly react to what others do and become part of the problem, not part of the solution.

Given that people who love us are going to treat us badly at times and that we take things way too personally, let me give you some tips on what to do about it.

Tip #1: Remember that people's actions are about them, not you. Marc and Angel Chernoff said, "Don't take other people's negativity personally. Most negative people behave negatively not just to you, but to everyone they interact with. What they say and do is a projection of their own reality – their own attitude. Even when a situation seems personal – even if someone insults you directly – it oftentimes has nothing to do with you. Remember, what others say and do, and the opinions they have, are based entirely on their own self-reflection." Tattoo this on your forehead: "How others treat me is about them, how I react is about me."

Tip #2: Try to hear the pain underneath people's mistreatment of you. When people treat you badly, they're usually acting out of the hurt and anger they feel in their own life. Everyone has some degree of woundedness in their lives, and, when they act out their woundedness at your expense, you need to be mature enough to see what's underneath their hurtful actions. Vironika Tugaleva wisely observed, "When someone is cruel, harsh, mean, to not take their words personally is one thing, but to hear the silent cry within those words is another. This sort of perspective can not only liberate us from crippling self-doubt in the face of criticism, it can also liberate us from automatically becoming blind participants in the interaction patterns that the cruel person has become accustomed to—a favour we do for the other person as much as for ourselves."

Tip #3: Know yourself. One of the most important keys to not taking things personally is to know yourself well enough that you can "metabolize" people's criticisms and attacks. Kovie Biakolo said, "Introspection and giving yourself adequate time to get to know yourself is also key to not taking things personally. You know your strengths and weaknesses; you know the things that you need to change and the things that you do well. When you know yourself better than anyone, you have clarity about whether the statements people make are honestly about you or are really just about them. In the wisdom of introspection, you'll find that what most people say reveals who they are, not who they think others are."

Tip #4: Square up with the degree of truth to what others say. It is important when others mistreat us that we listen for any truth in what they're saying while putting an assertive stop to how they're abusively saying it. Kim Giles said, "You should always be willing to take a look at yourself and honestly assess if there is any truth to what they say. If there is truth, you may want to learn from this, commit to doing better, and then let go of the offense because holding on to it won't serve anyone." Don't let how hurtfully people say things get in the way of honest self-examination and taking responsibility for what you need to work on in life. Always try to see what truth there is in the message while letting how the messenger talks to you be about them. Do otherwise, and you won't grow as much.

Munchkins, when you were a child, you thought and reasoned like a child. As you move from childhood to adulthood, put away childish things, especially the tendency to take everything personally. There's a great deal of emotional health and freedom waiting for you if do.

40

WALK ON THE SUNNY
SIDE OF THE STREET

The Lord has done it this very day; let
us rejoice today and be glad.
—Psalm 118:24

Why, my soul, are you downcast? Why
so disturbed within me?
—Psalm 42:5

We are all in the gutter, but some of
us are looking at the stars.
— Oscar Wilde

Even the darkest night will end and the sun will rise.
— Victor Hugo

Pop psychology has come up with a lot of good ideas that have helped people live better lives. At the same time, it has come up with some pretty bad ideas that have harmed people along the way. Let me give you an example.

The pop psychology notion that your thoughts should always be positive is, from my perspective, one of the worst ideas to ever come out of self-help land. Why? Because putting a positive spin on everything takes you away from being grounded in reality and dealing with life honestly. Let me give you a few examples of thoughts that are positive but not true.

"I can do anything I set my mind to!" No, actually, you can't. Nobody can. It's a positive idea, but a misguided one that can lead people to try to accomplish things they simply don't have the intellect, talent, resources, or ability to accomplish.

"The sky's the limit!" I take this to mean that there are no limits to the level of success we can achieve in life. That's simply not true given that there are internal and external factors beyond our control that put a ceiling over how much success we can have. For example, one external factor that impacts our success is that there are a lot of talented people out there competing for the same thing and not everyone can win.

"I'm awesome!" No, actually you're not. You're just as big of a mess as the rest of us. You don't want to stomp around the planet each day telling yourself how great you are at the expense of ignoring how great you aren't.

"Everything that happens to me is a wonderful blessing!" No, everything that happens to us in life isn't a blessing. Some things happen to us that are traumatic and bad and need to be seen that way. For example, if someone runs a red light, slams into your car, and cripples you for the rest of your life, that's not a wonderful blessing but a tragic thing to overcome.

"I'm special." Sorry, no you're not. None of us are. You're *unique* in that there is no one exactly like you on the planet, but unique and special are not the same thing. If you're special, then everyone is special. If everyone is special, then no one is special.

"I'm a good person." No, you're not, at least not according to the Bible: "As it is written: There is no one righteous, not even one" (Romans 3:10). The humanistic psychology idea that people are basically good is positive and makes us feel better about ourselves, but it flies in the face of world history and the painful biblical truth that we all have a natural bent to sinfully miss the mark of God's moral perfection.

You may think I've really gone off my rocker to say all this given that the title of this chapter is "Walk on the Sunny Side of the Street." As I've admitted before, I am certifiably off my rocker. But I'm trying to tell you something important here—don't focus on whether or not your thoughts are positive or negative, simply focus on whether or not they're true.

With that in mind, don't tell yourself something positive if it's not true. Don't tell yourself something negative if it's not true. Tell yourself the truth and try not to care about whether or not it's positive or negative. If a particular thought is true and left you feeling bad, so be it. If a particular thought is true and left you feeling good, so be it.

Let me give you an example of what I'm talking about from my own life. I was diagnosed with cancer before you wonderful munchkins got here. The last thing I needed to do was to put an *inaccurately* positive spin on it, like "Boy, this is awesome—I'm so lucky to have cancer." And I didn't need to put an *inaccurately* negative spin on it, like "I'm doomed and going to die a slow and painful death." Why? Because neither was grounded in reality.

What I needed to do in the midst of having cancer was to view it from the most truthful perspective possible. Once I did that, I needed to spend as much time as possible on the truthful positive side of the street (the sunny side) to navigate my way through it.

Here's what all this needed to sound like in my head and heart: "I've got cancer. That's true and bad. I have a lot of loving people around me who will help me through it. That's true and good. I might survive this or I might not, right now I don't know. I'm going to get the best medical help I can and do what they say is best. In the next few months, I'm going to hope for the best and prepare for the worst. I'm going to spend a lot of time thinking about how blessed I've been and how every second of my life was a gift from God. I'm going to try to avoid any whiff of bitterness or resentment about the fact that I have cancer and be grateful that I live during a time when medical science has advanced to the point they can do a lot to help me. I'm going to thank everyone I know for their love and support during this difficult time. I'm going to acknowledge that the cancer is treatable but not assume anything good, bad, or ugly. I'm going to let this remind me of just how precious every second of life is and try not to waste a single moment from here on out. I thank God that He deeply cares about what I'm going through and is doing everything He can to help me get through it."

Munchkins, dedicate your mind to the truth each day whether the truth is positive or negative. Spend as much time on the truthful "sunny" side of the street as you can, but make sure you spend some time on the truthful cloudy side as well. The truth, whether it's positive or negative, will set you free.

By the way, the song I based this chapter on, "On the Sunny Side of the Street," was composed by Jimmy McHugh with lyrics by Dorothy Fields. It came out in 1930 when our country entered the Great Depression, one of the worst times in American history.

REMEMBER PEOPLE'S NAMES

Now the Lord God had formed out of the
ground all the wild animals and all the
birds in the sky. He brought them to the
man to see what he would name them;
and whatever the man called each living
creature, that was its name.
—Genesis 2:19

Let love and faithfulness never leave you; bind
them around your neck, and write them on the
tablet of your heart. Then you will win favor and
a good name in the sight of God and man.
—Proverbs 3:4

A name represents identity, a deep feeling, and
holds tremendous significance to its owner.
— Rachel Ingber

Remember my name and you add to
my feeling of importance.
— Dale Carnegie

I have a terrible time remembering people's names, especially when I
don't see them very often. This isn't a function of getting older, it's a
function of the fact that I have a terrible time remembering people's

names when I don't see them very often. I identify with comedian Don Adams who said, "I am a quick study—I can memorize a script in an hour—but I can't remember a name three seconds. I've even forgotten my wife's name on occasion."

I've played all kinds of mind tricks to get myself to remember people's names, but then I can't remember the mind trick I used to do it. It's embarrassing to admit, but there have been times I've muttered something under my breath that I thought was the person's name just to try to appear like I knew what to call them. Did I say that I have a terrible time remembering people's names when I don't see them very often?

Dale Carnegie, author of *How to Win Friends and Influence People*, one of the most popular self-help books of all time, made a big deal out of remembering people's names, and rightly so. He said, "The name sets the individual apart; it makes him or her unique among all others. The information we are imparting or the request we are making takes on a special importance when we approach the situation with the name of the individual."

I'm bringing all this up because I want you munchkins to make sure to remember people's names as you go through life. So far, you seem to be doing a great job. When I ask you who your friends are at school, you rip off a lengthy list of your schoolmates' names rather than say, "I don't know, I just like 'em." Good for you. Make sure you keep it up.

I want to further encourage you about the name thing to avoid calling people derogatory names. There are four versions of this to avoid.

First, don't take someone's name and turn it into a derogatory nickname, like calling someone whose name is Bob, Slob or Blob.

Second, don't give someone with a distinguishing physical characteristic a derogatory nickname, like calling someone "Freckles" who has freckles or "Honker" for someone with a big nose or "Small Fry" for someone who's short.

Third, don't take where someone comes from and turn it into a derogatory nickname. There's actually a federal government task force that was commissioned to replace all derogatory names based on our country's geographic features. One of the first names they went after was "Squaw" given that it is both a racist and sexist slur.

And, fourth, don't call people overtly derogatory names. It's verbally abusive to call someone a derogatory name and leaves them feeling torn down, not built up.

Some people feel we are taking being "woke" to an unhealthy extreme these days, especially when it comes to the names we call people. I don't think we can be too woke about it. Names matter, and it is important to be respectful and not take someone's name and turn it into something abusive. If that's being too woke, I'm all for it.

The flip side of all this is I don't want you to allow people to call you derogatory names either. If someone calls you a derogatory name, bring it to their attention and ask them to stop. If they won't stop, tell someone in authority and let them deal with it. If someone in authority won't deal with it, don't have anything to do with the person.

Munchkins, I want to go on four bunny trails before I close.

First, I want to take this moment to apologize to all the people whose names I butchered when recording videos where I read each chapter of this book to my grandkids and posted these videos on YouTube. This book has literally hundreds of quotes in it, and, believe me, I did the best I could to find the proper pronunciation of everyone's names out of respect for their wisdom and insight. No matter how hard I tried, though, I couldn't find the right pronunciation for everyone, and I apologize.

Second, I want to challenge you not to do anything that would lead you to disgrace your own name. Golfer Ben Hogan said, "Your name is the most important thing you own. Don't ever do anything to disgrace or cheapen it." People can call us derogatory names all they want, but we don't want to act in ways that bring dishonor to our own name.

Third, while I want us to be more sensitive about the names we call each other, I don't want us to be too sensitive. For example, when I came into the world, one of my older brothers couldn't pronounce "Chris" and called me "Crick." That name stuck for years, and I actually liked it for a while. But, when I got to high school, I didn't like it as much and felt somewhat embarrassed being called Crick in public. So, I asked my family to switch back to Chris, and that's what they've called me ever since.

Finally, Dale Carnegie once said, "Names are the sweetest and most important sound in any language." I love that. I don't know about you, but when someone calls me by my name, it feels great, like I've been given something sweet to enjoy. Let's dedicate ourselves to calling people by their names and spread some sweetness around.

Okay, that's enough for now. I've been all over the map on the importance of remembering people's names and not calling them anything derogatory or disrespectful. I think you get the point.

FIND A GOOD FRIEND
. . . AND BE ONE

A friend loves at all times, and a brother
is born for a time of adversity.
—Proverbs 17:17

Two are better than one, because they
have a good return for their labor; If
either of them falls down, one can help
the other up. But pity anyone who falls
and has no one to help them up.
—Ecclesiastes 4:9-10

Don't walk in front of me . . . I may not
follow. Don't walk behind me . . . I may not
lead. Walk beside me . . . just be my friend.
— Albert Camus

There is no possession more valuable
than a good and faithful friend.
—Socrates

This chapter may seem like a repeat of the "Hang Around Good People"
chapter, but it's not. This is about a whole different ball of wax.

Not only do we need to hang around good people, but we also
need to develop close friendships with others. Without good friends,

navigating our way through all the madness of life becomes much more difficult. Let me walk you through some of the factors that play into a person being a good friend.

A good friend tends to look at life the way you do. Aristotle said, "What is a friend? A single soul dwelling in two bodies." A good friend doesn't think *exactly* the same way you do (that would be boring), but they fundamentally "get" how you view reality and think in similar ways.

A good friend often understands you better than you do. They are objective enough about you to see your strengths and weaknesses—things that you sometimes don't see about yourself. Vincent Van Gogh wisely observed, "Sometimes they know us better than we know ourselves. With gentle honesty, they are there to guide and support us, to share our laughter and our tears. Their presence reminds us that we are never really alone."

A good friend is willing to say things that are painful to hear. Proverbs 27:6 says, "Wounds from a friend can be trusted, but an enemy multiplies his kisses." Francis Ward Weller said, "A friend can tell you things you don't want to tell yourself."

A good friend moves toward you when others are moving away from you. When others abandon you, a good friend re-doubles their commitment to being with you through thick and thin. Shannon Alder said, "A best friend is the only one that walks into your life when the world has walked out."

A good friend accepts you, warts and all. They aren't there only for the good side of you, they're there for the messy side as well. Bernard Meltzer said, "A true friend is someone who thinks that you are a good egg even though he knows that you are slightly cracked." Elbert Hubbard said, "A friend is someone who knows all about you and still loves you."

A good friend stays committed. Not only does a good friend allow the friendship to develop over time, but, once it becomes a close bond, they remain committed to the friendship *over the long haul*. Socrates said, "Be slow to fall into friendship, but when you are in, continue firm and constant." William Penn noted, "A true friend unbosoms freely, advises justly, assists readily, adventures boldly, takes all patiently, defends courageously, and continues a friend unchangeably."

A good friend is someone who forgives you when you wound them. All relationships involve being wounded, but a good friend won't hold it against you. Jean de La Bruyere noted, "Two persons cannot long be friends if they cannot forgive each other's little failings." J. D. Redmerski put it this way, "Best friends, no matter what they do or how much they hurt you, it only hurts as much as it does because they are your best friend. And none of us are perfect. Mistakes were made for best friends to forgive; it's what makes being a best friend official."

A good friend believes in you. They believe in your potential to grow into a loving and mature human being, and they won't settle for you being anything less. Ralph Waldo Emerson said, "The glory of friendship is not the outstretched hand, not the kindly smile, nor the joy of companionship; it is the spiritual inspiration that comes to one when you discover that someone else believes in you and is willing to trust you with a friendship."

A good friend will strongly disagree with you. Timothy Keller said, "Friends become wiser together through a healthy clash of viewpoints." Proverbs 27:17 puts it this way, "As iron sharpens iron, so one person sharpens another." Good friends don't nod in disingenuous agreement just to get along. They respectfully challenge each other's viewpoints so that both people end up viewing life in a more accurate way.

A good friend isn't there just for himself or herself but for you. They are involved with you because of what they have to offer, not what they want to take. Charlotte Bronte wisely observed, "If we would build on a sure foundation in friendship, we must love our friends for their sakes rather than for our own."

Keep in mind that a good friendship is always a two-way street. I don't mean this to be critical, but make sure you're willing to offer the things we just talked about to someone so that your friendship is a mutual-giving experience rather than a mutual-taking one.

Munchkins, I leave you with one final quote. Henri Nouwen beautifully observed, "When we honestly ask ourselves which person in our lives means the most to us, we often find that it is those who, instead of giving advice, solutions, or cures, have chosen rather to share our pain and touch our wounds with a warm and tender hand. The friend who can be silent with us in a moment of despair or confusion, who can stay with us in an hour of grief and bereavement, who can tolerate not knowing, not curing, not healing and face with us the reality of our powerlessness, that is a friend who cares."

Stay in the game. If you have a good friend or two, hang on to them for dear life. If you don't, keep looking for a good friend while trying to be one in return.

DON'T JUDGE A BOOK
BY ITS COVER

Stop judging by mere appearances,
but instead judge correctly.
—John 7:24

By their fruit you will recognize them. Do people
pick grapes from thornbushes, or figs
from thistles? Likewise, every good tree bears
good fruit, but a bad tree bears bad
fruit. A good tree cannot bear bad fruit, and
a bad tree cannot bear good fruit.
—Matthew 7:16-18

Things are not always what they seem; the
first appearance deceives many;
the intelligence of a few perceives what
has been carefully hidden.
— Plato

What do we tell our children? Haste makes waste.
Look before you leap. Stop and think. Don't judge a
book by its cover. We believe that we are always better
off gathering as much information as possible and
spending as much time as possible in deliberation.
—Malcolm Gladwell

I used to play a lot of tennis when I was younger. I'll never forget one tournament I played in when I was in college. I was waiting for my opponent to arrive at the court for our match, wondering how good or bad of a player he might be.

After a few minutes, my opponent showed up. He was in his teens, had on a pair of raggedy jeans that were unevenly cut off to turn them into tennis shorts, was wearing a pair of high-top Converse tennis shoes, wore a ratty old t-shirt that looked like it hadn't been washed in a couple of months, and had a racquet that looked like it had been sitting in his parent's garage collecting dust for the last twenty years.

I, on the other hand, was wearing proper tennis attire—tennis shorts, a tennis shirt, tennis shoes, and a fairly expensive racquet. If we had played the match on appearance alone, I would have won, 6-0, 6-0. Unfortunately, you don't play a tennis match on appearance alone.

I started licking my chops, thinking I had an easy first-round win under my belt before we even hit a shot. As we started hitting balls to warm up, I began to grow a little bit concerned that this kid might have "game" (skill, talent, ability) and that the match might not be as easy as I first thought.

Once the match started, I grew even more concerned. This kid was really good—crisp groundstrokes, powerful serve, great volley, and quick around the court. I proceeded to get my fanny kicked that day and was out of the tournament after the first round.

I'll never forget driving back to my apartment after the match. I felt embarrassed that I had judged this guy by the clothes he was wearing and the racquet he used. I felt embarrassed I presumed to be the better player just because I was dressed in nicer clothes and had a more expensive racquet. How arrogant and shallow of me to fall into the age-old trap of judging a book by its cover.

Sadly, it is all too human to judge the outside of a man or woman and base how we view them on their external appearance. Rather than get to know a person and hold off making any judgments until we more fully understand their talents, abilities, personality, background, and character, we tend to assume positive things about people who look good on the outside and negative things about those who look less-than-good on the outside.

There are at least five major things wrong with judging a book by its cover.

First, the tendency to judge someone based on outside appearance causes us to fall into being overly influenced by the first moment we lay eyes on someone. In other words, our first, instantaneous reaction to how someone looks spins us into making assumptions about the person that often have no basis in reality. Ovid was right when he said, "First appearance deceives many."

Second, the fact that we judge people based on outside appearance reflects how shallow we are as human beings. The Dalai Lama said, "Even within one person, yesterday and today, there are differences. We must look at a deeper level." Far too many of us don't take the time to look at a deeper level at others, defaulting to quick, superficial assessments far too often. Shannon Hale put it this way, "Many times I have learned that you never judge a book by its cover. Like people, it is the inside that counts."

Third, since people over-emphasize their external appearance to cover up what's going on inside, we often miss the deeper pain and suffering they're experiencing internally. We interact with them as objects rather than human beings doing the best they can to make their way through life. Judging the outside of a person causes us to miss the humanity inside. As Steven Cosgroves put it, "Never judge someone by the way he looks or a book by the way it's covered; for inside those tattered pages, there's a lot to be discovered."

Fourth, judging others based on their external appearance is arrogant. Going back to my tennis experience, who was I to assume to know *anything* about a person based on their external appearance? How arrogant of me. I deserved the rump kicking I got that day if for no other reason than I presumed to judge someone based on how they looked on the outside.

Fifth, it's lazy. Judging people based on externals doesn't require any hard work on our part. We don't have to take the time to get to know people, we don't have to ask any questions, we don't have to go below the surface, and we don't have to fight our shallowness and arrogance. Judging a book by its cover is the slothful, lazy person's way of going through life.

Humorist Dave Barry said, "There's nothing wrong with enjoying looking at the surface of the ocean itself, except that when you finally see what goes on underwater, you realize that you've been missing the whole point of the ocean. Staying on the surface all the time is like going to the circus and staring at the outside of the tent." He's so right.

Munchkins, when we first notice someone, all we see is their surface, their outside. We can't afford to camp out there. Let's take the time to get to know what's underneath the surface of a human being before we make any judgments. And, when we judge, let's make sure it comes from a heart of humility and self-awareness that, in the grand scheme of things, we are no better. You don't want to get your fanny kicked by looking on the outside, do you?

SMILE MORE OFTEN

A happy heart makes the face cheerful . . .
—Proverbs 15:13

When I smiled at them, they scarcely believed it;
the light of my face was precious to them.
—Job 29:34

What sunshine is to flowers, smiles are to
humanity. These are but trifles, to be
sure; but scattered along life's pathway,
the good they do is inconceivable.
— Joseph Addison

When in doubt, smile.
— Gary Rudz

It's interesting how some of the most uplifting songs were written during the most depressing times. That's certainly the case with "When You're Smiling," written by Larry Shay, Mark Fisher, and Joe Goodwin in 1928, just before the start of the Great Depression.

The most memorable lyric in the song is, "When you're smiling, when you're smiling, the whole world smiles at you." The song has been recorded by everyone from Ella Fitzgerald to Louis Armstrong to Michael Buble' and has been used in numerous movies and television shows. It has even been used to sell beer.

There is something about smiling that does us and the world we live in a lot of good. Not that you need me to sell you on it, but here are some of the benefits of smiling. In no order of importance, they are:

- Smiling is associated with longer life
- Smiling helps you to stay positive
- Smiling can decrease stress
- Smiling makes you more attractive, youthful
- Smiling can elevate your mood
- Smiling reduces pain
- Smiling boosts your immune system

An expression I heard growing up was "Turn that frown upside down," something I needed to hear because I was prone to frowning. That was and is great advice. I'm not suggesting that you never frown or allow your face to be sad, I'm just saying that, whenever possible, try to go from a frown to a smile in the face of life's vicissitudes. As Genki Kawamura put it, "It's a little magic trick you can play on yourself. Whenever you feel sad and lonely, just smile and close your eyes. Do it as many times as you have to."

Not only is smiling life-enhancing for you, but it also leaves the world better off. H. Jackson Brown, Jr., said, "Today, give a stranger one of your smiles. It might be the only sunshine he sees all day." Thich Nhat Hanh noted, "Smiling is a kind of mouth yoga. When we smile, it releases the tension in our face. Others notice it, even strangers, and are likely to smile back. By smiling, we initiate a wonderful chain reaction, touching the joy in anyone we encounter. A smile is an ambassador of goodwill."

You munchkins laugh a lot, but I'm not sure how much you smile. I want to encourage you to smile a lot more often, even if it is an act of will on your part. When I tell you "No," like "No, you can't have three more bowls of ice cream and play nine more hours of video games," I want you to turn that frown upside down and respond with a huge smile, a smile that acknowledges Pop is actually looking out for you given that I'm unwilling to indulge your every wish and whim. Caroline Carr insightfully observed, "Decide to smile and keep upbeat. A scowling, bad-tempered face is far less attractive than a smiling, accepting one."

While we're talking about how smiling makes you more attractive, let me encourage you to follow Khalid Masood's advice, "Smile, it's free makeup." I had never thought of a smile that way, but we're saving ourselves a lot of money when we let a smile be makeup for our face. We could probably put all the cosmetic companies out of business if we just smiled more often.

The world we live in needs us to smile more often. So many people walk around with a perpetual frown or scowl on their faces. Not only do others notice, but they tend to return the same look back. Abhijit Naskar said, "A smile has no nationality, yet, with it, you can speak to people from all nationalities." The Dalai Lama noted, "A simple smile. That's the start of opening your heart and being compassionate to others."

As you try to smile more, make sure you do it with those you are the closest to. There's certainly nothing wrong with smiling at strangers (although some of them will wonder what you're up to), but we need to smile the most often at those who are in our inner circle. Make sure you reserve your biggest and most genuine smiles for those you share the greatest intimacy with—they probably need it the most.

A final thought. Try to make sure your smiles are as genuine as possible. Disingenuous smiles or those that mask darker, more sinister motives are harmful to the planet. If you feel you don't have a legitimate reason to smile, remind yourself of all the blessings you have in life. All your blessings in life are more than enough reason to genuinely smile more often.

You munchkins make me smile. Your energy, funny observations, interests, and way of reacting to things constantly put a smile on my face. Thank you for that. I hope how I interact with you puts a smile on your face as well.

As Thich Nhat Hanh noted, smiling is a form of "mouth yoga" that leaves us and the world we live in a lot better off. Use each and every day to turn that frown upside down and leave the world a better place.

BREAK FREE FROM EGYPT

Jesus replied, "Very truly I tell you,
everyone who sins is a slave to sin."
—John 8:34

It is for freedom that Christ has set us free.
—Galatians 5:1

The battle for self-control over an intense undesired habit
consists of an endless series of skirmishes, in which our
urges and our better angels clash several times each day.
— Matthew D. Lieberman

The dark night is a profoundly good thing. It
is an ongoing spiritual process in which we are
liberated from attachments and compulsions and
empowered to live and love more freely."
— Gerald G. May

Everyone on the planet is a slave to sin in some way, shape, or form.
What I mean is that everyone is addicted to unhealthily medicating the
spiritual, emotional, and physical pain they're in, pain that comes from
living in a fallen world where "Each day has enough trouble of its own"
(Matthew 6:34) and we human beings are hurtful to each other.

To put this differently, everyone has idols in their life, gods before
God if you will. We all fall into the sinful trap of loving people, places,

and possessions more than we love God. Loving a person, place, or possession more than we love God is the very definition of idolatry. When God commanded, "You shall have no other gods before me" (Exodus 20:3), He was making it clear that in our fallen state we have a natural tendency to love what's down here on earth more than we love Him.

St. Augustine said, "The essence of sin is disordered love," meaning that we fall into sin when we love someone or something more than we love God. If we love a person more than we love God, we have disordered love. If we love money more than we love God, we have disordered love. If we love power more than we love God, we have disordered love. If we love possessions more than we love God, we have disordered love.

I have numerous addictions. Everyone does. I've spent my life addicted to work, sports, approval, caffeine, ice cream, cleanliness, diet soda, criticalness, control, and self-righteousness, just to painfully name a few. You already have addictions of your own—video games, snacks, toys, and irritating Pop, just to name a few. I don't say all this to put any of us down but just to tell it like it is so that we don't walk around in denial. As they say, "Denial is not a river in Egypt," and we don't want to deny the fact that we are addicted to all kinds of things.

Not to rub our faces in it, but we're all addicted to certain thoughts and feelings as we go through life. I've spent my life addicted to erroneously thinking "I must be perfect" and "I must have everyone's love and approval." Emotionally, I've spent my life addicted to feeling angry and sometimes find myself looking for things to get mad about when I haven't been angry for a while. So, as strange as it may sound, we're all addicted to specific thoughts and feelings, and being addicted to them damages our lives and makes us miserable.

Even though you're young pups, you're already addicted to certain ways of thinking, feeling, and acting. For example, you're already addicted to thinking "Nonnie and Pop should give me everything I want," emotionally reacting in anger when we have the nerve to tell you no, and behaviorally reacting by stomping off when you don't get your way. This isn't unique to you given that every kid thinks, feels, and acts this way to some degree. But, it ain't good.

I'm writing all this to challenge you to become more consciously aware of the thoughts, feelings, and actions you're addicted to and to work harder to overcome them. If you wait too long to work on this stuff, it will be a lot harder when you're older to do much about it. That being said, no matter how old you are, you can break free from the destructive thoughts, feelings, and actions you're addicted to if you work hard enough and cooperate with God's supernatural grace and power.

Some final thoughts about addiction.

When you try to break free from an addiction, you're going to feel worse for a while. It's always darkest before the dawn in terms of the physical, emotional, and spiritual pain that comes from overcoming addictions. Because that's true, I want to encourage you to have other people around who can support your efforts to stay the course in overcoming them. Because things always get worse before they get better, you don't want to go through a painful process like that by yourself.

When you're addicted to anything down here on earth, you're actually longing for God. G. K. Chesterton said, "Every man who knocks on the door of a brothel is looking for God." All addictions are a substitute for what our heart longs for—closeness with our Maker. A notch below our longing for closeness with God is our longing for closeness with other people. Hannah Brencher wisely observed, "The opposite of addiction is not sobriety; the opposite of addiction is connection." A deeper, healthier connection with God and with other human beings is the most powerful way to overcome addiction.

Finally, please extend yourself grace and compassion about being an addict. God extends grace and compassion to us about the addictions we have, and we need to do the same. Please, don't go the shame and self-condemnation route when it comes to the fact that you have numerous addictions—you're going to need all the energy you waste on shame and self-condemnation to break the chains of your addictions.

Munchkins, I love you dearly, and it breaks my heart that you, like me and everyone else, are caught up in addictions that damage your life. I encourage you to re-order your love—God first, your neighbor and you second, and everything else a distant third. Metaphorically, leave Egypt, go through the wilderness, and get to the land of milk and honey as fast as you can.

EMBRACE THE
MYSTERY OF LIFE

"Can you fathom the mysteries of God? Can you probe
the limits of the Almighty? They are higher than the
heavens above—what can you do? They are deeper than
the depths below—what can you know? Their measure
is longer than the earth and wider than the sea."
—Job 11:7-9

Daniel replied, "No wise man, enchanter, magician or
diviner can explain to the king the mystery he has asked
about, but there is a God in heaven who reveals mysteries."
—Daniel 2:27

The mystery of life isn't a problem to
solve, but a reality to experience.
—Frank Herbert

Without mysteries, life would be very
dull indeed. What would be left to
strive for if everything were known?
—Charles de Lint

Most of us love a good mystery. The world's greatest mystery writers,
like Arthur Conan Doyle, Agatha Christie, and Dashiell Hammett, are

masters at weaving spell-binding stories that require wise and discerning sleuths to "crack the case."

Mystery cuts across all areas of life. Thankfully, there are men and women in various areas of intellectual endeavor who love a good mystery and have devoted their lives to figuring things out for the betterment of mankind. We stand in amazement as these intellectual sleuths solve one mystery after another, leaving the world better off in the process.

That being said, we sometimes erroneously think that all the mysteries of life are going to be solved someday. We believe that, given enough time, the super-bright folks on the planet are ultimately going to figure everything out and that nothing will be a mystery anymore.

Stephen Hawking, for example, desired to develop "the theory of everything" when he was a rising star in theoretical physics at Cambridge in the 1960s. His desire to discover a singular, master theory that fully explained and linked together all the physical aspects of the universe was audacious, to say the least. Truth be told, no one is ever going to come up with a "theory of everything" regardless of the field they are in or how smart they are.

Try as we might to fully understand things, mystery is an inescapable part of life. No finite human mind can comprehend the infinite, something that is reserved for an all-knowing God. The Apostle Paul was right to observe, "For the wisdom of this world is foolishness in God's sight" (1 Corinthians 3:19). Our wisest insights into objective reality are foolishness to God, something that far too many geniuses forget.

The most important matters in life will always be shrouded in mystery—God, spirituality, the soul, love and attachment, truth, morality, and the qualities of a well-lived life. We need to do everything we can to peel back the layers of knowledge and understanding in these areas along the way, but we never want to lose our sense of wonder about these matters and the mystery that always envelops them.

As human beings, we certainly need to question and study the things that mystify us. The pursuit of knowledge in an effort to understand things better is a wonderful thing. Neil Armstrong, the first person to step foot on the moon, noted "Mystery creates wonder and wonder is the basis of man's desire to understand." Thank goodness for mystery in life, because it is what compels us to seek greater understanding.

When it comes to the most important mystery of all, God, I want you to pursue knowing and understanding Him better as your life unfolds. At the same time, I want you to humble yourself and accept the fact that you will never come within a million miles of knowing God in all His glory. Nadia Bolz-Weber wisely observed, "I need a God who is bigger and more nimble and mysterious than what I could understand and contrive. Otherwise it can feel like I am worshipping nothing more than my own ability to understand the divine."

Mystery is your friend, not your enemy. The fact that there is always more to understand is a good thing because it continually fuels our efforts to put more puzzle pieces together about reality. Anais Nin stated, "The possession of knowledge does not kill the sense of wonder and mystery. There is always more mystery." Behind every mystery is another mystery, something that's not easy to accept at times.

I want you to accept that even the relatively unimportant things in life are shrouded in mystery. I, for example, find properly operating my television remote control to be a mystery. I'm constantly messing things up on my t.v. and have to call others for help. Just the other day, I spent almost two hours on the phone with a technician in central Europe getting help to turn my television channels back on. Thankfully, what I did wrong wasn't a mystery to him, and I was back in business after the call.

The Apostle Paul accurately observed, "For now we see only a reflection as in a mirror; then we shall see face to face. Now I know in part; then I shall know fully, even as I am fully known" (I Corinthians 13:12). All areas of life involve knowing in part, never knowing in full. When it comes to knowing in full, some of us humbly accept our limitations and peacefully live in wonder and amazement while pursuing a deeper understanding of things. Others let their pride get in the way, arrogantly thinking they are going to develop a theory of everything and never coming within a zillion miles of attaining their aspirations.

Munchkins, I want you to pursue a greater understanding of things as you go through life. But I want you to be okay with the fact that you will never fully understand what you study and that mystery will be your constant companion along the way. Harry Emerson Fosdick said, "I would rather live in a world where my life is surrounded by mystery than live in a world so small that my mind could comprehend it." That's the humble, wonder-producing attitude we're supposed to have in life, an attitude that gives energy and vitality to our brief time on the planet. Don't settle for anything less.

47

OBSERVE YOUR THOUGHTS
BUT DON'T TRUST THEM

Test me, Lord, and try me, examine my heart and my mind.
—Psalm 26:2

The mind governed by the flesh is death, but the
mind governed by the Spirit is life and peace.
—Romans 8:6

Eventually you will see that the real cause
of problems is not life itself. It's the
commotion the mind makes about life
that really causes the problems.
— Michael A. Singer

You have power over your mind - not outside
events. Realize this, and you will find strength.
—Marcus Aurelius

Your "thinker" is a lot more broken than you realize. To put it differently, your mind is always misfiring when it comes to seeing reality accurately. Every thought you've ever had is misaligned with how things really are, sometimes to a great degree. Not very encouraging, I know.

We have a tendency to assume our thoughts are accurate, but they aren't. Like it or not, the thoughts we have each day are always "off" in some way. Our minds constantly misinterpret and misperceive the things that happen to us. And, yet, we think our thoughts are accurate, and we often follow them right over the edge of the nearest emotional and behavioral cliff, much to our own demise and the demise of those around us.

Our thoughts are just that, thoughts. While they are not to be ignored, they are not to be fully trusted or allowed to determine our every action and choice. To become healthier people, we have to learn how to observe our thoughts as they pass through our minds while not assuming them to be true. Aristotle wisely noted, "It is the mark of an educated mind to be able to entertain a thought without accepting it." When it comes to what goes through our minds each day, we need to resist the urge to automatically believe our thoughts, much less act on them.

I'm getting a little Buddhisty and New Agey here, but people can't spiritually, psychologically, or relationally grow if they assume their thoughts to be spot-on interpretations of how things really are. Because our thoughts are always distorting reality in some way, we can't fully trust them.

While we tend to put a lot of stock in our thoughts, the Bible is pretty clear that they don't align with the thoughts of God all that much, saying "For the foolishness of God is wiser than human wisdom, and the weakness of God is stronger than human strength" (1 Corinthians 1:25). Let that soak in for a minute. At the risk of misinterpreting this verse, it seems that the shallowest of God's thoughts are far deeper and more accurate than the wisest, most accurate thoughts we human beings have. Ouch!

If God exists, and I believe He does, we need His thoughts to take the place of our thoughts if we are going to live life fully. As much as possible, we need to think the thoughts of God each day if we are going to see reality for what it is and deal with it in a mature and loving manner. Anything less than God's thoughts running through our mind is going to get in the way of us fulfilling the two greatest commandments— loving God with all our heart, mind, soul, and strength and loving our neighbor as ourselves.

God wasn't putting us down but simply shooting straight with us when He said, "For my thoughts are not your thoughts, neither are your ways my ways,' declares the LORD" (Isaiah 55:8). God thinks on a level that is infinitely higher than we can ever imagine, and His thoughts are always perfectly aligned with reality. If that weren't the case, God wouldn't be God, and He wouldn't be worthy of our devotion and worship.

God's thoughts being higher than our thoughts is why the Bible says, "Trust in the LORD with all your heart and lean not on your own understanding" (Proverbs 3:5). We're not to blindly trust our own or other people's thoughts about life, liberty, and the pursuit of happiness. Our job is to observe the thoughts that go through our minds each day, submit them to God for clarification on whether or not we're seeing things as they truly are, and humbly allow Him to renew our minds by helping us think the way He does.

God, through human hands, wrote down His most important thoughts in the Bible. You've probably heard it said, "Everything that's true isn't in the Bible, but everything that's in the Bible is true." Because everything that's true isn't in the Bible, we're supposed to read a wide variety of books to learn as much as we possibly can as we go through life, relying on God to help us discern what is true and what is false. Certainly, the Bible needs to be at the top of the list for what we study on a daily basis if we want to more fully understand the truth about why we're here and how to experience a life of purpose and meaning.

Hebrews 4:12 says, "For the word of God is alive and active. Sharper than any double-edged sword, it penetrates even to dividing soul and spirit, joints and marrow; it judges the thoughts and attitudes of the heart." If that's true, we're acting wisely if we read and study the Bible on a daily basis. If we want to see reality for what it really is, we need to read the Bible. If we want to see ourselves for who we really are, we need to read the Bible. If we want the wisest advice on how to live life, we need to read the Bible. As much as the Bible is criticized and mocked, it is the only book on earth that offers a truly accurate view of reality.

Munchkins, I want you to make a decision early in life about who you are going to turn to for how to view reality. Are you going to turn to yourself, the smartest people in human history, or God? I want to challenge you to observe the thoughts that go through your mind each day, have a healthy skepticism about whether or not they are true, and trust God to help you separate the wheat from the chaff. Let the thoughts of God run through your mind so that you are properly aligned with reality and cope with life in a mature and loving manner.

48

STAY BALANCED

Do not conform to the pattern of this world . . .
—Romans 12:2

But seek first his kingdom and his righteousness,
and all these things will be given to you as well.
—Matthew 6:33

Happiness is not a matter of intensity but of
balance and order and rhythm and harmony.
– Thomas Merton

Mature mental health demands, then, an
extraordinary capacity to flexibly strike and
continually restrike a delicate balance
between conflicting needs, goals, duties,
responsibilities, directions, et cetera.
—M. Scott Peck

It's all the rage today to talk about work-life balance. I think that's a false dichotomy given that work is a subset of life. So, in this chapter, I'd like to talk to you about *life balance*. Living your life in balance is one of the most important challenges you'll face while you're here, and whether or not you achieve it will determine the quality of your life on planet earth.

Sadly, the world we live in is dangerously out of balance. Individually, each of us is out of balance to some degree. Some of us work too much, party too much, eat too much, lay around too much, spend too much . . . I think you get the point. The flip side of this is that some of us are out of balance in that we work too little, party too little, eat too little, lay around too little, spend too little . . . I think you get the point.

The oldest of you munchkins learned to ride a bike recently. The primary challenge of learning to ride a bike is to maintain your balance, something you discovered quite often when you lost your balance and had a painful fall. Courageously, you were willing to get up, dust off, and climb back on your bike to give it another try. Because of your courage and determination, you now know how to balance as you ride your bike and can look forward to a life of enjoyable bike riding.

The balance you learned riding a bike is a good metaphor for the balance you'll need riding the bike of life. Life is constantly tugging on us from all different directions, and we have to learn when to say no and when to say yes if we want our lives to achieve a healthy degree of balance and equilibrium.

Along these lines and using a different metaphor, Brian Dyson, former vice-chairman and COO of Coca-Cola, said, "Imagine life as a game in which you are juggling some five balls in the air. You name them —work, family, health, friends and spirit and you're keeping all of these in the air. You will soon understand that work is a rubber ball. If you drop it, it will bounce back. But the other four balls — family, health, friends and spirit are made of glass. If you drop one of these, they will be irrevocably scuffed, marked, nicked, damaged or even shattered. They will never be the same. You must understand that and strive for balance in your life."

Using the metaphor of recipes, Stacey Ballis said, "Life is also about balance, just the way recipes are about balance. When your recipe isn't balanced, it doesn't taste right. Too much salt or too little can make all the difference. Lack of acid, too much bitterness or sweetness, if you don't find the balance your food will never be all it can be. The same is true of your life. You need it all. Work that makes you happy and fulfilled and supports you financially. Family and friends to lean on and celebrate with. Hopefully someone special to share your life with, and a family of your own if you want that. Some way of giving back, in honor of your own blessings. A sense of spirituality or something that keeps you grounded. Time to do the things you need for good health, eating right and exercising and managing your stress. If you have too much of one and not enough of another, then your life isn't balanced, and without that balance, nothing else will matter."

Achieving balance in life is a constant challenge, not something we achieve and then don't need to keep pursuing. Tina Hallis wisely observed, "Work-life balance is not something we can find. That's because we use words as if this balance were a noun when in reality it's an action verb. We cannot find balance because it's a continual action with ongoing adjustments, just like the tightrope walker who constantly moves his pole to keep from falling." She's right. Finding balance is a lifelong challenge where we are going to need to constantly adjust our "pole" to avoid falling off the tightrope.

Another way we can talk about balance is to see it as practicing moderation in life. Aristotle famously said, "Moderation in all things." Ralph Waldo Emerson humorously added, "Moderation in all things, especially moderation." The point they're both making is that we need to avoid excess if we want to experience a balanced life. Excess in any way will throw you out of balance and make for a very painful fall.

Munchkins, you're already being taught balance by those who love you. You're being taught how to strike a healthy balance between work, play, rest, exercise, eating right, and the like. While this is painful because it means not getting to overindulge the things you find more pleasurable (like playing video games or eating snacks all the time), it's for your own good.

Paul Boese humorously noted, "We come into this world head first and go out feet first; in between, it is all a matter of balance." That's right. Before you go out feet first, try to live your life with as much balance as possible. Your brief time on this beautiful blue orb will go so much better if you do.

MAKE MINISCULE
MODIFICATIONS

I can do all this through him who gives me strength.
—Philippians 4:13

Let us not become weary in doing good, for at the proper
time we will reap a harvest if we do not give up.
—Galatians 6:9

A very small shift in direction can lead to a
very meaningful change in destination.
— James Clear

Maturity is when you stop complaining and
making excuses, and start making changes.
—Roy T. Bennett

We all need to change. Unfortunately, too many of us have a "road to Damascus" attitude when it comes to making changes in life. What I mean is that a lot of us wait for someone or something outside of us to change who we are, expect the change to be radical, and demand that change takes place quickly.

First, while we often need an external event of some kind *to get the ball rolling*, change requires us to make an *internal commitment* if it is going to happen. God often works through external circumstances to turn up the heat on us to get us motivated to change, but He is too much of a gentleman to ever violate our free will and force us to change. If we're going to change, it has to come from an internal decision to cooperate with God's intervention, not fight it.

Second, change is rarely radical in nature. While some people experience the power of God's grace in such a way that they miraculously and radically change in a specific area of life, the radical transformation of our character defects doesn't happen this way. Transformation of our character requires daily "baby steps" that lead to noticeable change over time.

Finally, lasting change is rarely, if ever, fast. It's a lifelong process that requires a great deal of patience and perseverance. With God's help, we need to work on our character defects for *the rest of our lives* because they never completely go away. To put it differently, salvation is a moment in time, sanctification is a lifelong process.

Think back to the story I told you about the caterpillar becoming a butterfly. That's a great picture of the change process. The caterpillar had to force its way through the narrow opening of the cocoon rather than depend on an outside force to do it for him or her. The caterpillar didn't go from being a caterpillar to a butterfly in a quick, radical transformation way. And the caterpillar had even more challenges and difficulties ahead of him or her even after becoming a butterfly.

Remember, it was the person watching the caterpillar turn into a butterfly who struggled to accept the laws of change. He wasn't willing to let the change process unfold naturally for the caterpillar. He impatiently enlarged the narrow opening of the cocoon so the caterpillar could come out more easily and turn into a butterfly more quickly. What he did reflects how most of us approach change in our own lives—we rely too much on outside forces, expect it to be radical, and demand it be quick.

There are a lot of good books on change, and the best ones seem to agree that if we are going to change, we have to make an internal commitment, accept that the change process involves numerous small steps, and embrace that it's a lifelong process. Failure to accept these non-negotiable laws of change only leads to frustration, discouragement, and defeat.

In order to change, we need to *make minuscule modifications* to our thoughts, feelings, and actions each day and stick with this process over a long period of time. It's a lot like putting a small amount of money away each day and watching it grow over a long period of time. If we do that, years later, we will be in significantly better financial shape.

Munchkins, let me share a personal example of how a small change in my life made all the difference in the world. Years ago, I had fallen into a bad habit of staying up until 1 or 2 in the morning watching television and eating things that were bad for me (ice cream, chips, popcorn, and cookies were my biggest weaknesses). Year after year, I didn't make any effort to change this unhealthy habit, a habit that often left me exhausted and sluggish the next day.

God finally got through to me about needing to make a change in this area of my life. I didn't get a letter from Him saying, "Chris, thou shalt go to bed early and stop eating stuff that's bad for you." But, in His non-bullying and respectful way, God made it clear what He wanted me to do but that He wasn't going to force me to do it. Remember, God is too much of a gentleman to ever violate our free will.

I finally decided to comply with God's loving nudge and started going to bed at 10:30 p.m. and being more careful about what I ate. I gotta tell you, it was tough sledding for a while (remember, things get worse before they get better when you're trying to break bad habits). Night after night, I would haul myself off to bed at 10:30 p.m. but have trouble falling asleep. Nevertheless, God helped me hold my own feet to the fire. I made an internal commitment to take better care of myself and go from being a malformed caterpillar to a healthy butterfly, and I was going to stick to it no matter what.

I am happy to report that making that one small change years ago has paid great dividends. Now, I don't even want to stay up past 10:30 p.m. because of how beneficial getting a good night's sleep has become to my physical and emotional health (plus, at my age, I just can't do it anymore). I still struggle with poor eating habits before going to bed, but, with God's help and my internal commitment to stay the course, I'm going to keep making small changes in that area over time and get healthier there as well.

Munchkins, don't expect anyone or anything outside of you to change you. Don't expect change to be radical. And don't expect change to be quick. The rules of change apply to you just like they do to everyone else. Make an internal commitment to getting better, be okay with making minuscule modifications in your behavior, and stick with the process over time. It's the only way to go from a caterpillar to a butterfly.

KEEP YOUR HEART OPEN
AND YOUR SKIN THICK

Therefore if you have any encouragement from being united
with Christ, if any comfort from his love, if any common
sharing in the Spirit, if any tenderness and compassion,
then make my joy complete by being like-minded, having
the same love, being one in spirit and of one mind.
—Philippians 2:1-2

Create in me a pure heart, O God, and
renew a steadfast spirit within me.
—Psalm 51:10

It is only once we stop taking everything for
granted and fully open our hearts to the beauty that
surrounds us that we will understand the importance
of joining our hands in the construction of a better
world for the people of generations to come.
— Francisco Battiti

Status will get you nowhere. Only an open heart will
allow you to float equally between everyone.
— Mitch Albom

We talked in an earlier chapter about the importance of *guarding* your
heart. This may sound like I'm speaking out of the other side of my

mouth, but I want to challenge you to avoid *closing* your heart while developing thick enough skin to handle the slings and arrows of life that inevitably come your way.

We all have a tendency to close our hearts given how painful life on this side of Heaven can be at times. We close our hearts in an effort to protect ourselves from the pain of people's mistreatment, the setbacks and failures we experience, and the losses and disappointments that come our way. But closing our hearts only leads to more emotional and relational pain in the long run. Closing our hearts may protect us from pain in the short term, but it always unravels on us later in life.

A closed heart can take many forms. Let me mention two that are especially damaging to the quality of our relationships with others—a heart filled with resentment and bitterness and a heart filled with coldness and indifference. The notion of a hardened heart in the Bible (Proverbs 28:14) typically comes down to these two versions of closing off our hearts.

Admittedly, it's a risky thing to keep our hearts open. Keeping our hearts open makes us vulnerable to how people might hurt us (again), how life might disappoint us (again), and the inevitable losses that come our way (again). To hold on to empathy, compassion, tenderness, and kindness in our hearts in the face of the vicissitudes of life, especially toward the people who wounded us deeply, is a scary thing. Nevertheless, it is what we are called to do if we are going to be mature, loving human beings.

That being said, keeping an open heart isn't the only thing we're supposed to work on when interacting with others. We're also supposed to have thick skin. What I mean by this is we need to have thick enough skin to not take people's hurtful actions personally. We talked about this in an earlier chapter, but it's worth talking about again.

Jesus struck a perfect balance when it came to keeping an open heart while having thick skin. He never once closed his heart to others even though people treated Him horribly. His heart was always filled with compassion, kindness, and empathy. Yet, Jesus never took anything people did personally. Jesus knew how people treated Him was about them and the bad place their soul was at in that moment.

Jesus's open heart and thick skin is why He could die an agonizing death on a cross and still utter words that were mind-blowing, "Father, forgive them, for they do not know what they are doing" (Luke 23:34). Jesus could only have responded this way to such evil treatment because He never lacked compassion toward others but didn't take one single thing personally while He was here—not one.

An open heart and thick skin are essential for going through life in a loving and yet assertive manner in our relationships with others. As Alaric Hutchinson said, "There is no excuse good enough to ever be out of alignment with love. You're going to get hurt, and you will feel pain. Yet your purpose is to keep loving, anyway. Keep moving forward with an open heart. Love is a Divine gift given to humanity. Wasting it is no longer an option. Love is what brings light to a dark place. Love is what transforms a dying world into a thriving planet."

We sometimes falsely believe that the only way to heal a wounded heart is to shut it down. Just the opposite is true. Christine Evangelou wisely noted, "You can only heal a broken heart through allowing it to open again; a closed heart remains a wounded heart. Many battles may be lost but you are not broken and you are not your wounds."

A word of caution. While we're to keep our hearts open and not take what people do personally, we need to have firm boundaries with others if they won't stop mistreating us. The heart of Jesus was constantly loving and compassionate, but, on more than a few occasions, He asserted Himself, even to the point of turning over a few tables and ending relationships with people who were unrepentantly abusive to Him.

Munchkins, keep your heart open and your skin thick. Do everything you can to have compassion for others while not taking their actions as a personal affront. And, when someone won't stop mistreating you, draw firm and non-negotiable boundaries with them. The love God has for us isn't just an open heart, nor is it just thick skin. It's both. And it's the kind of love God wants us to have toward everyone we encounter.

51

KEEP YOUR HEAD UP

"When these things begin to take place, stand up and lift up
your heads, because your redemption is drawing near."
—Luke 21:28

Let your eyes look straight ahead; fix
your gaze directly before you.
—Proverbs 4:2

He who is silent and bows his head dies
every time he does so. He who
speaks aloud and walks with his head
held high dies only once.
— Giovanni Falcone

To everyone battling a difficulty or under
attack right now: smile, keep
your head up, keep moving and stay
positive, you'll get through it.
— Germany Kent

It's easy to get discouraged. We experience so many losses, setbacks, disappointments, and failures in life that it's easy to throw in the towel and walk away feeling defeated. In this, my final chapter of advice, I want to encourage you to keep your head held high and keep moving with confidence into the life God has laid out for you.

There are five things that I want to encourage you about, truths that can help you keep your head held high as you live your life from day to day.

First, God made you in His image. Be encouraged as you go through life that you are "fearfully and wonderfully made" (Psalm 139:14) by God in His image and possess complete and permanent worth the whole time you're here. Don't ever tell yourself or let others tell you you're worthless, 'cause it just ain't so.

Second, God has your back. God is always looking out for you, protecting you in ways that you will never fully understand on this side of Heaven. Proverbs 2:7-8 says, "He holds success in store for the upright, he is a shield to those whose walk is blameless, for he guards the course of the just and protects the way of his faithful ones." Don't ever tell yourself or let others tell you that God has abandoned you, 'cause it just ain't so.

Third, God has a plan for you that is uniquely tailored to how He created you. Jeremiah 29:11 says, "For I know the plans I have for you," declares the LORD, "plans to prosper you and not to harm you, plans to give you hope and a future." God will never force His plans for your life on you because He has too much respect for your freedom to choose your own path. But don't ever tell yourself or let others tell you that God doesn't have a plan for you, 'cause it just ain't so.

Fourth, God's love for you is broader, deeper, and higher than you can fully grasp, and it never changes. Ephesians 3: 17-19 says, "And I pray that you, being rooted and established in love, may have power, together with all the Lord's holy people, to grasp how wide and long and high and deep is the love of Christ, and to know this love that surpasses knowledge—that you may be filled to the measure of all the fullness of God." On earth, we only experience conditional love from others because human beings are incapable of unconditional love. Only God's love is full, complete, and unconditional. Don't ever tell yourself or let others tell you that God's love depends on how you act, 'cause it just ain't so.

Fifth, God is always ready, willing, and able to empower your efforts to live life in a healthy and upright manner. In other words, you don't have to fight temptation in your own power but can tap the power of

God to resist doing things that harm you and others. God is clear about this, saying, "No temptation has overtaken you except what is common to mankind. And God is faithful; he will not let you be tempted beyond what you can bear. But when you are tempted, he will also provide a way out so that you can endure it" (1 Corinthians 10:13). Don't ever tell yourself or let others tell you that you're on your own when it comes to battling temptation, 'cause it just ain't so.

These aspects of God's character are the primary reasons we never need to hang our heads. It's why the Bible says, "If God is for us, who can be against us?" (Romans 8:31). If God, who is unconditionally loving and "Omni" (all-knowing, all-powerful, and everywhere-at-once), is for us, we never have a reason to drop our heads. As Marvin Ashton put it, "As children of God we are somebody. He will build us, mold us, and magnify us if we will but hold our heads up, our arms out, and walk with him."

While all this is true, let me speak out of the other side of my mouth for a minute. While it's important to keep our heads up, we don't ever want to do so in an arrogant or prideful manner. Max Forman said, "Always hold your head up, but be careful to keep your nose at a friendly level." Comedian Jerry Seinfeld observed, "Keep your head up in failure and your head down in success." We don't want to allow failure to get the best of us such that we drop our heads, but we don't want to let success go to our heads such that we walk around with our noses up in the air.

Munchkins, one of the reasons I'm talking about the importance of keeping your head up is that every piece of advice we've covered in this book falls in the "easier said than done" category. You're going to get discouraged at times trying to act on the advice in this book. Consequently, you'll be tempted to throw in the towel and stop trying to grow as a human being. Be encouraged—with God's help and the help of loved ones, you have every reason to believe your life can be as fulfilling and abundant as you want it to be.

I close this chapter with one of my favorite verses in the Bible. I hope you are encouraged by it and that it will help you to keep your head up.

Even youths grow tired and weary,
      and young men stumble and fall;
but those who hope in the LORD
      will renew their strength.
They will soar on wings like eagles;
      they will run and not grow weary,
      they will walk and not be faint. (Isaiah 40:30-31)

52

PUTTING POP'S ADVICE
INTO ACTION

Do not merely listen to the word, and so deceive yourselves.
Do what it says. Anyone who listens to the word but does
not do what it says is like someone who looks at his face
in a mirror and, after looking at himself, goes away and
immediately forgets what he looks like. But whoever
looks intently into the perfect law that gives freedom,
and continues in it-not forgetting what they have heard,
but doing it—they will be blessed in what they do.
—James 1:22-25

What good is it, my brothers and sisters, if someone
claims to have faith but has no deeds?
Can such faith save them? Suppose a brother or
a sister is without clothes and daily food.
If one of you says to them, "Go in peace; keep
warm and well fed," but does nothing
about their physical needs, what good is it?
In the same way, faith by itself, if
it is not accompanied by action, is dead.
—James 2:14-17

If you truly feel that self-esteem and motivation
have to happen first before you can make
changes in your life, then we'll probably be
sharing walkers at a retirement home as we
talk over what might have been.
— Shannon Alder

Knowledge is power: You hear it all the time
but knowledge is not power. It's only
potential power. It only becomes power when
we apply it and use it. Somebody who
reads a book and doesn't apply it, they're at
no advantage over someone who's
illiterate. None of it works unless YOU
work. We have to do our part. If
knowing is half the battle, action is
the second half of the battle.
— Jim Kwik

We've come a long way together. We've looked at fifty pieces of advice, advice that is grounded in biblical wisdom. Each piece of advice we've explored is a pearl of great value, and we would all be wise to string these pearls together and wear them around our necks each day. That, of course, would make most of us look strange, but I think you get the point.

The hardest part of any endeavor is to apply the things we learn to our lives. If we don't, it pretty much goes to waste and our lives don't turn out the way God wanted them to. If we do, we give our lives a chance to be better than we could have ever imagined. Because applying what we've covered is crucial, I wrote *Pop's Advice Workbook* and asked you to complete it as you read through the book. You did do the workbook along the way, didn't you?

Poet Robert Frost's poem, *The Road Not Taken*, talks about the fact that as we go through life, we come to forks in the road where we have a choice between the wise, hard, healthy path and the foolish, easy, destructive path. Frost rightly noted in his poem that the tendency among we human beings is to take the more traveled path of foolishness, ease, and self-destruction. He writes:

> I shall be telling this with a sigh
> Somewhere ages and ages hence:
> Two roads diverged in a wood, and I—
> I took the one less traveled by
> And that has made all the difference.

The path we choose each day, be it the wise path or the foolish one, will dictate the overall quality of our lives. Every choice we make either enhances our lives in terms of helping us grow into more mature, loving people or diminishes our lives in terms of becoming more immature and selfish in how we live.

I've stood at the Frostian fork in the road thousands of times in my life, sometimes choosing the wise path that left me and others around me better off, and sometimes choosing the foolish path that left me and others around me worse off. Whatever it means to be a mature, loving human being, it has a lot to do with choosing the wise path more often than we choose the foolish path.

Regardless of the path we choose, suffering is always involved. The two paths available to us involve a choice between two kinds of suffering.

If we choose the path of following the advice in this book, what I believe to be the wise path, we are going to suffer, but it's the kind of suffering that helps us grow and leaves us better off in the long run. This is the path of healthy suffering.

If, on the other hand, we choose not to follow the advice in this book, what I believe to be the foolish path, we are going to suffer, but it's the kind of suffering that leaves us worse off in the long run. This path stunts our growth and leaves us a shell of a human being. This is the path of unhealthy suffering.

Don't let anyone ever tell you there is a non-suffering path in life. There isn't. Each day has all kinds of problems and difficulties wired into it, and, whether we face or avoid them, we are going to suffer.

The choice we get to make in life is which kind of suffering we want to experience—the kind that leaves us and the world we live in better off or the kind that leaves us and the world we live in worse off. The wisest people regularly choose the path of healthy suffering that leaves themselves and everyone else better off. The foolish regularly choose the path of unhealthy suffering that leaves themselves and everyone else worse off. I'm sure all the choices you've made in life confirm this "reap what you sow" reality.

Most of us bounce back and forth between these two paths, sometimes choosing the wise path and sometimes choosing the foolish one. That's why most people's lives are a combination of healthy and unhealthy suffering that leaves the world better off at times and leaves it worse off at other times. The only person to ever walk the planet who constantly chose the wise path of healthy suffering was Jesus Christ. Consequently, He is the only person who ever constantly left the world better off by everything He said or did.

All the advice I've given us in this book is going to go to waste if we don't find the courage and discipline to apply it. Applying this advice requires *courage* because we have to stand up to the lazy part of us that would settle for staying in our comfort zone and doing the same thing over and over again expecting a different result. Applying this advice requires *discipline* because it doesn't do much good to face our problems for a short period of time and then quit. We've got to be courageous and disciplined enough to persevere over a lifetime if we want to experience life in full.

We can't afford to postpone applying the advice in this book until we're emotionally ready and feeling motivated. If we do that, we'll wait a long, long time. Will Rogers rightly observed, "If you wait until you're ready, you'll wait forever." We have to act now, whether we feel ready or not. As Anthon St. Maarten put it, "No more excuses. No more self-sabotage. No more self-pity. No more comparing yourself to others. Time to step up. Take action right now and start living your life with purpose."

We've got to take full responsibility for the path we travel. How we live our lives is totally on us, and we need to own that while we're here. St. Augustine insightfully observed, "God provides the wind, but man must raise the sails." If we don't raise our sails and lazily expect the wind God provides each day to push our ships out to sea, we're fooling ourselves and going to stay anchored in the harbor of no growth for the rest of our lives.

We've got to learn to be okay with taking small steps every day. Peter Marshall was right when he said, "Small deeds done are better than great deeds planned." As we've talked about before, the smallest steps can lead to more steps until we've made quite a bit of progress. We need to humble ourselves to the fact the smallest actions are the least we can do to put each day to good use.

We've got to learn to be patient as well. Not only do we need to be okay with the smallest of steps in life, but we need to take them slowly and over a long period of time so we don't self-destructively rush our growth and development in life. There's an old Chinese proverb, "Be not afraid of going slowly. Be afraid only of standing still." Be afraid of inaction in life, not small steps of progress done over a long period of time.

We need to face the fact that inaction is one of our greatest enemies in life and that what we know is not near as important as whether or not we apply it. Norman Vincent Peale was right when he said, "Action is a great restorer and builder of confidence. Inaction is not only the result, but the cause, of fear." And Johann Wolfgang von Goethe wisely observed, "Knowing is not enough: we must apply. Willing is not enough; we must do."

Munchkins, you mean the world to me. I hope this book will be helpful to you, your munchkins, and your munchkin's munchkins long after I'm gone. Please take all the advice we've covered in this book to heart and teach it to your children and your children's children as well. Take the less traveled path in life and watch it make all the difference in the world to you and the generations to follow.

Pop's Advice Workbook
Putting Pop's Advice into Action

LESSON 1

Are You Ready to Change?

> . . . grit grows as we figure out our life philosophy,
> learn to dust ourselves off after rejection and
> disappointment, and learn to tell the difference between
> low-level goals that should be abandoned quickly and
> higher-level goals that demand more tenacity. The
> maturation story is that we develop the capacity for
> long-term passion and perseverance as we get older.
> —Angela Duckworth

Before you start doing the workbook, I want you to stop and ask yourself two questions: "Am I ready, willing, and able to make some changes in my life" and "Am I going to stay the course when things get tough?" I'm not bringing this up to discourage you. I'm bringing this up because a lot of us fall into what I call the "New Year's Resolution Problem."

The New Year's Resolution Problem is a common phenomenon among human beings. We get sick and tired of being sick and tired about certain things in our lives, and we resolve to turn things around in the weeks and months to come. The only problem is that our desire to change runs into what I call the "It Gets Worse Before It Gets Better Problem," and we often throw in the towel because our level of suffering worsens before positive results start to show. The It Gets Worse Before It Gets Better Problem torpedoes more personal change efforts than you can shake a stick at.

The last thing I want you to do is to start the workbook and bail out when the going gets tough. I'm sure you've heard the expression, "When the going gets tough, the tough get going." Well, it's time to assess that about yourself. So, before you go on, I want you to answer some questions about yourself.

Question #1: What changes do I want to make in my life?

_____

_____

_____

_____

_____

_____

Question #2: What are the costs personally and professionally if I make changes along the lines discussed in Pop's Advice?

_____

_____

_____

_____

_____

_____

Question #3: Who am I going to ask to hold me accountable for staying on the path of personal growth and development when I backslide?

_____

_____

_____

_____

_____

_____

Question #4: Are there any changes I'm trying to make that I don't have sufficient ability, accountability, or acumen to make?

_____

_____

_____

_____

_____

_____

Question #5: Am I willing to allow my efforts to grow into a more mature and loving person to humble me into patiently taking small steps over a long period of time?

_____

_____

_____

_____

_____

_____

_____

Throughout the workbook, I'm going to suggest books for you to read in your effort to drill down more deeply into the advice we've covered. I know you don't have all the time in the world, but I want to encourage you to do as much reading as possible in the areas where you struggle. To make lasting changes in your life, consider reading the books listed below.

Recommended Reading

- ★ *Atomic Habits: An Easy & Proven Way to Build Good Habits & Break Bad Ones* by James Clear
- ★ *Grit: The Power of Passion and Perseverance* by Angela Duckworth
- ★ *How People Change* by Timothy Lane and Paul David Tripp
- ★ *The Power of Habit: Why We Do What We Do in Life and Business* by Charles Duhigg
- ★ *The 7 Habits of Highly Effective People* (30th Anniversary Edition) by Stephen R. Covey

LESSON 2

Hang Around Good People

Associate yourself with people of good quality, for
it is better to be alone than in bad company.
—Booker T. Washington

The company we keep is one of the most important decisions we make in life. There are (at least) two groups of people to avoid, the chronically self-absorbed (narcissists) and the militant rule-breakers (sociopaths). Let me remind you why these folks are to be avoided as much as possible.

Narcissists are people who have a grandiose sense of self-importance, are preoccupied with fantasies of unlimited success and power, believe that they are special and can only be understood by other special people, require excessive admiration, have a strong sense of entitlement, take advantage of others to achieve their own ends, lack empathy for the pain others are in, often envy others and think others are envious of them and show arrogant and haughty behaviors and attitudes.

Sociopaths are people who refuse to conform to social norms, repeatedly lie, fail to plan ahead, act impulsively, are often irritable and aggressive, tend to disregard their own safety and the safety of others, act irresponsibly, and lack remorse when they hurt others.

Narcissism and sociopathy are on a continuum, from people who are not this way much at all to those who are diagnostically narcissistic personality disorder and anti-social personality disorder. Every human being, you and me included, have some degree of narcissism and sociopathy in us, something that is supposed to keep us humble when we interact with those around us.

In this lesson, I want you to think through the people in your life and humbly assess those who fall into what I call the "90% or higher" range of these two disordered ways of interacting with others. Who are the people in your life who are chronically self-absorbed and militantly

196

rule-breaking in how they interact with you? Even though you're not a psychologist, I want you to try to figure out who the people are in your life who act this way. In the space provided below and using a pseudonym, write the person's name and how they interact with you in narcissistic and/or sociopathic ways.

Person #1: _____

Ways they act narcissistic/sociopathic in how they interact with me:

_____
_____
_____
_____
_____
_____
_____
_____
_____
_____

Person #2: _____

Ways they act narcissistic/sociopathic in how they interact with me:

_____
_____
_____
_____
_____
_____
_____
_____
_____
_____

We aren't to assess narcissism and sociopathy about others out of a spirit of arrogance as if we are better than everyone else but out of a spirit of honesty and humility that some people are toxic for us to be around.

We need to wisely honor the command in Scripture, "Have nothing to do with such people" (2 Timothy 3:5).

Now that you have identified the people who are noticeably narcissistic or sociopathic in how they treat you, I want to turn you over to the experts when it comes to what you can do about it. These authors are far wiser and more discerning about how to deal with narcissists and sociopaths than I will ever be, and I want you to soak in their wisdom and expertise as you navigate your way through how to interact with these kinds of folks.

Recommended Reading/Viewing

★ *Disarming the Narcissist: Surviving and Thriving with the Self-Absorbed* by Wendy Behary, LCSW
★ *Enough About You, Let's Talk About Me* by Les Carter, Ph.D.
★ *Freeing Yourself from the Narcissist in Your Life* by Linda Martinez-Lewi, Ph.D.
★ Les Carter (https://www.youtube.com/c/SurvivingNarcissism)
★ *Outsmarting the Sociopath Next Door* by Martha Stout, Ph.D.
★ Ross Rosenberg (https://www.youtube.com/user/clinicalcareconsult)
★ *The Sociopath Next Door* by Martha Stout, Ph.D.
★ *Why Is It Always About You?: The Seven Deadly Sins of Narcissism* by Sandy Hotchkiss, LCSW

LESSON 3

Own Your Own Stuff

> Whenever we seek to avoid the responsibility
> for our own behavior, we do so by
> attempting to give that responsibility to
> some other individual or organization
> or entity. But this means we then give
> away our power to that entity.
> — M. Scott Peck

We all have a tendency to blame our feelings and actions on others. The flip side of this is that we allow others to blame their feelings and actions on us. Neither tendency enables us to experience higher levels of emotional health we can have as we go through life.

The tendency to blame others for how we feel and act leads to saying things like, "You really made me mad when you didn't get the report to me on time" and "It's your fault I yelled at you because you wouldn't stop driving so fast." If we want to experience greater emotional, relational, and spiritual health in life, we have to learn how to say things like "I felt angry when you didn't get the report to me on time" and "I was wrong to yell at you when you wouldn't stop driving so fast, and I want to apologize."

This may sound like semantics and much ado about nothing, but it's not. Learning to take full responsibility for what you feel and how you act each day is one of the most important steps you can take to experience a healthier life. Sadly, few people get there, but those who do will tell you it's worth the effort.

In this lesson, I want you to write down who you tend to blame for your feelings and actions, what feelings and actions you blame them for, and what they do that trigger (not cause) your reaction. After you do that, we're going to switch things around and get you to write down who you allow to blame you for their feelings and actions. Let's get started.

The person I blame for my feelings and actions: _____

The feelings and actions I blame them for: _____
_____
_____
_____

The things they do/don't do that trigger (not cause) my response: _____
_____
_____
_____

The person I blame for my feelings and actions: _____

The feelings and actions I blame them for: _____
_____
_____
_____

The things they do/don't do that trigger (not cause) my response: _____
_____
_____
_____

Now, let's flip this around. Who blames you for their feelings and actions, what feelings and actions do they blame you for, and what things do you do that trigger (not cause) their response?

The person who blames me for their feelings and actions: _____

The feelings and actions they blame me for: _____
_____
_____
_____

The things I do/don't do that trigger (not cause) their response: _____

_____

_____

_____

The person who blames me for their feelings and actions: _____

The feelings and actions they blame me for: _____

_____

_____

_____

The things I do/don't do that trigger (not cause) their response: _____

_____

_____

_____

_____

_____

_____

As with each lesson, I'm going to encourage you to do some deeper work on each piece of advice by turning you over to the experts for what you can do to grow further in that particular area. To take appropriate responsibility in life, consider reading the books below.

Recommended Reading

- ★ *But It's Not My Fault* by Julia Cook
- ★ *The Berenstain Bears and The Blame Game* by Stan and Jan Berenstain
- ★ *The Road Less Traveled* by M. Scott Peck
- ★ *The Untethered Soul* by Michael Singer

LESSON 4

Tell People What You Need

You aren't alive if you aren't in need.
—Henry Cloud

Everybody is needy. In this lesson, I want you to go through the list of psychological needs we covered earlier and assess how strongly you desire each particular need. In doing this exercise, try to get a sense of what your top three emotional needs are in your relationship with others.

Acceptance: being favorably received by others "warts and all"

1	2	3	4	5	6	7
Feel little desire		Feel moderate desire			Feel strong desire	
for this need		for this need			for this need	

Affection: care being expressed through physical touch

1	2	3	4	5	6	7
Feel little desire		Feel moderate desire			Feel strong desire	
for this need		for this need			for this need	

Affirmation: having positive character qualities confirmed

1	2	3	4	5	6	7
Feel little desire		Feel moderate desire			Feel strong desire	
for this need		for this need			for this need	

Appreciation: gratitude being expressed for your kind and caring actions

1	2	3	4	5	6	7
Feel little desire		Feel moderate desire			Feel strong desire	
for this need		for this need			for this need	

Attention: being given appropriate interest and focus by another

1	2	3	4	5	6	7
Feel little desire		Feel moderate desire			Feel strong desire	
for this need		for this need			for this need	

Comfort: being given consolation and sympathy when experiencing a loss or setback

1	2	3	4	5	6	7
Feel little desire		Feel moderate desire			Feel strong desire	
for this need		for this need			for this need	

Encouragement: being urged forward when you get discouraged about persevering

1	2	3	4	5	6	7
Feel little desire		Feel moderate desire			Feel strong desire	
for this need		for this need			for this need	

Respect: being treated with civility and decency

1	2	3	4	5	6	7
Feel little desire		Feel moderate desire			Feel strong desire	
for this need		for this need			for this need	

Security: knowing that others are "all in" and that the relationship is going to last and be safe

1	2	3	4	5	6	7
Feel little desire		Feel moderate desire			Feel strong desire	
for this need		for this need			for this need	

Support: help through acts of service with the physical and emotional "loads" you carry in life

1	2	3	4	5	6	7
Feel little desire		Feel moderate desire			Feel strong desire	
for this need		for this need			for this need	

Understanding: people know how we think and feel whether they agree with us or not

1	2	3	4	5	6	7
Feel little desire for this need		Feel moderate desire for this need			Feel strong desire for this need	

Look back through your answers and circle the psychological needs that you rated a "6" or "7." Those are the needs you feel the strongest desire for in your life. Now, think about the safest people in your life and consider asking them to meet those needs. They are not responsible for your needs or for meeting them, but it is okay to be "poor in spirit" and see if they might be willing to meet some of these needs. Now, ask the same people what needs they would like you to meet. Turnabout is fair play, and you want to be ready, willing, and able to meet the psychological needs of others.

To do a better job of asking people to meet your needs and meeting their needs in return, please consider reading the books listed below.

Recommended Reading

★ *Emotional Intelligence* by Daniel Goleman
★ *Emotional Intelligence 2.0* by Travis Bradberry and Jean Greaves
★ *Parenting from the Inside Out* by Daniel Siegel and Mary Hartzell
★ *The 5 Love Languages* by Gary Chapman

LESSON 5

Think the Right Thoughts

Don't believe everything you hear—even in your own mind.
—Daniel Amen

All of us suffer from "stinking thinking," faulty ways of looking at reality that lead to unhealthy emotional, relational, and spiritual suffering. Because that's true, we all need to work harder on overcoming the flawed "tapes" that play in our minds and replace them with better, more accurate ways of looking at reality.

Take a minute to complete the self-assessment below. Don't answer as you think you should, answer in terms of how you really think when it comes to how you view reality.

1	2	3	4	5	6	7
	Strongly		Neutral		Strongly	
	Disagree				Agree	

_____ 1. I must be perfect.

_____ 2. I must have everyone's love and approval.

_____ 3. It is easier to avoid problems than to face them.

_____ 4. I can't be happy unless things go the way I want them to.

_____ 5. My unhappiness is someone else's fault.

_____ 6. I can have it all.

_____ 7. My worth is determined by my performance.

_____ 8. Life should be easy.

_____ 9. Life should be fair.

_____ 10. People are basically good.

Each statement above is a distorted/irrational way to look at reality. Circle every statement you gave a "6" or "7." These are some of the faulty beliefs you agree with the most strongly and need to overcome.

Now, let's turn our attention to the other side of the coin, the truths we need to believe in order to be healthy human beings. Take a minute to complete the self-assessment below. Don't answer as you think you should, answer as you really think when it comes to how you view reality.

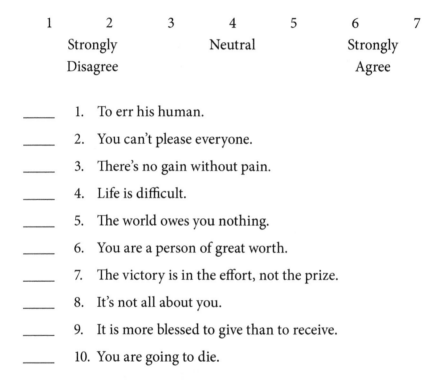

1	2	3	4	5	6	7
	Strongly		Neutral		Strongly	
	Disagree				Agree	

_____ 1. To err his human.

_____ 2. You can't please everyone.

_____ 3. There's no gain without pain.

_____ 4. Life is difficult.

_____ 5. The world owes you nothing.

_____ 6. You are a person of great worth.

_____ 7. The victory is in the effort, not the prize.

_____ 8. It's not all about you.

_____ 9. It is more blessed to give than to receive.

_____ 10. You are going to die.

Each statement above is a true/accurate way to look at reality. Circle every statement you gave a "6" or "7." These are some of the right beliefs you agree with the most strongly and need to hold on to.

We all need help being transformed by the renewing of our minds. Here are some books you might want to read to go more deeply into the issue of overcoming faulty thinking.

Recommended Reading

★ *A Liberated Mind* by Steven Hayes
★ *Feeling Good* by David Burns
★ *Mind Over Mood* by Dennis Greenberger and Christine Padesky
★ *The Lies Couples Believe* by Chris Thurman
★ *The Lies We Believe* (30th Anniversary Edition) by Chris Thurman
★ *The Lies We Believe About God* by Chris Thurman

LESSON 6

Practice Good Boundaries

When we fail to set boundaries and
hold people accountable, we feel
used and mistreated. This is why we
sometimes attack who they are, which
is far more hurtful than addressing
a behavior or a choice.
— Brené Brown

Healthy boundaries with others are a crucial issue in life. Specifically, healthy boundaries are important because we don't want to enable people to mistreat us. It is critical for us to get better at knowing when to say "no" and when to say "yes" in our interactions with others.

In light of the fact that we all need to have better boundaries with others, I want you to write down situations from your past or in the here and now where you allowed someone to mistreat you and how you didn't have healthy boundaries with that person.

Situation #1
How the person mistreated me: _____
_____
_____
_____

What I did about it that demonstrated a lack of good boundaries: _____
_____
_____
_____

How things played out in that relationship: _____

_____

_____

_____

Situation #2

How the person mistreated me: _____

_____

_____

_____

What I did about it that demonstrated a lack of good boundaries: _____

_____

_____

_____

How things played out in that relationship: _____

_____

_____

_____

Now, let's look at the other side of this issue. Write down situations where someone treated you badly where you had appropriate boundaries and how that situation played out.

Situation #1

How the person mistreated me: _____

_____

_____

_____

What I did about it that demonstrated good boundaries: _____

_____

_____

_____

How things played out in that relationship: _____

_____

_____

_____

Situation #2
How the person mistreated me: _____

_____

_____

_____

What I did about it that demonstrated good boundaries: _____

_____

_____

_____

How things played out in that relationship: _____

_____

_____

_____

As we go through life, we need to find the courage to stand up to mistreatment, draw clear lines in the sand for what we are not going to tolerate, and be assertive when people unrepentantly violate our boundaries. To practice better boundaries with others and let others practice better boundaries with you, please consider reading the books listed below.

Recommended Reading

- ★ *Boundaries* by Henry Cloud and John Townsend
- ★ *Boundaries in Marriage* by Henry Cloud and John Townsend
- ★ *Not Nice* by Aziz Gazipura
- ★ *The Assertiveness Workbook* by Randy J. Patterson
- ★ *The Emotionally Destructive Marriage* by Leslie Vernick
- ★ *The Verbally Abusive Relationship* by Patricia Evans

LESSON 7

Listen More Than You Talk

The most basic of all human needs is
the need to understand and be
understood. The best way to understand
people is to listen to them.
— Ralph G. Nichols

Listening deeply to others is a lost art form. In this lesson, I want you to choose someone from your life you deeply care about and work on becoming a better listener to the aches and pains of their soul.

Choose the person you're going to listen better to and ask them if they will talk to you for fifteen minutes about how they're doing. Let them know you are trying to work on improving your listening skills and that you would like them to assess how you did after the conversation is over. Let them know you want them to be completely honest and not sugarcoat things.

Once you've spent fifteen minutes listening to this person share from their heart, have them assess you along the following dimensions:

	Did This Poorly			Did This Okay			Did This Well
Asked probing, thoughtful questions	1	2	3	4	5	6	7
Listened for what was behind my words	1	2	3	4	5	6	7
Listened for what I *wasn't* saying	1	2	3	4	5	6	7
Made good eye contact	1	2	3	4	5	6	7
Used good/open body posture	1	2	3	4	5	6	7
Stopped all other activities/distractions	1	2	3	4	5	6	7
Nodded and smiled	1	2	3	4	5	6	7
Summarized and paraphrased my words	1	2	3	4	5	6	7
Didn't interrupt	1	2	3	4	5	6	7

Didn't assume anything about what I said	1	2	3	4	5	6	7
Didn't take what I said personally	1	2	3	4	5	6	7
Accepted what I said and didn't argue	1	2	3	4	5	6	7
Said "I understand" and "Please say more"	1	2	3	4	5	6	7

Try not to be defensive about how the person rated your performance. Use their ratings to see what you need to work on so that you can become a better listener over time.

Now, I want you to wait two weeks and get together with the same person for another fifteen-minute session of listening to them share from their heart. To get better at anything, we need to practice, practice, practice. This time when you're with them, think back to the input they gave you previously, especially where they rated you a "1" or a "2," and work on improving in that area. After the session, have them fill out the assessment below.

	Did This Poorly			Did This Okay			Did This Well
Asked probing, thoughtful questions	1	2	3	4	5	6	7
Listened for what was behind my words	1	2	3	4	5	6	7
Listened for what I wasn't saying	1	2	3	4	5	6	7
Made good eye contact	1	2	3	4	5	6	7
Used good/open body posture	1	2	3	4	5	6	7
Stopped all other activities/distractions	1	2	3	4	5	6	7
Nodded and smiled	1	2	3	4	5	6	7
Summarized and paraphrased my words	1	2	3	4	5	6	7
Didn't interrupt	1	2	3	4	5	6	7
Didn't assume anything about what I said	1	2	3	4	5	6	7
Didn't take what I said personally	1	2	3	4	5	6	7
Accepted what I said and didn't argue	1	2	3	4	5	6	7
Said "I understand" and "Please say more"	1	2	3	4	5	6	7

Compare this assessment to the previous one and see if, in their eyes, you did any better. Wherever they rated you a "1" or a "2" are areas you still need to work on. Don't get discouraged about the fact that you still have work to do on becoming a better listener—we all do and it's a lifelong process.

Learning to listen to people on a deeper level is one of the best things you can do to become a more loving person. There is something powerful about putting yourself aside, giving someone your undivided attention, and making your interactions all about them and how they are doing.

To help you become a better listener, consider reading the books listed below.

Recommended Reading

★ *Crucial Conversations* by Kerry Patterson, Joseph Grinny, Ron McMillan, and Al Switzler
★ *4 Essential Keys to Effective Communication* by Bento Leal
★ *I Hear You* by Michael Sorensen
★ *Just Listen* by Mark Goulston
★ *The Lost Art of Listening* by Michael Nichols and Martha Straus
★ *21 Days of Effective Communication* by Ian Tuhovsky
★ *You're Not Listening* by Kate Murphy

LESSON 8

Please Mind Your Manners

Good manners have much to do with
the emotions. To make them ring true,
one must feel them, not merely exhibit them.
— Amy Vanderbilt

Just as deep listening is a lost art in today's world, so are good manners.
Nevertheless, to grow into better people, we need to work on improving
our manners each day.

Take a few minutes to assess yourself along the following dimensions
of good manners. Try to be as honest as you can about how good or bad
you are at having the manners listed below when it comes to how you
interact with others.

	Do This Poorly			Do This Okay			Do This Well
Say "Yes, sir" and "No, mam"	1	2	3	4	5	6	7
Say "Excuse me, could you say that again?"	1	2	3	4	5	6	7
Say "Please" when I want something	1	2	3	4	5	6	7
Say "Thank you" when appropriate	1	2	3	4	5	6	7
Chew with my mouth closed	1	2	3	4	5	6	7
Pull up to the dinner table	1	2	3	4	5	6	7
Keep my elbows off the dinner table	1	2	3	4	5	6	7
Let others get served first	1	2	3	4	5	6	7
Don't reach across the table for food	1	2	3	4	5	6	7
Don't talk with my mouth full	1	2	3	4	5	6	7
Use a napkin	1	2	3	4	5	6	7
Don't slurp	1	2	3	4	5	6	7
Don't rush to eat and leave the table	1	2	3	4	5	6	7

Participate in dinner conversation	1	2	3	4	5	6	7
Use utensils rather than my fingers	1	2	3	4	5	6	7
Don't talk too loudly or too softly	1	2	3	4	5	6	7
Don't interrupt people	1	2	3	4	5	6	7
Don't dominate conversations	1	2	3	4	5	6	7
Don't use coarse or foul language	1	2	3	4	5	6	7
Don't burp or pass gas in public	1	2	3	4	5	6	7
Say "Excuse me" when getting by someone	1	2	3	4	5	6	7
Hold doors open for others	1	2	3	4	5	6	7
Arrive on time if not early	1	2	3	4	5	6	7
Pay attention to good hygiene	1	2	3	4	5	6	7
Offer my seat to the elderly or disabled	1	2	3	4	5	6	7
Don't chew gum in formal settings	1	2	3	4	5	6	7
Don't talk in movie theaters during a film	1	2	3	4	5	6	7
Don't put my feet on someone's seatback	1	2	3	4	5	6	7
Don't gossip	1	2	3	4	5	6	7
Don't take things that aren't mine	1	2	3	4	5	6	7
Clean up after myself	1	2	3	4	5	6	7
Don't invite myself over to others' homes	1	2	3	4	5	6	7
Stand up when adults enter the room	1	2	3	4	5	6	7
Maintain good eye contact	1	2	3	4	5	6	7
Shake hands firmly when meeting others	1	2	3	4	5	6	7
Smile at people rather than frown	1	2	3	4	5	6	7
Tell people what I like, not dislike	1	2	3	4	5	6	7
No negative comments on people's looks	1	2	3	4	5	6	7
Knock on closed doors and wait to go in	1	2	3	4	5	6	7
Cover my mouth when I cough	1	2	3	4	5	6	7
Cover my nose when I sneeze	1	2	3	4	5	6	7
Don't grumble when asked to do a favor	1	2	3	4	5	6	7
Return things I borrow	1	2	3	4	5	6	7
Hug and kiss my grandparents	1	2	3	4	5	6	7

That's a pretty extensive list of good manners, and, believe me, I could have added another fifty items for your consideration. All I'm trying to say here is that good manners matter and that you need to make sure you practice them each and every day. For further help in this area, consider reading the books listed below.

Recommended Reading

★ *A Kid's Guide to Manners* by Katherine Flannery
★ *Choosing Civility* by P.M. Forni
★ *Emily Post's Etiquette* by Emily Post
★ *Etiquette for Dummies* by Sue Fox
★ *George Washington's Rules of Civility* by Moncure Daniel Conway and George Washington
★ *How Rude!* by Alex Packer
★ *Miss Manners' Guide to Excruciatingly Correct Behavior* by Judith Martin

LESSON 9

Withdraw and Pray

> The only thing to seek in contemplative prayer is God;
> and we seek Him successfully when we realize that we
> cannot find Him unless He shows Himself to us, and
> yet at the same time that He would not have inspired
> us to seek Him unless we had already found Him.
> — Thomas Merton

We all need to get away from people at times and go to "lonely places" and pray (Luke 5:16). A lot of us, me included, get confused about how to pray, so let me walk you through different kinds of prayers and ask you to write a short prayer in each category.

Prayer of Praise and Adoration: praising God for His attributes.

_____

_____

_____

_____

Prayer of Thanksgiving: thanking God for your life and all your blessings.

_____

_____

_____

_____

Prayer of Faith: affirming that you have faith in God's will being done.

_____

_____

_____

_____

Prayer of Intercession: praying on someone's behalf for their well-being.

_____

_____

_____

_____

Corporate Prayer: praying in a group for God to bring unity and community.

_____

_____

_____

_____

Prayer of Consecration: taking communion, asking God to bless the bread and wine.

_____

_____

_____

_____

Prayer of the Holy Spirit: asking the Holy Spirit to help you when you don't know what to pray.

_____

_____

_____

_____

Prayer of Petition: putting your needs before God and asking Him to meet them.

_____

_____

_____

_____

Prayer of Confession: confessing your sins and defects to God.

_____

_____

_____

_____

Prayer of Blessing: asking God to bless your relationships, work, activities, efforts, etc.

_____

_____

_____

_____

Now, take a minute to figure out where you can pray that would be quiet and peaceful. Where would that place be?

_____

Finally, decide when you're going to pray and put it in your schedule. What times are you going to set aside for prayer?

_____

Withdrawing to lonely and quiet places to pray is essential in life. For further help in this area, please consider reading the books listed below.

Recommended Reading

- ★ *A Praying Life* by Paul E. Miller
- ★ *E. M. Bounds on Prayer* by E. M. Bounds
- ★ *Prayer* by Timothy Keller

LESSON 10

Laugh . . . a Lot

Always laugh when you can, it is cheap medicine.
— Lord Byron

Laughter is the best medicine, and I want you to healthily laugh as often as you can as you go through life. I say "healthily laugh" because we sometimes fall into unhealthy laughter—laughing derisively at other people's expense, laughing at crude/coarse joking, and laughing when something is not funny, to mention a few.

With that in mind, let me suggest a number of ways you can healthily laugh. Under each heading, write down your thoughts about how you could improve in this area of your life.

Watch sitcoms on television. What appropriate comedy shows might you watch on television?

_____
_____
_____
_____

Watch film comedies. What appropriate film comedies might you watch?

_____
_____
_____
_____

Watch stand-up comedians whose act is appropriate. Which comedians might you watch whose stand-up routine is, at worst, PG?

_____
_____
_____
_____

Write jokes. Try your hand at writing a joke in the space below.

_____

_____

_____

_____

Read the funnies. If you still read the newspaper, make sure you don't skip the funnies.

_____

_____

_____

_____

Make friends with funny people. Spend time hanging around people who have a good sense of humor.

_____

_____

_____

_____

Read humorous books. Again, drawing from appropriate literature, read humorous books.

_____

_____

_____

_____

Hang out with a little kid. Kids are incredibly funny, and nothing will put a smile on your face or trigger laughter in your heart more than being around them.

_____

_____

_____

_____

Play fun games. Play fun games with family and friends at least once every few months.

_____

_____

_____

_____

Write down funny things you hear people say. People say some pretty funny things, and it's a good thing to write them down when you hear them.

_____

_____

_____

_____

Watch funny YouTube clips. View some of YouTube's funniest videos (outtakes from shows, comedians doing their stand-up routine or being interviewed, funny movie clips, etc.).

_____

_____

_____

_____

It goes without saying that it is important to laugh as you go through life. Make sure laughter is a part of each day so you can keep your head up as you go through life. To help laugh more often, consider reading/ viewing the things listed below

Recommended Reading/Viewing

★ *Chicken Soup for the Soul: Laughter is the Best Medicine* by Amy Newmark
★ *Laughter Really is the Best Medicine* by Reader's Digest Editors
★ *Laughter Totally is the Best Medicine* by Reader's Digest Editors
★ *Funny YouTube Clips*

LESSON 11

Cry . . . a Lot

Heaven knows we need never be ashamed of
our tears, for they are rain upon the
blinding dust of earth, overlying our hard
hearts. I was better after I had cried,
than before—more sorry, more aware of
my own ingratitude, more gentle.
— Charles Dickens

There's a time for laughing, and there's a time for crying. Here, we need
to explore when it's time to cry.

Crying is tied to sadness, and sadness is tied to loss. Given how
many losses we experience in life, we are going to need to shed some
tears along the way. Losses come in all forms—the death of a loved one,
getting fired from a job, and a dream not being realized.

First, let's explore the notion of loss. In the space provided below,
list the most significant losses you've experienced in life.

Loss #1: _____
_____
_____
_____

Loss #2: _____
_____
_____
_____

Loss #3: _____
_____
_____
_____

Next, I want you to write down how you coped with each loss. Specifically, were you able to grieve the loss? If you didn't properly grieve the loss, how did you deal with it?

How I dealt with Loss #1: _____
_____
_____
_____
_____
_____
_____

How I dealt with Loss #2: _____
_____
_____
_____
_____
_____
_____

How I dealt with Loss #3: _____
_____
_____
_____
_____
_____
_____

If you didn't properly grieve some or all of the losses mentioned above, what would help you to do so? Let me offer you some ideas.

Read books by experts who have experienced the same loss or who can guide you through your loss: _____
_____
_____

Carefully select high-quality movies having to do with the loss you experienced and watch them a few times: _____

_____

_____

Share your loss with a safe, trustworthy friend: _____

Get into counseling with a professional who is an expert in doing grief work with those who have experienced significant losses/setbacks: _____

Participate in a grief recovery group related to the specific loss you have experienced and work on your grief there: _____

Watch highly viewed YouTube videos on dealing with grief and the healthy effects of having a good cry: _____

_____

_____

If you want to go further into how to properly grieve your losses, please consider reading the books listed below.

Recommended Reading

- ★ *Bearing the Unbearable* by Joanne Cacciatore
- ★ *Grief Day by Day* by Jan Warner
- ★ *It's Not Supposed to Be This Way* by Lysa TerKeurst
- ★ *It's OK that You're Not OK* by Megan Devine
- ★ *Shattered Dreams* by Larry Crabb

LESSON 12

Stay in the Here-and-Now

The true definition of mental illness is
when the majority of your time is
spent in the past or future, but rarely
living in the realism of NOW.
— Shannon L. Alder

It's hard to live in the moment. Given how many regrets we have about the past and how many fears we have about the future, it is a difficult thing to live as fully in the here-and-now as we need to.

That being said, let's focus in this lesson on how to live more fully in the moment. Here are some tips to consider as you begin each day. In the space provided, write down how you might take action on each tip provided.

Tip #1: Fully experience the sights, sounds, smells, touch, taste, and emotions of each moment. Experience each moment with your five senses as much as possible.

_____

_____

Tip #2: Remove unneeded possessions. Part of what gets in the way of living more fully in the here-and-now is that we are often encumbered with possessions we don't really need.

_____

_____

Tip #3: Forgive past hurts. A major hindrance to living in the moment is when we refuse to forgive people who have hurt us, holding on to bitterness and resentment instead.

_____

_____

Tip #4: Don't dwell on past failures or accomplishments. Living more fully in the moment requires that we stop ruminating about the setbacks and successes in our past.

_____

_____

Tip #5: Overcome your addictions. Addictions of any kind have a way of draining us of the energy and focus we need to live in the present.

_____

_____

Tip #6: Acknowledge the blessings you have. Take time throughout the day to be grateful for all the good things in your life.

_____

_____

Tip #7: Regulate your breathing. Take time throughout the day to take deep, cleansing breaths.

_____

_____

Tip #8: Bring your mind back when it wanders. When you find yourself thinking about the past or the future, bring your mind back to the moment.

_____

_____

Tip #9: Avoid trying to multitask. Try to fully focus on one activity at a time.

_____

_____

Tip #10: Look for ways to practice acts of kindness. Be kind to others by doing things that would be helpful or encouraging to them.

_____

_____

Tip #11: Look at your thoughts and feelings, not through them. Living in the present requires that we observe the thoughts and feelings we have as they pass by, not ruminate about them or allow them to dictate reality to us.

Tip #12: Spend time in silence. Try each day to quiet your thoughts and feelings and allow silence to take over.

Tip #13: Make some time for yourself. Make sure you set aside some time for yourself each day, even if it's only a few minutes, to check in with yourself.

Tip #14: Do a mindful body scan. Focusing on one part of your body at a time, pay attention to how that area of your body feels and any sensations you are having.

Tip #15: Practice mediation on a daily basis. Find a meditation practice that is healthy and geared toward keeping you in the here-and-now.

I hope you found these tips for living more fully in the moment helpful. To go deeper into this area of life, please consider reading the books below.

Recommended Reading

★ *Practicing Mindfulness* by Matthew Sockolov
★ *Right Here Right Now* by Amy Oden
★ *The Mindful Christian* by Irene Kraegal
★ *You Are Here* by Thich Nhat Hahn

LESSON 13

Be Grateful, Even for
Your Problems

Gratitude unlocks the fullness of life. It turns
what we have into enough, and more.
It turns denial into acceptance, chaos to
order, confusion to clarity. It can turn
a meal into a feast, a house into a
home, a stranger into a friend.
—Melody Beattie

It's far too easy to focus on what is going badly in our lives or what
we want that we don't have. In this lesson, let's work on developing an
"attitude of gratitude" so that our lives will be healthier and happier.

First, what are the things you are currently grateful for in your life
(Examples: my job, friendships, health, freedom, satisfying hobbies, etc.)?

_____

_____

_____

_____

_____

Second, what personal growth and development came out of the
painful and difficult things that have come your way in life (Example:
not getting a promotion when I wanted it helped me to be humble and
more patient)?

_____

_____

_____

_____

_____

Third, what bad things *haven't* come your way in life that you are thankful *didn't* occur (Examples: never had a serious health issue, never been laid off from a job, etc.)?

_____

_____

_____

_____

_____

Fourth, out of the abundance of what you've been blessed with in life, what can you give to others as a way to express gratitude (Examples: extra clothes you can give away, free time you can use to volunteer, etc.)?

_____

_____

_____

_____

_____

Fifth, who do you need to say "thank you" to, either verbally or in a written note, because of the positive impact they've had on your life (Examples: call my parents and thank them for loving me; write a "thank you" note to a college professor who taught me a lot, etc.)?

_____

_____

_____

_____

_____

Sixth, what silver linings have there been in the painful things that have happened to you that you need to be grateful for (Examples: diagnosed with cancer but had medical help that enabled me to thrive, got laid off at work but this led to getting a better job, etc.)?

_____

_____

_____

_____

_____

Seventh, write down some of the good things that happened today (Examples: someone let me into traffic, someone held a door open for me, a friend called to encourage me, etc.).

_____

_____

_____

_____

_____

_____

Finally, pray daily prayers of gratitude. Prayerfully express gratitude to God each hour of the day for all of the blessings He sent your way.

_____

_____

_____

_____

_____

_____

It is crucial that we have an attitude of gratitude as we go through life. To help you make further progress in this area, please consider reading the following books.

Recommended Reading

★ *365 Thank Yous* by John Kralik
★ *Choosing Gratitude* by Nancy DeMoss Wolgemuth
★ *The Little Book of Gratitude* by Robert Emmons

LESSON 14

Stay Humble

On the highest throne in the world, we
still sit only on our own bottom.
— Michel de Montaigne

There are a zillion ways to practice humility in life. Let me give you my "Top 15 Ways to Practice Humility" list for your consideration. With each entry, write a thought about who you might do this with and how you might go about it.

Ask others for feedback. Very few things will humble you faster than asking others to give you both positive and negative feedback on your character and performance.

_____

_____

Give people credit for their ideas, especially when you benefitted from them or improved on them. Practice humility by "giving credit where credit is due."

_____

_____

Admit when you're wrong about something you said or did. Humble yourself by acknowledging when you expressed an incorrect view/opinion or did an incorrect action.

_____

_____

Admit when you don't know something or understand something very well. Be humble enough to admit when you don't know very much about a given topic or area of life.

_____

_____

Acknowledge the superior talents and abilities of others. Don't be threatened by the fact that other people are more talented or gifted than you at certain things.

_____

_____

Apologize when you do something selfish or immature. We all act selfishly and immaturely at times and need to apologize and ask people to forgive us when we do.

_____

_____

Study biblical morality. Nothing will humble you faster than studying the perfect moral righteousness of God.

_____

_____

Acknowledge that your gifts, talents, and abilities are from God. Don't take credit for anything that you didn't give yourself in terms of these particular blessings.

_____

_____

Acknowledge that your talents, skills, and abilities have been developed and improved with the help of others. You didn't get better by yourself.

_____

_____

Pay your talents, abilities, and skills forward. Don't hoard what you have, pass it along to others to help them improve as well, even if it means they surpass you.

_____

_____

Remember that, compared to God, you are no better or worse than anyone else. Avoid looking down or up your nose at others.

_____

_____

Let others go first. Look out for others by letting them go ahead of you when possible.

_____

_____

Don't assume anything about others. Get to know people first before you make any assumptions or judgments about their character or abilities.

_____

_____

Practice an act of humility each day. Don't let a day go by without serving others in a humbling manner.

_____

_____

Stay in learning mode. We never master anything in life but always need to be in the classroom learning things along the way.

_____

_____

Talk about yourself as little as possible. Put your focus on letting others talk about themselves, and avoid bringing the focus back to you.

_____

_____

There are dozens of other ways to practice humility. Please, consider practicing those listed above each day. If you want to drill down into how to stay humble in life, please consider reading the books recommended below.

Recommended Reading

★ *Humility: The Journey Toward Holiness* by Andrew Murray
★ *Humility: The Forgotten Virtue* by Wayne Mack
★ *Humility: True Greatness* by C.J. Mahaney
★ *The Blessing of Humility* by Jerry Bridges
★ *The Freedom of Self-Forgetfulness* by Timothy Keller

LESSON 15

Have Compassion for Yourself and Others

Compassion is, by definition, relational.
Compassion literally means 'to suffer with,'
which implies a basic mutuality in the
experience of suffering. The emotion of
compassion springs from the recognition that
the human experience is imperfect.
— Kristin Neff

We need to have more compassion for others and for ourselves as we go through life. Life is difficult and painful for everyone, and we need to be ready, willing, and able to bathe our life and other people's lives in compassion along the way.

Listed below are various ways you can practice greater self-compassion and other person-compassion in life. In the space provided, write down your thoughts on how you might put each piece of advice into action.

Start with self-compassion. We need to offer ourselves compassion in light of the fact that our own lives are painful and each day presents challenges and difficulties.

_____
_____
_____
_____
_____
_____

Reach out with concern to someone you know is hurting and offer to spend time with them. People are often hesitant to ask for compassion, and, when it is appropriate to do so, reach out to those who are hurting and offer a compassionate heart.

Listen, really listen. When you're with someone, make sure there are no distractions and that you are paying attention to what they have to say.

When offering compassion, ask yourself how you would feel in their shoes. When people are hurting, we need to try to feel their pain and empathize with their suffering.

Keep the focus on them. Make the person who is hurting the center of attention and don't draw any attention to yourself.

Pause before you speak. Make sure the other person has finished expressing their thoughts and feelings before you express yours.

_____

_____

_____

_____

_____

_____

Speak from the heart. Make sure you respond out of a caring heart rather than an overly-analytical mind when speaking to a person who is hurting.

_____

_____

_____

_____

_____

Speak kind and encouraging words. When we do talk, we need to make sure our words are not only from our heart but aimed at comforting and encouraging the person who's hurting.

_____

_____

_____

_____

_____

Compassion is in short supply these days, both toward ourselves and toward others. If you want to drill down more deeply into the importance of self-compassion and compassion toward others, please consider reading the books listed below.

Recommended Reading

- ★ *Radical Compassion* by Tara Brach
- ★ *Self-Compassion* by Kristin Neff
- ★ *Tattoos on the Heart: The Power of Boundless Compassion* by Gregory Boyle
- ★ *The Mindful Path to Self-Compassion* by Christopher Germer and Sharon Salzberg
- ★ *The Mindful Self-Compassion Workbook* by Kristin Neff

LESSON 16

Do the Hard Things First

> If you have to eat two frogs, eat the
> ugliest one first." This is another
> way of saying that if you have two
> important tasks before you,
> start with the biggest, hardest, and
> most important task first.
> — Brian Tracy

Life is full of problems. The real issue is whether or not we're going to face these problems or run from them. Related to this is whether or not we are going to tackle the harder problems first or start with the easier ones and hope we get around to the hard ones.

In this lesson, think about areas of your life where you tend to do the easier, more enjoyable things first and often don't get around to doing the harder, more painful things (Examples: eat junk food before eating nutritious food, watch television before picking up around the house, buy things before paying all your bills, go out to eat rather than cook at home). After providing various examples, write down what price you paid (emotionally, relationally, financially, spiritually) for putting the harder thing off.

Example of doing the easier thing first: _____
_____
_____

The price I paid for doing this: _____
_____
_____

Example of doing the easier thing first: _____

_____

_____

The price I paid for doing this: _____

_____

_____

Example of doing the easier thing first: _____

_____

_____

The price I paid for doing this: _____

_____

_____

Example of doing the easier thing first: _____

_____

_____

The price I paid for doing this: _____

_____

_____

Now, write down the opposite. What are some examples of where you did the hard thing first and the positive benefits that came into your life?

Example of doing the harder thing first: _____

_____

_____

The benefit I received for doing this: _____

_____

_____

Example of doing the harder thing first: _____

_____

_____

The benefit I received for doing this: _____

_____

_____

Example of doing the harder thing first: _____

_____

_____

The benefit I received for doing this: _____

_____

_____

Example of doing the harder thing first: _____

_____

_____

The benefit I received for doing this: _____

_____

_____

The simple but important lesson here is that we need to get the harder things out of the way before we do the easier things in life. If this is a problem area for you, please consider reading the books below.

Recommended Reading

- ★ *Do Hard Things* by Alexi Harris and Brett Harris
- ★ *Do the Easy Hard Things First* by Scott Allan
- ★ *I Can Do Hard Things: Mindful Affirmations for Kids* by Gabi Garcia and Charity Russell
- ★ *The Road Less Traveled* by M. Scott Peck

LESSON 17

Strive for Excellence,
Not Perfection

I am careful not to confuse excellence with perfection.
Excellence, I can reach for; perfection is God's business.
— Michael J. Fox

A lot of us struggle with trying to be perfect. To put it in spiritual terminology, we pridefully try to be God's equal by demanding of ourselves that we be all-knowing (omniscient), all-powerful (omnipotent), and everywhere-at-once (omnipresent).

The effort to be perfect is self-destructive, whereas the effort to be excellent is growthful and constructive. In this lesson, I want you to address whether or not you lean toward perfectionism or excellence across four very important dimensions.

Idealistic or Realistic? Do you find yourself thinking about how things should be or how they actually are? Do you find yourself mentally stiff-arming painful reality or accepting it even if you don't like it?

_____

_____

_____

_____

Product-Minded or Process-Minded? Do you find yourself postponing happiness and contentment until you've achieved what you're working on or enjoying the journey as you move in the direction of achieving the things you want in life?

_____

_____

_____

_____

The Best or Your Best? Do you find that you compare yourself to others to see how you stack up or are able to simply focus on being the best version of you that you can be?

_____

_____

_____

_____

_____

Worth = Performance or Worth = Made in God's Image? Do you tie your worth as a human being to how well or poorly you perform in your various roles or to the fact that God fearfully and wonderfully made you in His image?

_____

_____

_____

_____

_____

Now, let's go back to trying to be God's equal as another example of trying to be perfect. Respond to the following questions below.

Do you beat yourself up for making mistakes, evidence that you expect yourself to be all-knowing (omniscient), or do you accept that you're going to make a lot of mistakes in life because you aren't all-knowing?

_____

_____

_____

Do you try to control others, evidence that you are trying to be all-powerful (omnipotent), or do you try to influence others by modeling how to do things in an excellent manner?

_____

_____

_____

Finally, do you try to get the work of 20 people done each day, evidence that you are trying to be everywhere-at-once (omnipresent), or do you try to get as much done each day as you can given that you're a finite human being?

_____

_____

_____

It is crucial we accept our limitations as human beings and humbly embrace the fact that we are not all-knowing, all-powerful, or everywhere-at-once. It is important that we accept reality as it is, focus on the process of moving in the direction of our goals, be the best we can be given who we are, and anchor our worth in being God's image bearers. For further help moving in these various directions, consider reading the books listed below.

Recommended Readings

★ *CBT Workbook for Perfectionism* by Sharon Martin
★ *How to Be an Imperfectionist* by Stephen Guise
★ *The ACT Workbook for Perfectionism* by Jennifer Kemp
★ *The Search for Significance* by Robert McGee
★ *The 7 Habits of Highly Effective People* by Stephen Covey
★ *When Perfect Isn't Good Enough* by Martin Antony and Richard Swenson

LESSON 18

Forgive Others . . .
and Yourself

Forgiveness is an act of the will, and the will can
function regardless of the temperature of the heart.
— Corrie Ten Boom

Forgiveness is a two-sided coin in the sense that we need to forgive
others for the wrongs they do to us and we need to forgive ourselves for
the wrongs we do to others.

In this lesson, I want you to work on both sides of the forgiveness
coin. First, I want you to work on who in your life you haven't
forgiven for what they did to you. Second, I want you to work on
not having forgiven yourself for the wrong things you've done along
the way.

There are people in your life who have deeply hurt you. In the space
provided below, I want you to write down the names of the people who
hurt you the most, what they did that was hurtful, and what has gotten
in the way of you forgiving them for what they did.

_____

_____

_____

_____

_____

_____

_____

_____

_____

There are people in your life who you have been hurtful toward. In
the space provided below, who, in your estimation, have you hurt the

most, what did you do that was hurtful to them, and what has gotten in the way of you forgiving yourself for what you did?

_____

_____

_____

_____

_____

_____

_____

_____

Next, let's walk through some of the core issues behind why we don't forgive others. These are the unhealthy beliefs inside each of us that get in the way of forgiving others for their hurtful actions. In the spaces provided, write down where you are on each of these issues.

Not forgiving others because the person in question isn't sorry for what they did. This is the lie that forgiveness is tied to whether or not the person is truly sorry for their hurtful actions and that we should withhold forgiveness until they are.

_____

_____

_____

_____

_____

_____

_____

_____

Not forgiving others because we erroneously think it means we're saying that what they did wasn't a big deal or didn't hurt. If we need to forgive someone, we're acknowledging that what they did was a big deal and hurt, otherwise we don't need to forgive them.

_____

_____

_____

_____

Not forgiving others because we erroneously think that if we do we have to resume having a relationship with them. Forgiving others doesn't automatically mean we are supposed to be around the person. In fact, there are times we need to permanently stay away from someone who hurt us even though we've forgiven them.

We're only hurting ourselves when we don't forgive others who hurt us or forgive ourselves for hurting others. There are no valid reasons for not forgiving others or ourselves, just prideful things inside of each of us that are unhealthy and toxic. If you want to go deeper into the issue of forgiving others and yourself, consider reading the books listed below.

Recommended Reading

- ★ *Forgiving What You Can't Forget* by Lysa TerKeurst
- ★ *How to Forgive Ourselves—Totally* by R. T. Kendall
- ★ *The Art of Forgiving* by Lewis Smedes
- ★ *The Forgiveness Journal* by Lysa TerKeurst
- ★ *The Gift of Forgiveness* by Charles Stanley
- ★ *Total Forgiveness* by R. T. Kendall

LESSON 19

Stand Up to Evil

The only thing necessary for the triumph of
evil is for good men to do nothing.
—Edmund Burke

Throughout human history, there have been evil people who have caused a great deal of harm to the world we live in. Sometimes this takes place on a global scale, and, other times, it takes place on a local level.

Some of us feel called to confront evil when it takes place on a global level, like when an autocratic despot invades another country and tries to take it over. Some of us feel called to confront evil on a local level, like when racism leads to people of color being singled out for mistreatment in our community.

There is a difference between an evil person and an evil action. An evil person is someone who militantly refuses to acknowledge their "dark side" and unrepentantly continues to act in immoral and unethical ways. An evil action, something we've all committed and will do again, is any action that doesn't square with the teachings of the Bible regarding God's moral laws.

In the space provided below, I want you to write down if you feel you are being called to oppose evil people who are causing harm to their country, countries around them, or countries around the world. If so, what practical ways can you oppose these individuals?

_____

_____

_____

_____

_____

_____

_____

_____

_____

In the space provided below, what specific evil actions have you witnessed in your community that you feel called to do something about? Write down what the specific evil action was, who did it, and what practical ways you can do something about it.

_____

_____

_____

_____

_____

_____

_____

_____

_____

_____

There are times we're supposed to stand up against the evil people and evil actions God wants us to stand up to. What I mean by this is that there are so many evil people in the world and so many evil actions committed each day that we can't possibly stand up to all of them. It is important for each of us to wisely discern what our particular calling is when it comes to standing up to evildoers and evil deeds. In the space provided below, do you have any specific sense of what this looks like for you?

_____

_____

_____

_____

_____

_____

_____

_____

_____

Courageous people throughout human history stood up to evil people and evil actions, many of whom paid an incredibly high price for doing so. In the space below, to what degree are you willing to pay the price (emotionally, financially, occupationally, spiritually) for standing up to evil?

_____

_____

_____

_____

_____

_____

_____

_____

_____

_____

Make a choice to stand up to evil people and evil actions when you're supposed to do so. If this is an area of your life you want to explore further, please consider reading the books listed below.

Recommended Reading

★ *Glittering Vices* by Rebecca Konyndyk DeYoung
★ *On Evil* by Thomas Aquinas
★ *People of the Lie* by M. Scott Peck
★ *Respectable Sins* by Jerry Bridges
★ *The Anatomy of Evil* by Michael Stone
★ *The Covert Passive-Aggressive Narcissist* by Debbie Mirza
★ *The Sociopath Next Door* by Martha Stout

LESSON 20

Read a Lot of Really
Good Books

Read the best books first, or you may not
have a chance to read them all.
—Henry David Thoreau

We've already talked about how important it is to read a lot of good
books while you're here. In this lesson, I'm going to push you to get your
reading list put together and make plans for when and where you are
going to read these books.

First, let's compile your reading list. We're going to do this a little
backward. I want you to go to the recommended reading lists at the end
of this lesson and pull up each of the articles mentioned. From each
article, list one book you will try to read before this year is over.

Books of the Bible I'll read in the next 365 days: _____
_____
_____

A classic I'll read in the next 365 days: _____
_____
_____

A book of poetry I'll read in the next 365 days: _____
_____
_____

A biography I'll read in the next 365 days: _____
_____
_____

A self-improvement book I'll read in the next 365 days: _____
_____
_____

A novel I'll read in the next 365 days: _____
_____
_____

A Christian classic I'll read in the next 365 days: _____
_____
_____

Now, let's turn our attention to a reading plan for how you're going to read as many books as possible in the years to come. Look your schedule over and figure out how many times you are going to read each week, how long you're going to read each time, and where you are going to read.

I'm going to read on these days _____
_____ at these times _____
_____ for this long _____
_____ and at this location _____
_____.

Don't forget that you can "read" a book on audio and can listen to books on audio when you're driving to work, in the shower, working out, etc. There are numerous ways to get a lot of reading done. Please make sure you invest yourself in becoming a voracious reader of the good books that are out there.

Confucious said, "You must find time for reading, or surrender yourself to self-chosen ignorance." Do yourself a big favor and read as much as you can so that you don't surrender yourself to self-chosen ignorance.

Recommended Reading

- ★ *How to Read the Bible for All Its Worth* by Gordon Fee and Douglas Stuart
- ★ 50 Best Classic Books of All Time (Content Writing Jobs): https://contentwritingjobs.com/blog/best-classic-books
- ★ 60+ Best Poetry Books of All-Time (Reedsy): https://reedsy.com/discovery/blog/best-poetry-books
- ★ The 30 Best Mystery Books of All Time (Reedsy): https://reedsy.com/discovery/blog/best-mystery-books
- ★ The 70 Best Biography Books of all time (The Art of Living): https://theartofliving.com/best-biographies/
- ★ The 100 Best Self-Improvement Books of All Time (Shortform): https://www.shortform.com/best-books/genre/best-self-improvement-books-of-all-time
- ★ The Best Novels of All Time (Ranker): https://www.ranker.com/crowdranked-list/best-books-of-all-time-_fiction_
- ★ Top 100 Christian Books of All Time (Worldview Institute): https://www.goodreads.com/list/show/19595.Top_100_Christian_Books_Worldview_Institute

LESSON 21

Accept Yourself and
Others, Warts and All

> One thing is clear to me: we, as human
> beings, must be willing to accept people
> who are different from ourselves.
> — Barbara Jordan

Accepting others and ourselves, warts and all, is a hard thing. In this
lesson, I want you to spend some time working on what it is about
yourself that you don't accept and what it is about other people that you
don't accept.

First, let's start with you. What are some of the flaws and defects
you don't accept about yourself?

_____

_____

_____

_____

_____

_____

_____

_____

_____

_____

_____

_____

_____

_____

_____

Second, what are some of the flaws and defects you don't accept about others?

_____
_____
_____
_____
_____
_____
_____
_____
_____
_____
_____
_____
_____
_____
_____

Third, is there any overlap between these two lists?

_____
_____
_____
_____
_____
_____
_____
_____
_____
_____
_____
_____
_____
_____
_____
_____

Fourth, what's getting in the way of you accepting the "warts and all" you and other people have?

_____

_____

_____

_____

_____

_____

_____

_____

_____

_____

_____

_____

_____

_____

Finally, what price have you paid emotionally and relationally for not accepting your flaws and other people's flaws?

_____

_____

_____

_____

_____

_____

_____

_____

_____

_____

_____

_____

_____

We need to accept our defects and the defects of others. Failure to do so is going to keep us down on ourselves and the rest of the human race. If you want to go deeper into this issue, please consider reading the books listed below.

Recommended Reading

- ★ *Get Out of Your Mind and Into Your Life* by Steven Hayes
- ★ *The Gifts of Acceptance* by Daniel Miller
- ★ *The Gift of Being Yourself* by David Benner
- ★ *The Gifts of Imperfection* by Brene Brown

LESSON 22

Stop Shoulding All Over Yourself

Shoulds' come only from leftover thinking. If
we are truly in this moment (the only
one there really is), we don't should on
ourselves. It's a great freedom. Next
time you feel a should coming at you, ask
yourself if it really belongs to you!
— Kelly Corbet

We all have toxic shoulds and shouldn'ts run through our minds each
day. In this lesson, I want you to explore whether or not you fall into
any of the shoulds and shouldn'ts I explore in my book, *Stop Shoulding
All Over Yourself.*

In the self-assessment questionnaire below, rate the degree to which
you agree or disagree with each statement. Try to be as honest as you can
about whether or not you think in these particular ways.

	Strongly Disagree						Strongly Agree
I shouldn't make mistakes	1	2	3	4	5	6	7
I should be able to get more done	1	2	3	4	5	6	7
I should be able to control my circumstances	1	2	3	4	5	6	7
I should know more than I do	1	2	3	4	5	6	7
I should be happier than I am	1	2	3	4	5	6	7
I shouldn't do embarrassing things	1	2	3	4	5	6	7
I shouldn't be addicted to anything	1	2	3	4	5	6	7
I should be more sensitive to others	1	2	3	4	5	6	7
I shouldn't forget things	1	2	3	4	5	6	7
I should be more successful	1	2	3	4	5	6	7
I should like everything about the way I look	1	2	3	4	5	6	7

I should be more intelligent relationally	1	2	3	4	5	6	7
I should be in a better mood	1	2	3	4	5	6	7
I should know what I want to do with my life	1	2	3	4	5	6	7
I shouldn't have any bad habits	1	2	3	4	5	6	7
I shouldn't be losing a step	1	2	3	4	5	6	7
I shouldn't have a bad bent	1	2	3	4	5	6	7
I should be a better communicator	1	2	3	4	5	6	7
I shouldn't have unlikeable qualities	1	2	3	4	5	6	7
I should have high self-esteem	1	2	3	4	5	6	7

Now, look back through your answers and see which statements you gave a "6" or a "7." These are the shoulds and shouldn'ts you agree with the most strongly and are causing the greatest damage to your emotional health and relationships with others. In the space provided below, write these statements down and why they are untrue.

Should/Shouldn't #1: _____

Why It's Not True: _____

_____

_____

_____

_____

Should/Shouldn't #2: _____

Why It's Not True: _____

_____

_____

_____

_____

Should/Shouldn't #3: _____

Why It's Not True: _____

_____

_____

_____

_____

Should/Shouldn't #4: _____

Why It's Not True: _____

_____

_____

_____

_____

It is important that we eliminate our shoulds and shouldn'ts as we go through life. They cause nothing but harm to our emotional well-being and our relationships with others. To explore this area more deeply, consider reading the books listed below.

Recommended Reading

★ *It's Your Attitude* by Chris Thurman
★ *Stop Shoulding All Over Yourself* by Chris Thurman
★ *Winning the War in Your Mind* by Craig Groeschel

LESSON 23

Be Angry but Don't
Act the Fool

Angry people are not always wise.
— Jane Austen

We feel angry when something blocks or frustrates our goal (getting stuck in a traffic jam when we need to get across town) or someone mistreats us (cuts us off in traffic). Some of us were raised to think that anger is always bad, but that's simply not true. There are three primary problems with the anger most of us feel: 1) we become angry about things that don't warrant getting angry; 2) we become angry too often; and 3) we express our anger in hurtful and sinful ways toward others.

First, write down the kinds of events that trigger (not cause) your anger.

Event #1 that triggers my anger is: _____
_____

Event #2 that triggers my anger is: _____
_____

Event #3 that triggers my anger is: _____
_____

Event #4 that triggers my anger is: _____
_____

Event #5 that triggers my anger is: _____
_____

Second, for each event listed above, write down how you typically respond.

I usually respond to Event #1 by: _____
_____

I usually respond to Event #2 by: _____
_____

I usually respond to Event #3 by: _____

_____

I usually respond to Event #4 by: _____

_____

I usually respond to Event #5 by: _____

_____

Third, there are five destructive types of reactions we have to the events that trigger our anger. With each type of response, write down how you tend to react that way in a given situation.

Passively: the tendency to stuff your anger and do nothing about it.

_____

_____

_____

_____

Aggressively: the tendency to spew your anger and explode at the external world.

_____

_____

_____

_____

Passive-Aggressively: the tendency to let your anger leak out indirectly at others' expense.

_____

_____

_____

_____

Self-Medicate: the tendency to soothe your anger with things that will make you feel good in the moment.

_____

_____

_____

_____

Try Harder: the tendency to try to be perfect so that people will treat you better.

_____

_____

_____

_____

We are going to get angry in life—that's a given. The real issue is whether or not we are going to be angry at the right time and in the right way. We can respond to our anger in the five destructive ways listed above, or we can learn to respond to our anger in assertive and healthy ways. To go further into the issue of handling your anger better, please consider reading the books listed below.

Recommended Reading

- ★ *Anger: Taming a Powerful Emotion* by Gary Chapman
- ★ *Anger Management Workbook for Kids* by Samantha Snowden
- ★ *Anger Management Workbook for Men* by Aaron Karmin
- ★ *Anger Management Workbook for Women* by Julie Catalano
- ★ *The Cognitive-Behavioral Workbook for Anger* by William Knaus and Robert Alberti

LESSON 24

Practice Generosity

The most truly generous persons are those who
give silently without hope of praise or reward.
— Carol Ryrie Brink

It is important to practice generosity as we go through life. Being generous takes many forms, but it certainly involves giving in a way that has an "ouch" to it and giving to others with no desire to be given anything back.

Let's walk through areas of life where we can give generously to others: time, talents, and treasures.

In the space provided below, write down how you can generously give your time to others. Examples include giving your time by volunteering for a good cause, meeting with someone who needs comfort and encouragement, helping someone move, and going over to someone's house to help them with a project.

_____

_____

_____

_____

_____

_____

_____

_____

_____

_____

_____

_____

_____

_____

In the space provided below, write down how you can generously give your talents to others. For example, if you are a talented tennis player, you could teach someone how to play tennis. If you are talented with technology, you could help someone with the technology problems they're having. If you're a talented painter, you could teach someone how to paint.

_____

_____

_____

_____

_____

_____

_____

_____

_____

_____

_____

_____

_____

_____

_____

_____

In the space provided below, write down how you could generously share your "treasures" with others. For example, you could give money to charitable organizations. If you have several automobiles, you could give someone a car who needs it. If you know a person or a group of people who are in legitimate financial need, how might you help?

_____

_____

_____

_____

_____

_____

_____

_____

_____

_____

_____

_____

_____

_____

Keep in mind that your time, talents, and treasures are on loan from God and not really yours anyway. When you give generously of the three, you're simply acknowledging God's goodness and trying to "pay it forward" to others. Also, keep in mind that you can't take anything with you once you exit the planet.

If you want to drill down more deeply into the importance of generosity, please consider reading the books listed below.

Recommended Reading

★ *Human Kind: Changing the World One Small Act at a Time* by Brad Aronson

★ *Money, Possessions, and Eternity: A Comprehensive Guide to What the Bible Says about Financial Stewardship, Generosity, Materialism, Retirement, Financial Planning, Gambling, Debt, and More* by Randy Alcorn

★ *The Generosity Factor: Discover the Joy of Giving Your Time, Talent, and Treasure* by Ken Blanchard and S. Truett Cathy

★ *The Genius of Generosity: Generous Living is Joyful Living* by Chip Ingram

★ *The Legacy Journey: A Radical View of Biblical Wealth and Generosity* by Dave Ramsey

LESSON 25

Seek Wise Counsel

Spiritual mentors or peers who are mature in
their relationship with God and whose present
walk with God we trust can seek God with us
and provide us with a sort of "safety net."
If we feel the Spirit is leading us to do something
but recognize that much is at stake if
we are wrong, we may do well to talk the matter
over with other mature Christians.
Proverbs advised rulers that wisdom rests
in a multitude of counselors, and that
advice remains valid for us as well. In the end,
we may not always settle on the counsel
others give us - like us, they too are fallible -
but if they are diligent students of the
Scriptures and persons of prayer, we should
humbly consider their counsel.
—Craig Keener

We all need wise counsel. The last thing we want to do in life, especially when the decisions we face are important ones, is lean only on our own understanding. Not that we don't have some valid thoughts about things, but tapping a variety of people and sources for what they think is the best way to end up making a good decision.

With that in mind, let's focus on three primary sources of wise counsel: the wisdom of God, the wisdom from books that agree with God, and the wisdom from people who are mature in their understanding of how to live life properly.

The wisdom of God permeates the Bible, especially in the books of Job, Proverbs, and Ecclesiastes. If you want wise counsel, it would be appropriate for you to study the Bible for all its worth, especially these three books. What wisdom have you gleaned from the Bible?

_____

_____

_____

_____

_____

_____

_____

_____

_____

_____

_____

_____

_____

The wisdom of God permeates the writings of authors who lean on Him for an understanding of truth and how to wisely apply it to your life. Who are some of your favorite authors when it comes to becoming wiser about how to live life well? What have you learned from them?

_____

_____

_____

_____

_____

_____

_____

_____

_____

_____

_____

_____

_____

Who do you turn to for counsel in your day-to-day life when you're trying to be wise about a decision you need to make or a problem you need to face?

_____

_____

_____

_____

_____

_____

_____

_____

_____

_____

_____

_____

_____

_____

_____

Truly wise people live in the world but don't practice the foolish ways of the world. Please consider reading the books listed below to become wiser in how to apply biblical truth to your problems as you go through life.

Recommended Readings

★ *Celebration of Discipline: The Path to Spiritual Growth* by Richard Foster
★ *Chesterton Spiritual Classics: Orthodoxy, Heretics, and The Everlasting Man* by G.K. Chesterton
★ *Everyone's a Theologian: An Introduction to Systematic Theology* by R. C. Sproul
★ *God's Wisdom for Navigating Life: A Year of Daily Devotions in the Book of Proverbs* by Tim Keller with Kathy Keller
★ *In Search of Wisdom: Life-Changing Truths in the Book of Proverbs* by Joyce Meyer
★ *Instruments in the Redeemer's Hands: People in Need of Change Helping People in Need of Change* by Paul David Tripp

★ *Knowing God* by J. I. Packer

★ *Living Life Backwards: How Ecclesiastes Teaches Us to Live in Light of the End* by David Gibson

★ *The Divine Conspiracy: Discovering Our Hidden Life in God* by Dallas Willard

★ *The Gospel According to Job: An Honest Look at Pain and Doubt from the Life of One Who Lost Everything* by Mike Mason

★ *The Knowledge of the Holy* by A. W. Tozer

LESSON 26

Be Anxious, Don't Worry

Worrying is carrying tomorrow's load with
today's strength—carrying two days
at once. It is moving into tomorrow
ahead of time. Worrying doesn't
empty tomorrow of its sorrow, it
empties today of its strength.
— Corrie Ten Boom

There is a difference between anxiety and worry. Anxiety is the emotion we experience when something or someone poses a genuine threat to our physical, financial, relational, emotional, and spiritual well-being. Worry is the unhealthy tendency to look into the future and ruminate about the bad things that might happen and whether or not we will be able to handle them.

In the space provided below, write down a list of things in your life that pose a genuine threat to you in some way and what you can do to address the problem directly.

Genuine Threat #1 and What I Can Do About It: _____
_____
_____
_____
_____

Genuine Threat #2 and What I Can Do About It: _____
_____
_____
_____
_____

Genuine Threat #3 and What I Can Do About It: _____

_____

_____

_____

_____

Genuine Threat #4 and What I Can Do About It: _____

_____

_____

_____

_____

Now, write down the things you worry about in the future and what, if anything, you can do about them if they were to happen.

Future Worry #1 and What, If Anything, I Can Do About It: _____

_____

_____

_____

_____

Future Worry #2 and What, If Anything, I Can Do About It: _____

_____

_____

_____

_____

Future Worry #3 and What, If Anything, I Can Do About It: _____

_____

_____

_____

_____

Future Worry #4 and What, If Anything, I Can Do About It: _____

_____

_____

_____

_____

Anxiety is a healthy reaction to things that pose a genuine threat to us. Worry is an unhealthy reaction that reflects the human tendency to "borrow problems from the future," many of which never happen. For a deeper dive into dealing with anxiety and worry, please consider reading the books listed below.

Recommended Reading

* ★ *Anxious for Nothing: Finding Calm in a Chaotic World* by Max Lucado
* ★ *A Liberated Mind: How to Pivot Toward What Matter* by Steven Hayes
* ★ *Don't Give the Enemy a Seat at Your Table: It's Time to Win the Battle of Your Mind . . .* by Louie Giglio
* ★ *The Worry Trick: How Your Brain Tricks You into Expecting the Worst and What You Can Do About It* by David Carbonell and Sally Winston
* ★ *The Anxiety and Worry Workbook: The Cognitive Behavioral Solution* by David Clark and Aaron Beck
* ★ *The Dialectical Behavior Therapy Skills Workbook for Anxiety: Breaking Free from Worry, Panic, PTSD, and Other Anxiety Symptoms* by Alexander Chapman, Kim Gratz, and Mathew Tull

LESSON 27

Don't Play to the Crowd

A truly strong person does not need the approval of others
any more than a lion needs the approval of sheep.
— Vernon Howard

We all have an approval junkie living inside of us. To one degree or
another, we find ourselves looking to others for approval when only the
approval of God truly matters.

Acceptance and approval are two different breeds of cats. Acceptance
is the healthy desire that others accept us "warts and all" rather than
reject us or mistreat us because we have flaws. Approval is an unhealthy
desire to get validation from others no matter what we have to do to
attain it.

Let's start with the issue of acceptance. What are some flaws and
defects you've hidden from others because you thought they wouldn't
accept you if they knew you had these imperfections?

_____
_____
_____
_____
_____
_____
_____
_____
_____
_____
_____
_____

Now, let's turn to approval. What are some of the ways you've
violated your own integrity to get the approval of others? What changes

have you made to your thoughts, feelings, and actions to get others to approve of you?

_____

_____

_____

_____

_____

_____

_____

_____

_____

_____

Not to rub your face in it, but what's the biggest flaw or defect you've hidden from others out of fear they wouldn't accept you if they knew about it?

_____

_____

_____

_____

_____

Again, not to rub your face in it, but what's the most serious way you have violated your integrity as a human being to gain the approval of others?

_____

_____

_____

_____

_____

Finally, what have you wanted people to approve of about you that you know, at some deeper level, isn't something anyone should approve of?

_____

_____

_____

_____

_____

We all have a need to be accepted "warts and all." That's normal and healthy. Sadly, many of us also have an unhealthy need for people's approval that leads us to alter who we are to get the validation of others. To go further into this issue, please consider reading the books listed below.

Recommended Reading

★ *Approval Addiction: Overcoming Your Need to Please Everyone* by Joyce Meyer

★ *Co-Dependent No More: How to Stop Controlling Others and Care for Yourself* by Melody Beattie

★ *Not Nice: Stop People Pleasing, Staying Silent, & Feeling Guilty . . . And Start Speaking Up, Saying No, Asking Boldly, and Unapologetically Being Yourself* by Aziz Gazipura

★ *Stop Checking Your Likes: Shake Off the Need for Approval and Live an Incredible Life* by Susie Moore

★ *When People are Big and God is Small: Overcoming Peer Pressure, Codependency, and the Fear Of Man* by Ed Welch

LESSON 28

Be Content with Little

He who is not contented with what he has, would not
be contented with what he would like to have.
— Socrates

In a world where many people have more than they could have ever
hoped for, contentment seems to be at an all-time low.

Contentment is tied to several things, but it is certainly tied to what
you expect from life. In the space provided below, write down what your
expectations are when it comes to being content with life (a good job,
getting married, a nice home, etc.).

My contentment is tied to expecting the following in life: _____
_____
_____
_____
_____
_____
_____
_____
_____
_____
_____
_____
_____
_____
_____
_____
_____
_____

Some people have wisely reduced contentment to having the bare necessities of life (food, clothing, shelter, companionship). If these bare necessities were met in your life, would you be content? If yes, say why. If no, say why not.

_____

_____

_____

_____

_____

_____

_____

_____

_____

_____

_____

_____

_____

_____

_____

_____

Who do you know that strikes you as a content individual? What is it about him or her that seems to make them content with their life?

_____

_____

_____

_____

_____

_____

_____

_____

_____

_____

_____
_____
_____
_____
_____
_____
_____

If you aren't content with your current situation, what one or two things added to your life do you think would lead you to feel more content?

_____
_____
_____
_____
_____
_____
_____
_____
_____
_____
_____
_____
_____
_____
_____
_____
_____

What might you be lacking *internally* that is keeping you from being content with what you already have externally?

_____
_____
_____
_____

For many of us, internal peace and contentment are hard to come by these days. If you want to go further into this topic, consider reading the books listed below.

Recommended Reading.

★ *Calm My Anxious Heart: A Woman's Guide to Finding Contentment* by Linda Dillow
★ *Contentment: The Secret to Lasting Calm* by Richard Swenson
★ *The Rare Jewel of Christian Contentment* by Jeremiah Burroughs

LESSON 29

Watch Your Mouth

Words: So innocent and powerless as they are,
as standing in a dictionary, how potent
for good and evil they become in the hands of
one who knows how to combine them.
—Nathaniel Hawthorne

The words we say matter because they have the power to build people up or tear them down. Apart from how our words impact others is the nature of the words themselves in terms of whether or not they're crude and foul or refined and decent.

Looking back in time, what was the worst thing you ever said to someone, words that tore them down and demeaned them?

_____

_____

_____

_____

_____

_____

_____

_____

_____

_____

_____

_____

_____

_____

_____

_____

_____

On the flip side, what's the kindest thing you have ever said to someone, words that built them up and left them encouraged?

_____

_____

_____

_____

_____

_____

_____

_____

_____

_____

_____

_____

_____

_____

_____

If you could, what words would you take back that you said to someone you cared about, and what words would you put in their place?

_____

_____

_____

_____

_____

_____

_____

_____

_____

_____

_____

_____

_____

When it comes to individual words (as opposed to the ones you string together), what are the ten foulest, crudest, coarsest words that have come out of your mouth in the last week?

1. _____
2. _____
3. _____
4. _____
5. _____
6. _____
7. _____
8. _____
9. _____
10. _____

When it comes to individual words (as opposed to the ones you string together), what are the ten purest, cleanest, most pleasant words that have come out of your mouth in the last week?

1. _____
2. _____
3. _____
4. _____
5. _____
6. _____
7. _____
8. _____
9. _____
10. _____

We all know that words matter and matter a lot. Keep working on eliminating the bad ones and saying more of the good ones. For further help in this area, please consider reading the books listed below.

Recommended Reading

★ *The Emotionally Destructive Marriage: How to Find Your Voice and Reclaim Your Hope* by Leslie Vernick

★ *The Verbally Abusive Relationship: How to Recognize It and How to Respond* by Patricia Evans

★ *Watch Your Mouth: Understanding the Power of the Tongue* by Tony Evans

★ *Watch Your Mouth Interactive Workbook: Understanding the Power of the Tongue* by Tony Evans

LESSON 30

Ask Others to Correct You

To admonish is better than to reproach
for admonition is mild and
friendly, but reproach is harsh and
insulting; and admonition corrects
those who are doing wrong, but
reproach only convicts them.
— Epictetus

We all need to be corrected. We're far too human to be above reproach when it comes to our words and deeds.

The problem most of us have is that we don't like others to correct us because it's a blow to our ego. Because this is true, we're prone to criticize others, beating them to the punch by correcting them before they can correct us.

Take a minute to think about people in your life who can give you corrective feedback on how to improve your interpersonal style, work performance, physical health habits, and spiritual growth and development. Make sure you choose people who genuinely care about you, are reasonably healthy in the areas they are going to provide feedback, and can provide fairly accurate input. Set up a meeting with each of these folks and ask them to give you input. In the spaces provided below, write down what they told you.

The person I turned to for feedback/correction about my interpersonal style said:

_____

_____

_____

_____

_____

The person I turned to for feedback/correction about my work performance said:

_____

_____

_____

_____

_____

_____

The person I turned to for feedback/correction on my physical health habits said:

_____

_____

_____

_____

_____

The person I turned to for feedback/correction on spiritual growth and development said:

_____

_____

_____

_____

_____

_____

Write down any themes that cut across the feedback you received:

_____

_____

_____

_____

_____

_____

What was the hardest feedback to hear?

_____

_____

_____

_____

_____

_____

_____

However painful it is, we all need to receive feedback and be corrected at times. Try to make receiving corrective feedback a regular part of your life so that you can grow into a healthier, more loving human being. To explore this area further, please consider reading the books listed below.

Recommended Reading

★ *Emotional Intelligence 2.0* by Travis Bradberry and Jean Greaves
★ *Crucial Conversations: Tools for Talking When the Stakes are High* by Kerry Patterson, Joseph Grenny, Ron McMillan, and Al Switzler
★ *Difficult Conversations: How to Discuss What Matters the Most* by Douglas Stone, Bruce Patton, and Sheila Heen
★ *Thanks for the Feedback: The Science and Art of Receiving Feedback Well* by Douglas Stone and Shelia Heen

LESSON 31

Listen To a Lot of
Really Good Music

If I had my life to live over again, I
would have made a rule to read
some poetry and listen to some music
at least once every week.
— Charles Darwin

Music is important for your emotional and spiritual health. If you make
sure you listen to the really good stuff, you will enrich your life.

Let's start on the bad side of the equation. Think back through
your music listening habits. What music left your soul worse off
and why?

_____

_____

_____

_____

_____

_____

_____

_____

_____

_____

Now, let's turn to the good side of the equation. Look back through
your music listening habits. What music left your soul better off
and why?

_____

_____

_____

_____

_____

_____

_____

_____

_____

_____

_____

Even if a song made your spirit soar, which songs have you liked that had lyrics that were *not* good for you, and what were they?

_____

_____

_____

_____

_____

_____

_____

_____

_____

_____

Even if you didn't like a particular song, which songs had lyrics that were good for you, and what were they?

_____

_____

_____

_____

_____

_____

_____

_____

_____

_____

What songs do you find yourself listening to over and over, and why do you think you're drawn to these songs?

_____

_____

_____

_____

_____

_____

_____

_____

_____

_____

_____

There are many wonderful benefits to listening to good music. Just like we need to be careful about what we eat and make sure what we consume is nutritious, we need to be careful about the music we listen to and make sure it is "nutritious" for our soul and spirit. To go deeper into the importance of listening to good music and how it can benefit you, consider reading the books listed below.

Recommended Reading

★ *Listen to This* by Alex Ross
★ *Music and the Mind* by Anthony Storr
★ *Music, Language, and the Brain* by Aniruddh Patel
★ *Musicophilia: Tales of Music and the Brain* by Oliver Sacks
★ *The Tao of Music: Using Music to Change Your Life* by John Ortiz
★ *This is Your Brain on Music: The Science of a Human Obsession* by Daniel Levitin

LESSON 32

Face Your Death

The fear of death follows from the fear of life. A man
who lives fully is prepared to die at any time.
—Mark Twain

Death is the ultimate fear for many of us. Yet, the reason people fear
death is often tied to the fact that they are not living their lives in a rich
and meaningful way.

To face death and live life more fully, I want you to play the "If I only
had ten years to live" game. In the spaces provided below, write down
your honest thoughts and feelings related to each question being asked.

If you only had ten years to live, how would you rearrange your priorities?
(Example: I would spend more time with family and friends and spend
less time trying to acquire wealth.)

_____

_____

_____

_____

_____

If you only had ten years to live, what things would you stop doing or
restrict doing that don't add value to your life? (Example: I would limit
my television watching to one hour a night.)

_____

_____

_____

_____

If you only had ten years to live, how would you live more fully in the present rather than postpone experiences until some point in the future? (Example: I would travel more often.)

_____

_____

_____

_____

_____

If you only had ten years to live, how would you more fully appreciate the elemental facts of life like the changing of seasons, autumn leaves turning colors, and holiday joyousness? (Example: I would take a weekly walk in nature and focus more deeply on the sensations I experience.)

_____

_____

_____

_____

_____

If you only had ten years to live, how would you communicate more frequently and deeply with loved ones? (Example: I'd call my parents and siblings more often and talk more deeply about how they are doing.)

_____

_____

_____

_____

_____

If you only had ten years to live, how would you live with less fear of rejection and take greater (healthy) risks interpersonally and professionally? (Example: I'd let someone I like know I want to get to know them better; I'd pursue a new role at work that would help me grow.)

_____

_____

_____

_____

_____

If you only had ten years to live, what would you do that would leave the world better off? (Example: I'd join an organization that serves a specific population in need like the homeless, people in recovery, first-time parents, empty nesters, newly marrieds, etc.)

_____

_____

_____

_____

_____

Facing your death is crucial if you are going to live more fully. Facing death doesn't mean becoming morbid about the fact that you're going to die but living life more fully in the face of it. For further help in this area, consider reading the books listed below.

Recommended Reading

★ *Facing Death: Finding Dignity, Hope, and Healing at the End* by Jim deMaine
★ *O Love That Will Not Let Me Go: Facing Death with Courageous Confidence in God* edited by Nancy Guthrie
★ *On Death and Dying: What the Dying Have to Teach Doctors, Nurses, Clergy & Their Own Families* by Elizabeth Kubler-Ross
★ *Staring at the Sun: Overcoming the Terror of Death* by Irvin Yalom
★ *The Denial of Death* by Ernest Becker

LESSON 33

Guard Your Heart

> While God does want us to be open with others, he
> also encourages us to put boundaries in place as we
> do. He talks repeatedly about guarding our hearts. So
> what's the difference? Hiding is a response out of fear,
> while guarding is a proactive choice to protect what
> matters most. In other words, we're not to deliberately
> put something of worth where it won't be valued.
> —Holley Gerth

Guarding your heart goes well beyond guarding your emotions.
Guarding your heart means to healthily protect your body, mind,
will, emotions, relationships, and spiritual longings from anyone
or anything that would presume to harm you in these areas, you
included.

In the spaces provided below, write down how you can guard your
heart in these various aspects of who you are. Be completely honest
with yourself about what it would take to guard your heart in these
important areas.

How I can guard my body against harm (Examples: eat better, exercise
regularly, get away from people who are physically abusive).

_____

_____

_____

_____

_____

_____

How I can guard my mind against thinking or believing things that are not true (Examples: study the Bible, read books on right thinking, keep a "self-talk" journal where I observe my thoughts without letting them determine how I view reality).

_____

_____

_____

_____

_____

_____

How I can guard my feelings against toxic emotions like bitterness, resentment, and contempt toward others (Examples: forgive others who have hurt me, extend grace to those who have mistreated me, and have a deeper level of humility that I'm not any better than anyone else).

_____

_____

_____

_____

_____

_____

How I can guard my will against repetitively committing sinful actions (Examples: join a 12-step group, get an accountability partner, confess my sins rather than hide them from people).

_____

_____

_____

_____

_____

_____

How I can guard my relationships with others (Examples: not having anything to do with those who unrepentantly hurt me, drawing firm boundaries with others when they mistreat me, having "speak the truth in love" conversations with those who don't treat me respectfully).

_____

_____

_____

_____

_____

_____

How I can guard my spiritual life (Examples: get involved in a Bible study group, develop a better understanding of spiritual warfare, practice spiritual disciplines, join a local fellowship).

_____

_____

_____

_____

_____

_____

Your heart, properly understood, is the wellspring of your life. Guard it with everything you've got. For a better understanding of how to guard your heart, consider reading the books listed below.

Recommended Reading

★ *Every Young Man's Battle: Strategies for Victory in the Real World of Sexual Temptation* by Stephen Arterburn and Fred Stoeker
★ *Every Young Woman's Battle: Guarding Your Mind, Heart, and Body in a Sex-Saturated* by Shannon Ethridge and Stephen Arterburn
★ *Guarding Your Child's Heart* by Gary Smalley
★ *Guarding Your Heart* by A. W. Pink
★ *Rebuilding the Real You: The Definitive Guide to the Holy Spirit's Work in Your Life* by Jack Hayford

LESSON 34

Wait for It, Wait for It

Patience is bitter, but its fruit is sweet.
— Aristotle

It's hard to be patient, and it's even harder to be patient in developing patience as you live your life. I saw a bumper sticker once that said, "I want patience . . . and I want it now!" That's how a lot of us feel, isn't it?

With that being said, I want to give you some tasks to do that will help you become a more patient person. These are easier-said-than done but will help you respond more patiently to things life throws your way.

Identify things in life that trigger your impatience: _____
_____
_____
_____
_____

Reframe the things that slow you down or block your goals as good things given that they can lead to having more patience: _____
_____
_____
_____
_____

Entertain the possibility that your impatience could be trying to tell you that what you're after may not be in your best interest: _____
_____
_____
_____
_____
_____

When something slows you down or blocks a goal, take a deep breath and try to generate potential solutions to the problem you face: _____

_____

_____

_____

_____

Before impatience can become a problem, make sure you have a good plan in place for what you are trying to do and the length of time it will take to execute that plan: _____

_____

_____

_____

_____

However painful this might be, take some time to view your impatience as a symptom of your "narcissism" in that a part of you wrongly believes things shouldn't ever slow you down or block your goals: _____

_____

_____

_____

_____

Count the cost of being impatient in that it almost always negatively impacts the quality of the work you're doing: _____

_____

_____

_____

_____

Some people seem to be born with a patient spirit. For those of us who aren't, we need to roll up our sleeves and work on developing one. If you're in the latter group, consider reading the books listed below.

Recommended Reading

★ *A Small Book About a Big Problem: Meditations on Anger, Patience, and Peace* by Ed Welch

★ *A Little SPOT of Patience: A Story About How to Enjoy Waiting* by Diane Alber

★ *Patience: The Art of Peaceful Living* by Allan Lokos

★ *The Book of Patience: 250 Ways to a More Patient You* by Courtney Ackerman

★ *The Power of Patience: How This Old-Fashioned Virtue Can Improve Your Life* by M. J. Ryan

LESSON 35

Go Fly a Kite

Try new hobbies. Develop new interests.
Pursue new experiences. When
you expand your interests, you increase
your opportunities for happiness.
— Richelle E. Goodrich

It is important for each of us to have a hobby or two along the way, something that can take us away from the heavy responsibilities we carry in life. There are numerous benefits from having hobbies—they help relieve stress, offer new experiences, help you better understand yourself, make you focus on the moment, improve your self-esteem, make you more interesting, help you become more physically healthy, improve your memory, allow you to meet new people, and strengthen your relationships with others.

You may currently have some hobbies you enjoy doing. If that's the case, skip this lesson and go on to the next one. If you don't, I want to get the ball rolling in that direction by giving you a lengthy list of hobbies to choose from that you might enjoy. There are hundreds and hundreds of hobbies available to us. Look through the list below and put a checkmark by anything you think you might find interesting and enjoyable to do.

__ Hiking	__ Backpacking	__ Camping	__ Hunting
__ Fishing	__ Archery	__ Canoeing	__ Kayaking
__ Running	__ Growing Vegetables	__ Composting	__ Astronomy
__ Beekeeping	__ Metal Detecting	__ Kite Flying	__ Meteorology
__ Antiquing	__ Coin Collecting	__ Toy Collecting	__ Cooking
__ Baking	__ Stamp Collecting	__ Art Collecting	__ Toy Collecting
__ Sewing	__ Home Brewing	__ Wine Making	__ Drawing
__ Quilting	__ Calligraphy	__ Crocheting	__ Painting
__ Photography	__ Scrapbooking	__ Knitting	__ Embroidery

__ Pottery	__ Jewelry Making	__ Welding	__ Wood Carving
__ Cobbling	__ Model Railroads	__ Board Games	__ Video Games
__ Card Games	__ Furniture Building	__ Trivia	__ Chess
__ Puzzles	__ Metal Working	__ Table Tennis	__ Juggling
__ Billiards	__ Home Improvement	__ Genealogy	__ Journaling
__ Book Club	__ Language Learning	__ Thrifting	__ Makeup Art
__ Dancing	__ Creative Writing	__ Hula Hooping	__ Scuba Diving
__ Travel	__ Adult Coloring	__ Scuba Diving	__ Volunteering
__ Jump Roping	__ Mountain Biking	__ Cosplaying	__ Basketball
__ Golf	__ Running	__ Volleyball	__ Badminton
__ Soccer	__ Pilates	__ Yoga	__ Meditation
__ Swimming	__ Figure Skating	__ Roller Skating	__ Rugby
__ Tai Chi	__ Stretching	__ Bowling	__ Ice Hockey
__ Racquetball	__ Gardening	__ Surfing	__ Baseball
__ Gymnastics	__ Horse Racing	__ Karate	__ Snowboarding
__ Cycling	__ Skateboarding	__ Fencing	__ Waterskiing
__ Skiing	__ Jet Skiing	__ Windsurfing	__ Kickboxing
__ Boxing	__ Sky Diving	__ Weight Lifting	__ Cross Country
__ Sculpture	__ Paint-by-Number	__ Stained Glass	__ Candle Making
__ Star Gazing	__ Designing Graphics	__ Floral Design	__ Hair Styling
__ Acting	__ Home Decorating	__ Felt Arts	__ Miniatures
__ Nail Art	__ Painting Rocks	__ Puppetry	__ Tie Die
__ Sudoku	__ Going to Museums	__ Blogging	__ Checkers
__ Grilling	__ Listening to Music	__ Writing Lyrics	__ Joining a Band
__ Coding	__ Public Speaking	__ Survey Taking	__ Pet Sitting
__ Engraving	__ Social Media	__ Tutoring	__ Coaching
__ Decluttering	__ Dog Training	__ Archeology	__ Car Racing

Obviously, choosing a hobby is going to be affected by how much time, energy, and financial resources you have as well as the area of the country you live in (you probably can't take up surfing as a hobby if you live in Kansas, take up car racing if you can't afford how expensive it is, or take up boxing if you have a glass jaw).

Now, go back through the list of hobbies you checked as being of interest to you. What one hobby off the list might you pursue further, either on your own or by getting together with others who share a similar interest in that hobby? What do you need to do to move in the direction of becoming more fully involved in that particular hobby so that it doesn't become an unfulfilled regret?

Most of us feel that we don't have time to get involved in a hobby. Let me suggest that you don't have time not to get involved in a hobby. Given the dozens of physical, emotional, mental, and spiritual health benefits of having a hobby, you can't afford to not have a hobby or two that helps you take a much-needed break from the demands of life.

If you want to go further into this issue, please consider reading the books listed below.

Recommended Reading

★ *101 Fun Things to Do in Retirement* by Stella Reingold
★ Dozens of books on specific hobbies such as coin collecting, cross-stitching, whittling, macrame', coloring, crochet, lettering, cooking, sewing, leather crafting, etc.

LESSON 36

Never Give Up

> Never quit. It is the easiest cop-out in the world. Set a goal
> and don't quit until you attain it. When you do attain it, set
> another goal, and don't quit until you reach it. Never quit.
> —Bear Bryant

It's easy to get discouraged and throw in the towel when we run into one roadblock after another. Yet, those who achieve the greatest success in life are the ones who keep trying to achieve their goals regardless of the setbacks they encounter.

Let's go back to the acronym we looked at earlier, **PERSEVERANCE**. Think about a current goal you have that is important to you and respond to the questions below. This will help you wisely decide whether or not to stay the course in pursuing this goal or move on to a different goal that is in your "wheelhouse" and be successfully accomplished.

Patience: We have to be patient and allow things to play out in their own time frame. Are you willing to be patient in achieving this goal?

_____

_____

Endurance: We have to bear the pain along the way to achieving what we want. Are you willing to endure pain and suffering along the way in achieving this goal?

_____

_____

Resilience: We have to bounce back up when we experience a setback. Are you willing to get back on the horse when you get bucked off in pursuit of this goal?

_____

_____

Sacrifice: We have to be willing to sacrifice time, energy, and talent to achieve what we want. Are you willing to sacrifice time, energy, and talent to achieve this goal?

Effort: We have to put in a lot of effort and avoid laziness at all costs. Are you willing to put in the effort necessary to achieve this goal?

Vision: We have to have a clear vision of what we're trying to accomplish. Do you have a clear vision of the goal you're trying to accomplish?

Experience: We have to execute our plan and learn from setbacks along the way. Are you willing to go through trial and error and learn along the way to achieving this goal?

Relationships: We need to involve others in our efforts to accomplish our goals. Are you willing to involve others in the pursuit of this goal?

Attitude: We have to have a realistic attitude in pursuing our aspirations. Do you have a realistic attitude when it comes to achieving this goal?

Necessity: We need to do whatever it takes, within moral and ethical constraints, to achieve this goal. Are you willing to ethically and morally do whatever it takes to achieve this goal?

Courage: Pursuing our goals always involves setbacks, and we have to courageously press on. In the face of setbacks, do you have the courage it takes to pursue this goal?

_____

_____

Enthusiasm: We need to be optimistic and passionate about our goals. Are you enthusiastic and passionate about the goal you are trying to achieve?

_____

_____

We are to never give in when pursuing a *valid, reasonable, ethical* goal in life. For help in this area, consider reading the books listed below.

Recommended Reading

★ *Grit: The Power of Passion and Perseverance* by Angela Duckworth
★ *Resilient: How to Grow an Unshakable Core of Calm, Strength, and Happiness* by Rick Hanson and Forrest Hanson
★ *The Daily Stoic: 366 Meditations on Wisdom, Perseverance, and the Art of Living* by Ryan Holliday and Stephen Hanselman
★ *The Grit Guide for Teens: A Workbook to Help You Build Perseverance, Self-Control, and a Growth Mindset* by Caren Baruch-Feldman

LESSON 37

Keep Your Promises

> Some people still make promises
> and keep their word. When they
> do, they help make life around
> them more stably human.
> —Lewis B. Smedes

Growing up I heard the expression, "A man's word is only as good as his bond." It meant that a real man (or woman) never fails to follow through on their promises once they make them.

Not to rub your face in it, but what promises have you made in your life that you failed to keep? And, when you broke your promise, what were the relational consequences?

Promise I Made and Negative Consequences When I Broke It: _____

_____

_____

_____

_____

Promise I Made and Negative Consequences When I Broke It: _____

_____

_____

_____

_____

Now, let's look at the other side of the coin. What promises have you kept and what were the positive consequences of doing so?

Promise I Made and Positive Consequences When I Kept It: _____

_____

_____

_____

_____

Promise I Made and Positive Consequences When I Kept It: _____

_____

_____

_____

_____

Let's turn this around again. What promises have been made to you, and what were the negative consequences when that promise was broken?

Promise Made to Me and Negative Consequences When It Was Broken:

_____

_____

_____

_____

Promise Made to Me and Negative Consequences When It Was Broken:

_____

_____

_____

_____

Finally, what promises have been made to you, and what were the positive consequences when someone kept their promise?

Promise Made to Me and Positive Consequences When It Was Kept: ____

_____

_____

_____

_____

Promise Made to Me and Positive Consequences When It Was Kept: ___

_____

_____

_____

_____

Promise Made to Me and Positive Consequences When It Was Kept: ___

_____

_____

_____

_____

Following through on your promises in life is crucial. And, when you break your promise, it is important to apologize, ask for forgiveness, and make amends to the person to whom you broke your promise. To go deeper into this important issue, please consider reading the books listed below.

Recommended Reading

★ *A Promise Made: A Charming Children's Book About Love and the Power of Keeping a Promise* by Jonathan Lau and Mike Lee
★ *Integrity Ninja: A Social, Emotional Children's Book About Being Honest and Keeping Your Promises* by Mary Nihn and Jelena Stupar

LESSON 38

Let Others Toot Your Horn

Who knows himself a braggart, let him fear this, for it will
come to pass that every braggart shall be found an ass.
— William Shakespeare

It's human to want to toot your own horn, to praise yourself for your
accomplishments and successes in life. But, it's never a good idea.

In this lesson, I want to take you into three issues related to tooting
your own horn versus letting others do it for you. Here goes.

First, think back to various times you tooted your own horn in
front of others. What did you brag about, and what kind of reaction
did you get?

I tooted my own horn (bragged) about _____
_____,
and the reaction from others was _____
_____

I tooted my own horn (bragged) about _____
_____,
and the reaction from others was _____
_____

I tooted my own horn (bragged) about _____
_____,
and the reaction from others was _____
_____

Second, think back to times when someone tooted your horn for you.
What did they brag about regarding your successes/accomplishments,
and how did that feel?

_____ tooted my horn about _____
_____
and I felt _____

311

_____ tooted my horn about _____

_____

and I felt _____

_____ tooted my horn about _____

_____

and I felt _____

Think back to a time when no one tooted your horn about an accomplishment or success you had. When that accomplishment or success went untooted, how did you feel?

No one tooted my horn about _____

_____ and it felt _____

_____

No one tooted my horn about _____

_____ and it felt _____

_____

No one tooted my horn about _____

_____ and it felt _____

_____

Another thing I want to push you on is when you tooted your own horn in a way that wasn't true ("I earned the Nobel Peace Prize today!" when you weren't even being considered) or was over-the-top ("I caught a catfish today that weighed 106 pounds" when you caught a catfish that weighed 16 pounds). Write down examples where you inaccurately tooted your own horn.

I falsely/inaccurately bragged about _____

_____ when the truth was _____

_____

_____

I falsely/inaccurately bragged about _____
_____ when the truth was _____
_____
_____

I falsely/inaccurately bragged about _____
_____ when the truth was _____
_____
_____

There are authors and speakers who teach that you should toot your own horn in life if nobody else is going to. I don't agree. I would rather something you did go untooted altogether than for you to presume to brag about it yourself. Bragging is bragging, and, in general, no one likes a braggart. Humility, even if it means an accomplishment of yours goes completely unnoticed, is the right ticket. For further help in this area, consider reading the books below.

Recommended Reading

★ *Confident Humility: Becoming Your Full Self Without Becoming Full of Yourself* by Dan Kent
★ *Humble Ninja: A Children's Book About Developing Humility* by Mary Ninh and Jelena Stupar
★ *The Berenstain Bears and the Biggest Brag* by Mike Berenstain
★ *The Power of Humility: Living Like Jesus Did* by R. T. Kendall

LESSON 39

Don't Take Things Personally

Not taking things personally is a true sign of maturity.
— Robert Celner

To cut us all a little slack, we come into the world taking everything personally. It's called *egocentric thinking*, and it means that we wrongly believe how others treat us is all about us.

In this lesson, I want you to think through the things you've taken personally and build a case that the event that happened wasn't about you *at all*—it was about the person who treated you the way they did. Let me put it this way. Even if you are going 5 miles per hour in the fast lane on a major highway, the fact that people honk their horns, make hand gestures, and swerve in front of you to aggressively tell you to move over is about them. What's about you is that you're going 5 miles per hour in the fast lane on a major highway (not smart).

In the space provided below, write down what things people do to you that you take personally and how their actions are about them, not you.

I take it personally when people _____

_____,

and, when they do this, it is about them in that _____

_____

I take it personally when people _____

_____,

and, when they do this, it is about them in that _____

_____

I take it personally when people _____

_____,

and, when they do this, it is about them in that _____

_____

I take it personally when people _____

_____,

and, when they do this, it is about them in that _____

_____

I take it personally when people _____

_____,

and, when they do this, it is about them in that _____

_____

I take it personally when people _____

_____,

and, when they do this, it is about them in that _____

_____

I take it personally when people _____

_____,

and, when they do this, it is about them in that _____

_____

Now, take each of these examples and write down how what you were doing in the situation was about you, not them. For example, if you're going 5 miles per hour in the fast lane on a major highway, that's about you, not the other motorists.

Me doing _____
is about me in that _____

_____

Me doing _____
is about me in that _____

_____

Me doing _____
is about me in that _____

_____

Me doing _____
is about me in that _____
_____

Me doing _____
is about me in that _____
_____

One of the biggest signs we are no longer thinking and acting like a child is that we let how others act be about them and how we act be about us. To go deeper into this important issue, consider reading the books listed below.

Recommended Reading

★ *Ego is the Enemy* by Ryan Holiday
★ *The Drama of the Gifted Child: The Search for the True Self* by Alice Miller
★ *The Freedom of Self-Forgetfulness: The Path to True Christian Joy* by Tim Keller
★ *The Highly Sensitive Person: How to Thrive When the World Overwhelms You* by Elaine Aron
★ *Unoffendable: How Just One Change Can Make All of Life Better* by Brant Hansen

LESSON 40

Walk on the Sunny Side of the Street

Remember, happiness doesn't depend upon
who you are or what you have; it
depends solely upon what you think. So start
each day by thinking of all the things
you have to be thankful for. Your future will
depend very largely on the thoughts
you think today. So think thoughts of hope
and confidence and love and success.
— Dale Carnegie

We've talked about how important it is that your thoughts are based on reality and that they don't inaccurately ugly up or pretty up your experiences. That being said, it is important to mentally "walk on the sunny side of the street" each day in terms of trying to stay focused on the things about your life that are positive, optimistic, and hopeful.

To move in that direction, I want you to write down all the positive things going on in your life right now. No matter how dark certain things may be, we can always walk on the sunny side of the street when it comes to thinking about the things we can be thankful for in life.

Positive Person, Place, or Thing in My Life: _____
_____

Positive Person, Place, or Thing in My Life: _____
_____

Positive Person, Place, or Thing in My Life: _____
_____

Positive Person, Place, or Thing in My Life: _____

_____

Positive Person, Place, or Thing in My Life: _____

_____

Positive Person, Place, or Thing in My Life: _____

_____

Positive Person, Place, or Thing in My Life: _____

_____

Positive Person, Place, or Thing in My Life: _____

_____

Positive Person, Place, or Thing in My Life: _____

_____

Positive Person, Place, or Thing in My Life: _____

_____

Positive Person, Place, or Thing in My Life: _____

_____

Positive Person, Place, or Thing in My Life: _____

_____

Positive Person, Place, or Thing in My Life: _____

_____

Positive Person, Place, or Thing in My Life: _____

_____

Positive Person, Place, or Thing in My Life: _____

_____

Positive Person, Place, or Thing in My Life: _____

_____

Positive Person, Place, or Thing in My Life: _____

_____

I don't believe in positive thinking if it leads to ignoring the reality of painful things in life or leads us to mentally create positives that aren't true. I do believe in positive thinking if, by that, we are talking about focusing our thoughts mostly on the true positives of life and being grateful for them. For more help with this challenge, please consider reading the books below.

Recommended Reading

★ *Authentic Happiness: Using the New Positive Psychology to Realize Your Potential for Lasting Fulfillment* by Martin Seligman

★ *Learned Optimism: How to Change Your Mind and Your Life* by Martin Seligman

★ *Positivity: Discover the Upward Spiral That Will Change Your Life* by Barbara Fredrickson

★ *The Happiness Advantage: How a Positive Brain Fuels Success in Work and Life* by Shawn Achor

LESSON 41

Remember People's Names

First you forget names, then you forget
faces. Next you forget to pull your zipper
up and finally, you forget to pull it down.
—George Burns

Understandably, it can be bothersome when we don't remember a person's name or they don't remember ours. Remembering people's names may not be a problem for you. Just in case it is, let's work on it here.

Step #1: Think about all the people you know, especially those you run into fairly often, and identify those whose names you can't remember. Describe this person and where you run into them:

Person #1: _____
_____
_____

Person #2: _____
_____
_____

Person #3: _____
_____
_____

Step #2: The next time you run into them, humbly admit you've forgotten their name (chalk it up to a bad memory or getting older, or both) and ask them to tell you what it is. What is this person's name?

Person #1's Name: _____
Person #2's Name: _____
Person #3's Name: _____

320

Next, associate the person's name with something meaningful to you. For example, if the person's name is "William," associate their name with William the Conqueror or William Wallace.

Association I Made with Person #1's Name: _____
_____

Association I Made with Person #2's Name: _____
_____

Association I Made with Person #3's Name: _____
_____

Next, find something in the person's appearance you can associate with their name. For example, if the person's name is "Jim" and you run into them in the gym and they are wearing gym shorts, make that association.

Physical Appearance Association I Made with Person #1's Name: _____
_____

Physical Appearance Association I Made with Person #2's Name: _____
_____

Physical Appearance Association I Made with Person #3's Name: _____
_____

Finally, repeat the person's name over and over in your mind.

Person #1's Name Repeated Ten Times: _____
_____
_____

Person #1's Name Repeated Ten Times: _____
_____
_____

Person #1's Name Repeated Ten Times: _____

_____

_____

It can be uncomfortable to admit when we forget someone's name because it can communicate to them that their name wasn't important enough to remember. If you want to do a better job remembering people's names, consider reading from the books listed below.

Recommended Reading

★ *How to Remember People's Names* by Matt DiMaio
★ *Remember Every Name Every Time* by Benjamin Levy
★ *7 Simple Tricks to Remembering Names: How to Recall Names of People You Meet* by Travis Tyler

LESSON 42

Make Good Friends
. . . and Be One

I think if I've learned anything about friendship, it's to
hang in, stay connected, fight for them, and let them
fight for you. Don't walk away, don't be distracted, don't
be too busy or tired, don't take them for granted. Friends
are part of the glue that holds life and faith together.
—Jon Katz

Friendships are crucial as we go through life. If we have a best friend (or
two), we are truly blessed and need to do whatever we can to properly
take care of that friendship

In this lesson, I want to focus on how to improve your friendships
with others by posing a series of questions and having you respond to
them as honestly as you can.

Who is your best friend?

_____

On average, how much time do the two of you spend interacting each week?

_____

How much of that time is face-to-face?

_____

How honest are you with each other about what's really going on in
your lives?

_____
_____
_____
_____

How empathic are the two of you toward each other in terms of feeling each other's pain about difficult issues in your lives?

_____

_____

_____

_____

Is your word your bond with each other, meaning do you follow through when you make a promise or commitment to each other?

_____

_____

_____

_____

In the relationship, what flaws and defects do each of you bring into the relationship?

_____

_____

_____

_____

How accepting are the two of you when it comes to your respective flaws and defects?

_____

_____

_____

_____

How present are the two of you when you're in each other's company?

_____

_____

_____

_____

How committed, through thick and thin, are the two of you to each other?

_____

_____

_____

_____

Being able to both cry and laugh with each other is crucial in a friendship. Are you able to do both with your best friend?

_____

_____

_____

_____

Close friendships take commitment and hard work. We have to spend enough time together, "keep things real" by honestly sharing what's going on, have empathy for the painful things the other person is going through, be "present" when we are in their company, and be able to laugh and cry through the ups and downs of life. To drill down more deeply into this important area of life, please consider reading the books listed below.

Recommended Reading

★ *How to Win Friends and Influence People* by Dale Carnegie
★ *Messy Beautiful Friendship: Finding and Nurturing Deep and Lasting Relationships* by Christine Hoover
★ *The Relationship Cure: 5 Steps to Strengthening Your Marriage, Family and Friendships* by John Gottman

LESSON 43

Don't Judge a Book
by Its Cover

Things are not always what they seem; the
first appearance deceives many;
the intelligence of a few perceives what
has been carefully hidden.
— Plato

We're all prone to use a person's observable appearance, mannerisms, quirks, strengths, and weaknesses to make superficial judgments about them. More often than not, this leads to misperceiving who people really are and interacting with them in a watered-down manner.

In this lesson, I want you to take a few minutes to explore this issue further. In the space provided below, write down the kinds of negative judgments you make about people across these various dimensions.

I negatively judge people by their *observable appearance* in the following ways: _____

_____

_____

_____

_____

_____

_____

_____

_____

_____

_____

_____

_____

I negatively judge people by their *observable mannerisms* in the following ways: _____

_____

_____

_____

_____

_____

_____

_____

_____

_____

_____

_____

_____

I negatively judge people by their *observable quirks* in the following ways: _____

_____

_____

_____

_____

_____

_____

_____

_____

_____

_____

_____

_____

I negatively judge people by their *observable strengths* in the following ways: _____

_____

_____

_____

_____
_____
_____
_____
_____
_____
_____
_____

I negatively judge people by their *observable weaknesses* in the following ways: _____

_____
_____
_____
_____
_____
_____
_____
_____
_____
_____
_____

The person I misjudged the most by their appearance, mannerisms quirks, strengths, and weaknesses is _____.
I judged them as _____

_____
_____
_____, and they turned out to be _____
_____
_____

It's hard not to judge a person by what we see, but we need to avoid doing so because it often leads to misperceiving who they really are as human beings. For more help with this issue, consider reading the books listed below.

Recommended Reading

★ *Don't Judge Me: Teaching Children Not to Judge Others Based on Appearance* by Jennifer Lescano
★ *Unoffendable: How Just One Change Can Make All of Life Better* by Brant Hansen

LESSON 44

Smile More Often

What sunshine is to flowers, smiles are to
humanity. These are but trifles, to be
sure; but scattered along life's pathway,
the good they do is inconceivable.
— Joseph Addison

Most of us need to smile more often. Even in the midst of serious problems in our lives and around the world, we need to make sure we smile at those we encounter each day.

In this lesson, I want you to make this week "Smile Week." Here's what I want you to work on in having a successful go at it.

Step #1: Practice smiling in front of a mirror for five minutes today. Make your smile as genuine and warm as possible. In the space provide below, write down how this affected your mood, stress level, and physiological reaction.

_____
_____
_____
_____
_____

Step #2: Smile at everyone you see. When you make eye contact with others, smile at them. In the space provided below, write down how that affected you and what reaction you got from the people you smiled at.

_____
_____
_____
_____
_____

Step #3: Make external triggers a cue to smile. Here are some examples: every time your phone rings, smile; every time you get into or exit your car, smile; every time you go into a store, smile, especially at the people who work there. In the space provided below, write down what are you going to use as a cue or trigger to smile more often.

_____

_____

_____

_____

_____

_____

Step #4: Think of things you like and smile. Here are some examples: think about an enjoyable trip you took and smile; think about a close friend who has been supportive over the years and smile; think about acts of kindness people have done to you and smile. In the space below, write down the people, places, and things that make you smile when you think about them.

_____

_____

_____

_____

_____

_____

Step #5: Think about someone who never smiles at you and smile at them. Most of us have someone in our life who rarely, if ever, smiles at us. Figure out who this person is and make sure you smile at them every time you see them. In the space below, write down how this impacts your interactions with this person.

_____

_____

_____

_____

_____

_____

The world needs more smilers, and I want to encourage you to become one—someone who genuinely and warmly smiles as often as possible. For further help on this important issue, consider reading the books below.

Recommended Reading

★ *Runaway Smile: An Unshared Smile is a Wasted Smile* by Nicholas Rossis

★ *Smile: Say It with a Smile* by Vince Cleghorne

★ *Smile: The Astonishing Powers of a Simple Act* by Ron Gutman

LESSON 45

Break Free from Egypt

Every form of addiction is bad, no matter whether
the narcotic be alcohol, morphine or idealism.
— Carl Gustav Jung

We're all addicts. We're all addicted to not just one thing but many things, and, far too often, we either deny that we have these addictions or rationalize their existence in our lives.

In this lesson, I want you to take a minute to assess what you might be addicted to. Below, put a checkmark by anything that may be an addiction for you.

__ television	__ exercise	__ caffeine	__food
__ texting	__ gaming	__ drugs	__ work
__ internet	__ romance	__ plastic surgery	__ lying
__ risky behavior	__ music	__ piercings	__ tattoos
__ sugar	__ tanning	__ lip balm	__ chewing ice
__ water	__ social media	__ rejection	__ hoarding
__ sniffing fumes	__ vaping	__ approval	__ anime
__ applause	__ cannabis	__ chocolate	__ codependency
__stubbornness	__drama	__diuretics	__energy drinks
__fantasizing	__fame	__isolating	__joking
__junk	__ lust	__laziness	__MSG
__prayer	__pornography	__perfectionism	__religion
__smoking	__sleeping	__therapy	__self-help
__therapy	__travel	__wealth	__exercise

Now, put a circle around any check mark where you are doing something to overcome that particular addiction (counseling, 12-step work, rehab, accountability partner, etc.). In the space provided below, write down your thoughts about how your efforts to overcome these addictions are going.

_____

_____

_____

_____

_____

_____

_____

_____

_____

_____

Finally, in areas of addiction where things are not going well, what can you do to raise the bar about getting the help you need to break free?

_____

_____

_____

_____

_____

_____

_____

_____

_____

All addictions are bad and cause damage to your physical, emotional, relational, and spiritual health. To go further into this issue, consider reading the books listed below.

Recommended Reading

★ *Addiction and Grace* by Gerald May
★ *Addictions: A Banquet in the Grave* by Ed Welch
★ *Breathing Under Water: Spirituality and the Twelve Steps* by Richard Rohr

★ *Celebrate Recovery 365 Daily Devotionals: Healing from Hurts, Habits, and Hang-Ups* by John Baker, Johnny Baker, and Mac Owen
★ *Clean: Overcoming Addiction and Ending America's Greatest Tragedy* by David Sheff
★ *Unbroken Brain: A Revolutionary New Way of Understanding Addiction* by Maia Szalavitz

LESSON 46

Embrace the Mystery of Life

Until we accept the fact that life itself is founded
in mystery, we shall learn nothing.
—Henry Miller

Merriam-Webster defines "mystery" as "something not understood or beyond understanding." If we accept that definition, there are a lot of things in life that are a mystery.

Related to the "people, places, or things" listed below, write down what you find most mysterious. Here are some examples: "I believe God is loving, but I don't understand how he can allow such horrible things to happen"; "I know people fall in love, but I don't understand why we're drawn to some people and not to others"; "I believe we are made body, soul, and spirit, but I don't understand how these interact with and impact each other."

God: _____
_____
_____
_____

Creation: _____
_____
_____
_____

Romantic Love: _____
_____
_____
_____

Life: _____

_____

_____

_____

Death: _____

_____

_____

_____

Meaning/Purpose: _____

_____

_____

_____

Evil: _____

_____

_____

_____

Body/Soul/Spirit: _____

_____

_____

_____

Beauty: _____

_____

_____

_____

Pain and Suffering: _____

_____

_____

_____

Kindness: _____

_____

_____

_____

All of these—God, creation, love, life, death, meaning/purpose, evil, body/soul/spirit, and beauty—are great mysteries that, on our best day, we will only partially understand. Nevertheless, we need to keep learning as much as we can while accepting that we will never know fully or completely. For help with some of these areas, consider reading the books listed below.

Recommended Reading

★ *Everyday Mysteries: A Handbook of Existential Psychotherapy* by Emmy van Deurzen
★ *Life Lessons: Two Experts on Death and Dying Teach Us About the Mysteries of Life and Living* by Elisabeth Kubler-Ross and David Kessler
★ *Man's Search for Meaning* by Viktor E. Frankl
★ *Reflections on the Existence of God: A Series of Essays* by Richard E. Simmons III
★ *The Mystery of Marriage: Meditations on the Miracle* by Mike Mason
★ *The Seven Mysteries of Life: An Exploration of Science and Philosophy* by Guy Murchie

LESSON 47

Observe Your Thoughts but Don't Trust Them

It is the mark of an educated mind to be able to
entertain a thought without accepting it.
— Aristotle

It is important to take our thoughts seriously, but there is a big difference between taking our thoughts seriously and allowing them to determine our view of reality. Thoughts are just that—thoughts—and just because we have them doesn't mean we have to believe them or let them run our lives.

Emotional health involves a lot of different things, but it certainly involves being more aware of what we think, objectively observing our thoughts, being curious that our minds often misfire when it comes to how we perceive reality, and thinking about what is true, lovely, pure, and worthwhile throughout the day.

For the next seven days, I want you to keep a "self-talk" journal where you write down the "false, ugly, impure, and worthless" thoughts that go through your mind that left you feeling emotionally disturbed (enraged, bitter, resentful, miserable). Once you write those thoughts down, I want you to write down the "true, lovely, pure, and worthwhile" thoughts you needed to have about the same situation. In the space provided below, write down some examples from your journal

Untrue, ugly, impure, and worthless thoughts that led to emotional turmoil: _____
_____
_____
_____
_____

True, lovely, pure, and worthwhile thoughts about the situation: _____

_____

_____

_____

_____

Untrue, ugly, impure, and worthless thoughts that led to emotional turmoil: _____

_____

_____

_____

_____

True, lovely, pure, and worthwhile thoughts about the situation: _____

_____

_____

_____

_____

Untrue, ugly, impure, and worthless thoughts that led to emotional turmoil: _____

_____

_____

_____

_____

True, lovely, pure, and worthwhile thoughts about the situation: _____

_____

_____

_____

_____

Untrue, ugly, impure, and worthless thoughts that led to emotional turmoil: _____

_____

_____

_____

True, lovely, pure, and worthwhile thoughts about the situation: _____
_____
_____
_____
_____

One of the most important skills we need to develop in life is the ability to observe our thoughts, not let them determine how we view reality and move our minds in the direction of accurate thoughts about what is true. For further help in this area, consider reading the books listed below.

Recommended Reading

★ *A Liberated Mind: How to Pivot Toward What Matters* by Steve Hayes
★ *Get Out of Your Mind and Into Your Life: The New Acceptance and Commitment Therapy* by Steven Hayes with Spencer Smith
★ *The Lies We Believe* by Chris Thurman
★ *The Obstacle is the Way: The Art of Turning Trials into Triumph* by Ryan Holiday
★ *The Untethered Soul: The Journey Beyond Yourself* by Michael Singer
★ *Winning the War in Your Mind: Change Your Thinking Change Your Life* by Greg Groeschel

LESSON 48

Stay Balanced

> Mature mental health demands, then, an
> extraordinary capacity to flexibly strike and
> continually restrike a delicate balance between
> conflicting needs, goals, duties, responsibilities,
> directions, et. cetera. The essence of this
> discipline of balancing is "giving up."
> —M. Scott Peck

Striking the right balance across the day-to-day demands of life is a difficult challenge. Every "Yes" we say to one thing is a "NO" to something else, requiring that we make difficult decisions about not only what to do but what not to do.

One of the more popular notions today is "achieving a healthy work-life balance" as if work isn't part of your life. In this lesson, I want to challenge you to put some effort into balancing your life as best you can.

In the space provided below, write down what healthy balance looks like in each of the areas mentioned. Given that we have *finite* amounts of time and energy each day, try to be wise in determining how much of each you give to these important areas. We're not going to strike a perfect balance in how we live our lives, but we can try to get close enough for horseshoes.

Work: _____

_____

_____

_____

_____

Deepening your relationships with loved ones: _____

_____

_____

_____

_____

Personal growth and development: _____

_____

_____

_____

_____

Spiritual growth and development: _____

_____

_____

_____

_____

Physical fitness: _____

_____

_____

_____

_____

Hobbies: _____

_____

_____

_____

_____

Rest/Relaxation: _____

_____

_____

_____

_____

Entertainment: _____

_____

_____

_____

_____

You may have heard the expression, "People don't plan to fail, they fail to plan." In light of all these areas of life (and others that require our time and energy), come up with a schedule for how a week would need to go for you to achieve a healthy balance in your life. Try to give each area a reasonable amount of time given the responsibilities you have in that area.

We all know that balance is important in life, and we all know how physically, emotionally, relationally, and spiritually exhausted we get when we don't strike that balance. For more help in this area, consider reading the books listed below.

Recommended Reading

★ *At Your Best: How to Get Time, Energy, and Priorities Working in Your Favor* by Cary Nieuwhof
★ *Find Balance: Thriving in a Do-It-All World* by Shaunti Feldhahn
★ *Having a Mary Heart in a Martha World: Finding Intimacy with God in the Busyness of Life* by Joanna Weaver
★ *In Over Your Head: Creating Balance and Finding Peace in the Busy* by Susie Larson
★ *In Search of Balance: Keys to a Stable Life* by Richard Swenson
★ *Margin: Restoring Emotional, Physical, Financial, and Time Reserves to Overloaded Lives* by Richard Swenson

LESSON 49

Make Miniscule Modifications

All big things come from small beginnings. The seed of
every habit is a single, tiny decision. But as that decision
is repeated, a habit sprouts and grows stronger. Roots
entrench themselves and branches grow. The task of
breaking a bad habit is like uprooting a powerful oak
within us. And the task of building a good habit is
like cultivating a delicate flower one day at a time.
— James Clear

A lot of us "swing for the fences" when we try to make changes in our lives. Rather than make small changes, we try to make huge alterations in how we do things so that change comes quickly and radically.

In this lesson, I want you to fight that particular part of your psychological makeup. I'm going to mention some areas of life that are important to work on, and I want you to write down what making the *smallest positive change* would look like in that area.

Let me give you a personal example of what I'm talking about related to my spiritual life. My prayer life had been bad for a while (like, not praying at all), so I decided I was going to get on my knees and pray *one minute a night* before going to bed. Once I made that small change, it led to praying more frequently and for longer periods of time.

With this example in mind, write down how you could make minuscule modifications in each of the areas of life listed below. Remember, start really small in each of these areas and trust that bigger changes are coming your way.

Reading: _____
_____
_____

Exercise: _____

_____

_____

Eating: _____

_____

_____

Praying: _____

_____

_____

Journaling: _____

_____

_____

Meditating: _____

_____

_____

Resting: _____

_____

_____

Organizing: _____

_____

_____

Hobbies: _____

_____

_____

Playing: _____

_____

_____

Cleaning: _____

_____

_____

Interacting: _____

_____

_____

Entertainment: _____

_____

_____

The purpose of this lesson is not to get you to be even busier and more overwhelmed by life. The purpose is to get you to take each area of life where you'd like to make some changes and encourage you to take a minor step of improvement in that area. For further help in doing this, consider reading the books listed below.

Recommended Reading

★ *Atomic Habits: An Easy & Proven Way to Build Good Habits & Break Bad Ones* by James Clear
★ *The Power of Habit: Why We Do What We Do in Life and Business* by Charles Duhigg
★ *Tiny Habits: The Small Changes That Change Everything* by B. J. Fogg

LESSON 50

Keep Your Heart Open
and Your Skin Thick

It is only once we stop taking everything for
granted and fully open our hearts to the beauty that
surrounds us that we will understand the importance
of joining our hands in the construction of a better
world for the people of generations to come.
— Francisco Battiti

It is tempting to close your heart to people given how hurtful they can sometimes be. The interpersonal wounds we accrue along the way often lead us to protect our hearts by shutting them down in an effort to avoid further harm.

In this lesson, I want you to take some steps to open your heart back up to others if you have shut it down to a certain degree. If you feel your heart is significantly shut down, don't respond to these questions. Instead, consider getting into counseling with a competent trauma specialist who can help you work through the wounds you've experienced and help you heal from them.

In the space provided below, write down your thoughts in response to each suggestion. Be as honest and transparent as you can be in your response.

Who has hurt you the most, and what did they do/not do that was hurtful to you?

_____

_____

_____

_____

Have you let yourself feel the emotional pain related to what they did? If not, take a few minutes to feel the hurt, anger, and sadness you feel about how they wounded you.

_____

_____

_____

_____

Have you given yourself compassion about what happened? If not, take a few minutes to offer yourself compassion, empathy, and kindness about how painful the situation was for you.

_____

_____

_____

_____

Have you forgiven this person for what they did? If not, what do you think is getting in the way of forgiving them and setting yourself free from their actions?

_____

_____

_____

_____

How much progress have you made in terms of seeing that what happened was about the person who mistreated you and not about you?

_____

_____

_____

_____

Have you shared this with anyone else? If so, was it helpful? If not, who might you turn to for help to heal this particular wound?

_____

_____

_____

_____

To open your heart and toughen your skin requires acknowledging the hurt someone caused you, letting yourself feel the pain of what happened, having compassion for yourself about what took place, allowing what happened to be about the person who caused the wound and not you, forgiving them for what they did whether they're sorry or not, and working through your wounds with caring and competent people so you can put it behind you and live the life you're meant to live. All easier said than done but critically important to do.

For further help with opening your heart and toughening your skin, consider reading the books listed below.

Recommended Reading

- ★ *Emotional First Aid: Healing Rejection, Guilt, Failure* by Guy Winch
- ★ *Forgiving What You Can't Forget: Discover How to Move On, Make Peace with Painful Memories, and Create a Life That's Beautiful Again* by Lysa TerKeurst
- ★ *It Didn't Start with You: How Inherited Family Trauma Shapes Who We Are and How to End the Cycle* by Mark Wolynn
- ★ *Healing for Damaged Emotions* by David Seamands
- ★ *Healing the Soul of a Woman: How to Overcome Your Emotional Wounds* by Joyce Meyer
- ★ *Suffering and the Heart of God: How Trauma Destroys and Christ Restores* by Diane Langberg
- ★ *The Art of Forgiving: When You Need to Forgive and Don't Know How* by Lewis Smedes
- ★ *Total Forgiveness* by R. T. Kendall

LESSON 51

Keep Your Head Up

> You've got to keep your head up, keep
> fighting, and do the best you can.
> —Pablo Sandoval

It's so easy to get discouraged, drop your head, and give up when life continues to throw hard things your way. In this lesson, I want to challenge you to not give in to discouragement in life and keep your head up no matter how hard things are.

First, write down a specific thing you currently feel discouraged about in life. You may feel discouraged about a number of things, but try to pick one that is especially discouraging to you.

_____

_____

_____

_____

_____

Second, write down the internal and external things getting in the way of being successful in this particular area of your life.

_____

_____

_____

_____

Third, of the things getting in your way, which ones can you do something about, and which ones are beyond your control?

_____

_____

_____

_____

Fourth, when it comes to the things you can do something about, what do you need to do to go around them, under them, over them, or through them?

_____

_____

_____

_____

_____

Fifth, who can you bring into this struggle who can provide wise counsel and expertise to help you stay the course?

_____

_____

_____

_____

_____

Sixth, related to the issue you feel discouraged about, what minor steps can you take that will encourage you?

_____

_____

_____

_____

_____

Seventh, what healthy way can you reward yourself when you take small steps in the direction of your goal?

_____

_____

_____

_____

_____

Eighth, what can you do spiritually to anchor yourself in the attributes of God, His promises, and His power to help you overcome this obstacle in life?

_____

_____

_____

_____

_____

While it is easy to get discouraged and throw in the towel, it is important to keep our heads up, keep trying to make progress toward the goals we have in life, and not grow weary of persevering when setbacks come our way. For further help in this area, consider reading the books listed below.

Recommended Reading

★ *Get Out of Your Head: Stopping the Spiral of Toxic Thoughts* by Jennie Allen

★ *Get Out of Your Own Way: Overcoming Self-Defeating Behavior* by Marl Goulston and Philip Goldberg

★ *Girl, Wash Your Face: Stop Believing the Lies About Who You Are So You Can Become Who You Were Meant to Be* by Rachel Hollis

★ *Make Your Bed: Little Things That Can Change Your Life . . . and Maybe the World* by Admiral William H. McRaven

LESSON 52

Putting Pop's Advice into Action

"The thief does not come except to steal,
and to kill, and to destroy. I have
come that they may have life, and that
they may have *it* more abundantly."
—Jesus Christ

The abundance of our lives is not determined
by how long we live, but how
well we live. Christ makes abundant life
possible if we choose to live it now.
—Barbara Brown Taylor

Living the abundant life is different than knowing about it.
It's time to begin practicing the life we were made for.
—Mark Beeson

We live in a world that defines the "good life" as one overflowing with power, possessions, and pleasure and that equates happiness to how well your external circumstances are going. That's not the abundant life. In fact, it's just the opposite.

The abundant life is an internal state, a life overflowing with love, joy, peace, patience, enthusiasm, confidence, humility, kindness, self-control, and faithfulness. It has little to do with how well your circumstances are going. Consequently, the abundant life can't be taken from you by a reversal of fortune in your day-to-day experiences.

The abundant life is life to the full, not merely existing. It's not flashy, glamorous, or impressive to the outside world. It is not obtained quickly but by the patient application of God's wisdom throughout life. It centers around growing, learning, maturing, enduring, and overcoming.

The abundant life is the result of many things, but, as it has been laid out in this book, it comes from following God's guidance. Rather than foolishly doing things our way, God asks us to do things His way. God knows that if we will do things His way our lives will be internally abundant no matter how good or bad things are going externally.

To move in the direction of abundant life, we have to choose to follow God's wisdom and apply it to our lives. That means not just being "hearers" of what He has to say but "doers" of what He asks us to do.

In the space provided, write down one small change you can make in each of the fifty areas of advice we have covered. Remember, don't be grandiose about the changes you are suggesting—keep them minuscule and manageable so you can accomplish them and put them in the "win" column for improving your life. Pride goes before destruction, and you don't want to pridefully "get over your skis" when it comes to the changes you're wanting to make in your life.

Hang Around Good People

_____

_____

_____

Own Your Own Stuff

_____

_____

_____

Tell People What You Need

_____

_____

_____

Think the Right Thoughts

_____

_____

_____

Practice Good Boundaries

_____

_____

_____

Listen More Than You Talk

_____

_____

_____

Please Mind Your Manners

_____

_____

_____

Withdraw and Pray

_____

_____

_____

Laugh . . . a Lot

_____

_____

_____

Cry . . . a Lot

_____

_____

_____

Stay in the Here-and-Now

_____

_____

_____

Be Grateful, Even for Your Problems

_____

_____

_____

Stay Humble

_____

_____

_____

Have Compassion for Yourself and Others

_____

_____

_____

Do the Hard Things First

_____

_____

_____

Strive for Excellence, Not Perfection

_____

_____

_____

Forgive Others . . . and Yourself

_____

_____

_____

Stand Up to Evil

_____

_____

_____

Read a Lot of Really Good Books

_____

_____

_____

Accept Yourself and Others, Warts and All

_____

_____

_____

Stop Shoulding All Over Yourself

_____

_____

_____

Be Angry but Don't Act the Fool

_____

_____

_____

Practice Generosity

_____

_____

_____

Seek Wise Counsel

_____

_____

_____

Be Anxious, Don't Worry

_____

_____

_____

Don't Play to the Crowd

_____

_____

_____

Be Content with Little

_____

_____

_____

Watch Your Mouth

_____

_____

_____

Ask Others to Correct You

_____

_____

_____

Listen to a Lot of Really Good Music

_____

_____

_____

Face Your Death

_____

_____

_____

Guard Your Heart

_____

_____

_____

Chris Thurman, Ph.D. A.K.A. "Pop"

Wait for It, Wait for It

_____

_____

_____

Go Fly a Kite

_____

_____

_____

Never Give Up

_____

_____

_____

Keep Your Promises

_____

_____

_____

Let Others Toot Your Horn

_____

_____

_____

Don't Take Things Personally

_____

_____

_____

Walk on the Sunny Side of the Street

_____

_____

_____

Remember People's Names

_____

_____

_____

Make Good Friends . . . and Be One

_____

_____

_____

Don't Judge a Book by Its Cover

_____

_____

_____

Smile More Often

_____

_____

_____

Break Free from Egypt

_____

_____

_____

Embrace the Mystery of Life

_____

_____

_____

Observe Your Thoughts but Don't Trust Them

_____

_____

_____

Stay Balanced

_____

_____

_____

Make Miniscule Modifications

_____

_____

_____

Keep Your Heart Open and Your Skin Thick

_____

_____

_____

Keep Your Head Up

_____

_____

_____

Now that you've come up with a minor change you can make in each of these areas, choose three that you are willing to commit to doing with no ifs, ands, or buts.

Issue #1 That I'm Committing to Work on and the Minor Change I'm Going to Make

_____

_____

_____

Issue #2 That I'm Committing to Work on and the Minor Change I'm Going to Make

_____

_____

_____

Issue #3 That I'm Committing to Work on and the Minor Change I'm Going to Make

_____

_____

_____

_____

If you have reached this point in *Pop's Advice*, I want to pat you on the back and say "Well done!" You've done a lot of good work to get here, and I'm excited about the positive benefits coming your way. I want to encourage you to stay the course in working on the advice you've been given in this book so that you can experience a fuller taste of the abundant life, leave the world you live in better off, and bring honor and glory to the God who made you in His image.

Acknowledgments

Holly, thank you for being such a loving and devoted wife, mom, and grandmother. I have learned so much over the years by watching you compassionately and graciously interact with others. You are the wife of noble character talked about in Proverbs, and I am a very rich man because of you.

Matt, Ashley, and Kelly, thank you for being such incredible kids. I won the lottery when you came into my life. You've taught me more about how to live life well than I've ever taught you, and I'm so proud of you that I could bust my buttons. You are a great blessing to my soul.

Scout, Leni, and Luke, thank you for being the most amazing grandkids on the planet. It's hard to describe how much joy you have brought into my life. From the day you arrived, you have blessed me beyond what I could have ever hoped for or imagined. You are the icing on the cake of my life, and I will never be able to thank you enough. I hope in some small way this book tells you how much I love and appreciate you.

God, thank you for unconditionally loving this particular mess of a human being. As if adopting me into your family wasn't enough, you've blessed me with a wonderful family of my own, a career as a psychologist that has been more than I could have ever hoped for, and so many wonderful opportunities and experiences to enjoy. Every good and perfect gift in my life comes from you. From the bottom of my heart, thank you.

About the Author

Dr. Chris Thurman is a psychologist, bestselling author, and popular speaker. He has a doctorate in counseling psychology from the University of Texas and has been in private practice for over thirty years. Chris has authored numerous books, including the bestseller *The Lies We Believe* (over 250,000 in print) and conducted hundreds of personal growth seminars for churches and corporations around the country.

Chris and his wife, Holly, have been married for over forty years and have three grown children and three absolutely wonderful grandchildren. In his spare time, Chris loves to play golf, follow his beloved Texas Longhorns, and, most importantly, teach others how to become more emotionally healthy human beings.

For more information concerning Dr. Thurman's seminars, please contact him at his website, drchristhurman.com.

CPSIA information can be obtained
at www.ICGtesting.com
Printed in the USA
JSHW082117041122
32650JS00001B/2

9 781664 278226